ENCYCLOPEDIA OF SHARKS

ENCYCLOPEDIA OF SHARKS

By Barbara Taylor

Miles Kelly

First published in 2016 by Miles Kelly Publishing Ltd
Harding's Barn, Bardfield End Green, Thaxted, Essex, CM6 3PX, UK

Copyright © Miles Kelly Publishing Ltd 2016

10 9 8 7 6 5 4 3 2 1

Publishing Director Belinda Gallagher
Creative Director Jo Cowan
Editorial Director Rosie Neave
Senior Editor Sarah Parkin
Editor Amy Johnson
Cover Designer Jo Cowan
Design Manager Joe Jones
Senior Designer Rob Hale
Image Manager Liberty Newton
Indexer Indexing Specialists (UK) Ltd
Production Elizabeth Collins, Caroline Kelly
Reprographics Stephan Davis, Jennifer Cozens, Thom Allaway
Contributor Anna Claybourne

All rights reserved. No part of this publication may be reproduced, stored in a retrieval system, or transmitted by any means, electronic, mechanical, photocopying, recording or otherwise, without the prior permission of the copyright holder.

ISBN: 978-1-78617-021-7

Printed in China

British Library Cataloguing-in-Publication Data
A catalogue record for this book is available from the British Library

Made with paper from a sustainable forest

www.mileskelly.net

SHARK TRUST

www.sharktrust.org

Contents

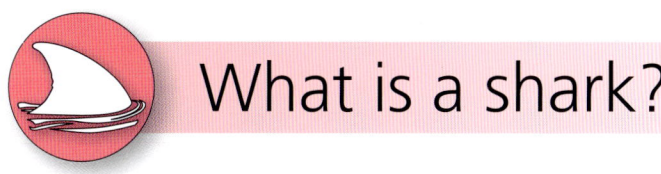

What is a shark?

All about sharks	12	Big and small	16
Records and statistics	14		

Where sharks live

Around the world 22
Shallows to the deep 24
Life on the bottom 28
Tropics to poles 30
Reef sharks 34

How sharks work

Shark shapes	38	Digesting food	70
Shark fins	42	Eyes and vision	72
Shark tails	44	Sensing smells	76
Sandpaper skin	48	Hearing sounds	78
A look inside	50	Touch and taste	80
Flexible skeleton	54	The sixth sense	84
Teeth and jaws	56	Smart sharks	86
Breathing underwater	60		
Heart and blood	64		
Muscles for moving	66		

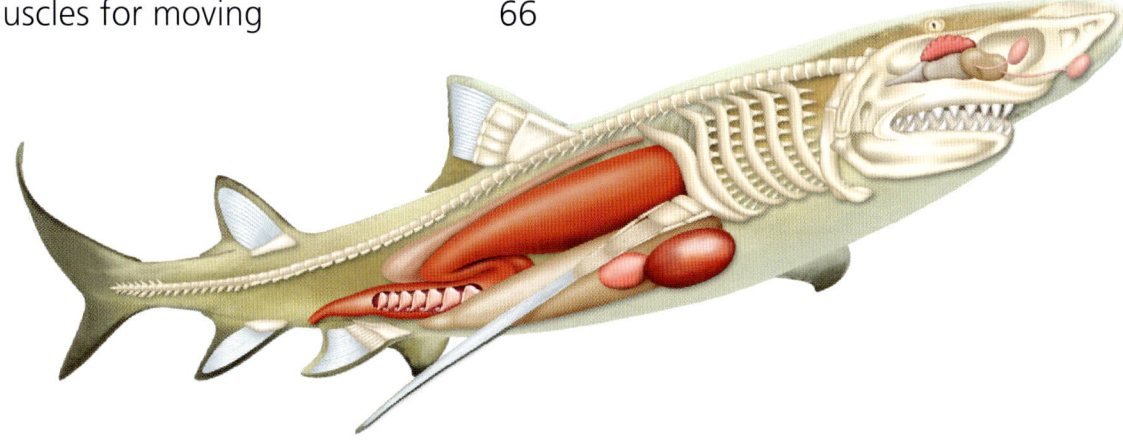

Life in the water

On the move	90	Filter-feeding	112
Swimming skills	94	Scavenging food	114
Fast sharks	96	Lighting up	118
Long-distance travel	100	Staying safe	120
Food and feeding	102	Spikes and spines	122
Going hunting	106	In disguise	124
Pack hunters	108	Loners and groups	128
		Sending messages	130
		Male and female sharks	132
		Meeting and mating	134
		Laying eggs	138
		Giving birth	142
		Newborn sharks	144
		Growing up	148
		Friends and enemies	150

Shark families

Types of shark	154	Sixgill and sevengill sharks	160
Frilled shark	158	Prickly and bramble sharks	164

Dogfish sharks

Dogfish sharks	168	Kitefin shark	190
Mandarin dogfish	170	Pygmy sharks	192
Spurdog sharks	172	Cookie-cutter sharks	194
Gulper sharks	176		
Lanternsharks	178		
Sleeper sharks	182		
Greenland shark	184		
Roughsharks	188		

Angelsharks

Angelsharks	198	Types of angelshark	202

Sawsharks

Sawsharks	206	Longnose sawshark	208

Bullhead sharks

Bullhead sharks	214	Port Jackson shark	220
Horn shark	216		

Carpet sharks

Carpet sharks	226	Bamboo sharks	236
Epaulette sharks	228	Nurse sharks	240
Blind sharks	230	Tawny nurse shark	242
Wobbegongs	232	Zebra shark	244
		Whale shark	248

Mackerel sharks

Mackerel sharks	254	Sand tiger shark	258
Goblin shark	256	Thresher sharks	260
		Megamouth shark	262
		Crocodile shark	266
		Basking shark	268
		Great white shark	272
		Champion hunter	274
		Mako sharks	278
		Salmon shark	282
		Porbeagle shark	284

Ground sharks

Catsharks	288	Tope shark	300
Swellsharks	292	Smoothhound sharks	304
Houndsharks	296	Leopard shark	306
Whiskery shark	298	Weasel sharks	310

Requiem sharks

Requiem sharks	314	Dusky shark	350
Blacknose shark	318	Sandbar shark	352
Silvertip shark	320	Night shark	354
Grey reef shark	324	Tiger shark	356
Spinner shark	328	River sharks	360
Bronze whaler shark	330	Lemon shark	362
Silky shark	332	Blue shark	366
Galapagos shark	334	Whitetip reef shark	370
Bull shark	338	Sharpnose sharks	372
Blacktip reef shark	340		
Blacktip shark	344		
Oceanic whitetip shark	346		

Hammerhead sharks

Hammerhead sharks	376		
Winghead shark	378	Scalloped hammerhead	382
Bonnethead shark	380	Great hammerhead	386

Shark relatives

Shark relatives	392	Skates	406
Rays	396	Guitarfish	408
Manta rays	398	Sawfish	412
Electric rays	400	Chimaeras	414
Stingrays	402	Elephant fish	418

Sharks and people

Living with sharks	422	Tourist attractions	440
Dangerous or not?	424	Sharks in captivity	444
Attacks	428	Shark products	446
Survival stories	430	Sharks and medicine	448
Staying safe	434	Legends and beliefs	450
Fishing for sharks	438	Books and films	452

Shark science

Studying sharks	458	Early sharks	472
Shark scientists	460	Shark fossils	474
Observation	464	Sharks in trouble	476
Discoveries and mysteries	468	Endangered species	478
Evolution of sharks	470	Saving sharks	482
Glossary	486	Acknowledgements	511
Index	500		

 # What is a shark?

All about sharks

- **Sharks are a type of fish**. They live and breathe underwater and most of them are brilliant swimmers.

- **Most fish have a skeleton** made from bone, but a shark's skeleton is made of a lightweight, rubbery material, called cartilage.

- **All sharks are carnivores**. This means that they eat meat. Many kinds are fierce hunters and chase after their prey.

- **Most sharks** are not dangerous to people. Only a few types attack people, including the great white shark, tiger shark and bull shark.

- **Sharks are mostly found** in seas and oceans, although a few rare sharks live in rivers.

- **A species** is the name for a particular type of living thing. Sharks of the same species can mate and have offspring (young).

What is a shark?

- **There are more than** 500 different species of shark, and more than 550 types of batoids (rays, skates, sawfish and guitarfish), which are their close relatives.

- **Many shark species** look similar, with long bodies, triangular fins and lots of sharp teeth. They can range greatly in size – from about the length of a banana to bigger than a bus.

- **Some sharks lay eggs**, but many give birth to live young, which are called pups.

- **Many sharks and rays** are very rare and over 30 percent are in danger of dying out soon, especially river sharks.

◀ Blue sharks have long, slender bodies and pointed snouts, which slide easily through the water, helping them to swim fast.

Records and statistics

- **The most widespread shark** is the blue shark, found in most of the world's seas and oceans.

- **The brightest** luminescent shark is the cookie-cutter. Its glow is as bright as a reading lamp.

- **The sharks with the flattest bodies** are wobbegong sharks and angelsharks.

- **The bigeye thresher shark** has the biggest eyes in relation to its body size.

- **Shortfin makos** make the highest leaps. They can jump more than 5 m out of the water.

▼ *A thresher shark's tail is up to 1.5 m long. When flicked from side to side, the tail makes a powerful weapon for catching prey.*

What is a shark?

- **The fussiest eaters** of the shark world are bullhead sharks. The diet of some bullheads consists of sea urchins and nothing else.

- **The common thresher shark** has the longest tail compared to its body size. The tail can be up to half of the shark's body length.

- **The fastest shark** is the shortfin mako shark, which reaches speeds of over 50 km/h.

- **The shark** with the most poisonous flesh is the Greenland shark.

- **The longest lifespans** for sharks range from 75 years for the spiny dogfish to perhaps over 100 years for the whale shark and Greenland shark.

> **DID YOU KNOW?**
> Thresher sharks are the second most threatened shark family, after angelsharks.

Big and small

- **The biggest shark ever**, *Megalodon*, is now extinct. This means the species has completely died out. Scientists think *Megalodon* may have weighed almost twice as much as a whale shark.

- **The whale shark** is the biggest living shark. It can measure over 15 m in length – that's as long as two buses end-to-end.

- **Whale sharks** are gentle fish that feed by filtering tiny food particles from the water.

- **The biggest hunting shark** is the great white. Its mouth can measure up to 1.2 m wide – big enough to swallow a seal whole.

- **Most sharks** are medium-sized, measuring 1–3 m in length.

- **The average size for a shark** is very similar to the average size of a human.

▼ Pygmy sharks are no more than 27 cm long.

What is a shark?

▲ The gigantic whale shark is the biggest fish in the world.

- **Although some types** are small, most sharks are still bigger than other kinds of fish.

- **The smallest types** are the spined pygmy shark and the dwarf lanternshark.

- **The hammerhead shark** with the biggest 'hammer' is the winghead shark. The width of its hammer is about 50 percent of its body length.

- **The widest batoid** is the manta ray, which is 6.7 m wide across its enormous fins.

What is a shark?

▼ The colossal whale shark is a harmless giant with a wide mouth over one metre across. It is a very fast swimmer and lives for 70 years or more.

Where sharks live

Around the world

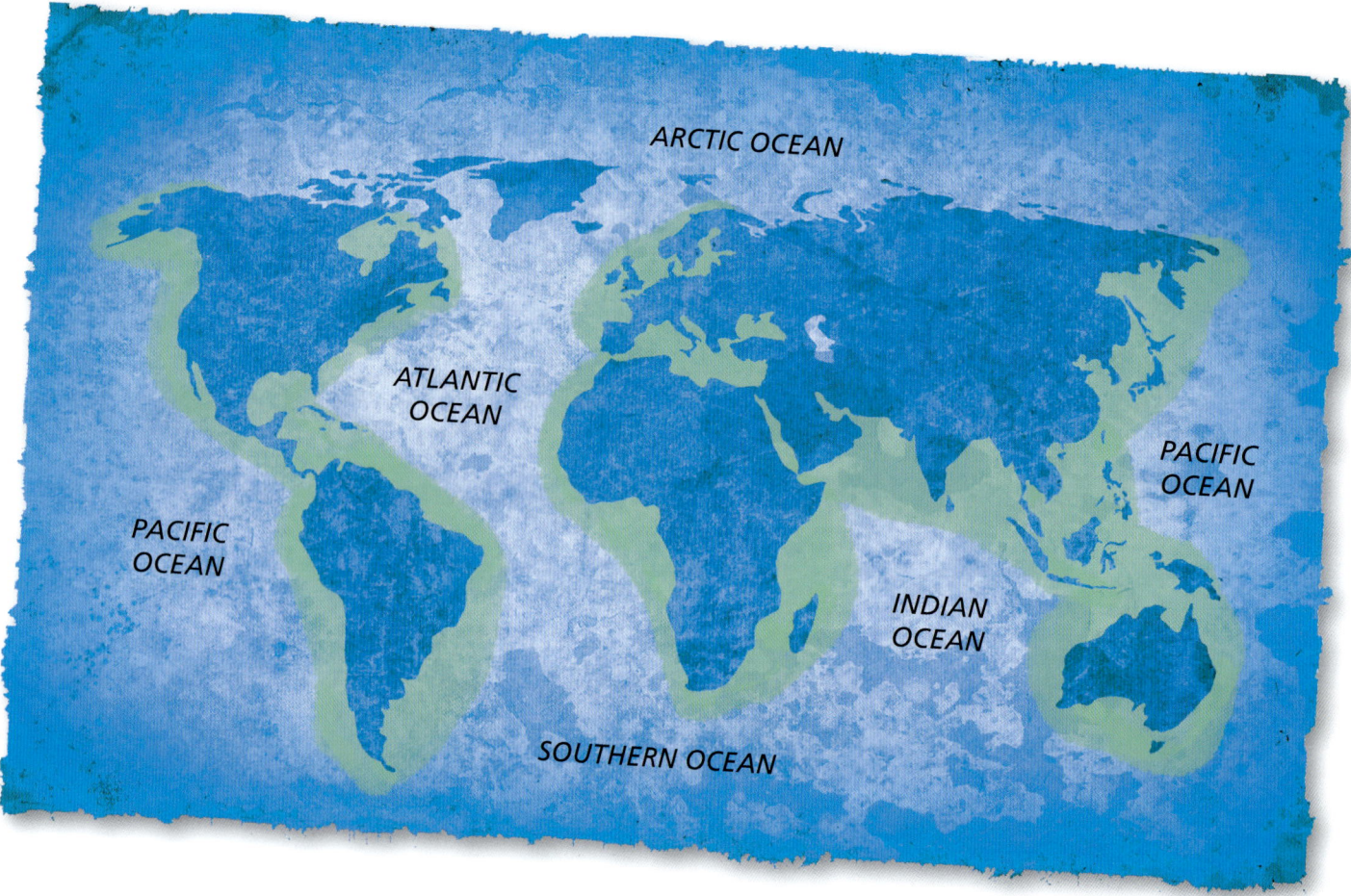

▲ The green areas on this world map show the parts of the oceans where sharks are most common.

- **Sharks are found** in seas and oceans around the world. They are almost all marine fish, which means they live in the salty seas rather than in fresh water.

- **They are most common** around coasts. Many species live in shallow sandy bays, near coral reefs or in the medium-deep water a few kilometres from the shore.

- **Coral reefs** and seaweed forests are good homes for young sharks. They provide them with food and shelter.

Where sharks live

- **Species that live** in the open ocean, such as blue sharks and great whites, are known as pelagic sharks.

- **Sharks living on** the ocean floor are called benthic sharks.

- **Lots of species live** in warm waters, but a few, such as the Greenland shark, inhabit cold water around the Arctic.

- **Sharks are hardly ever found** in the Southern Ocean around Antarctica – probably because it is too cold.

- **Epaulette sharks** are often found in rockpools. They can move from one pool to another across land by dragging themselves with their strong pectoral fins.

- **Cold water sharks**, such as the frilled shark and goblin shark, often live in very deep water.

- **Some sharks are warm-blooded**. This means they can control their body temperature, so they are able to live in a greater variety of water temperatures than other sharks. The great white shark is warm-blooded.

> **DID YOU KNOW?**
> A few sharks, such as bull sharks and river sharks, can survive in fresh (not salty) water. They are able to swim in rivers and lakes.

▲ *The great white shark has an inner heating system, which recycles body heat and keeps the shark warmer than the water around it.*

Shallows to the deep

- **Different species of sharks** live at different levels in the oceans, from the warm surface waters to the cold ocean depths.

- **The mackerel and requiem** shark families cruise the sunlit surface waters looking for prey. These sharks include mako sharks, porbeagle sharks, tiger sharks and bull sharks.

- **Basking sharks and whale sharks** swim near to the surface in order to scoop up floating plankton.

- **Catsharks and prickly sharks** live at middle depths in the oceans, in water below about 1000 m.

- **A few deep-sea sharks**, such as cookie-cutter sharks, spend the day in deep water, but rise up to the surface to feed at night.

- **Spiny dogfish and porbeagle sharks** spend the winter sheltering in deep water, but they move to shallow waters near the coast in spring and autumn.

- **Portuguese sharks** have been found at depths of nearly 3700 m below the sea's surface. They live at such great depths scientists don't know much about them.

▼ *Sixgill sharks have large eyes to help them capture as much light as possible in deep, dark waters. This shark is only a pup.*

Where sharks live

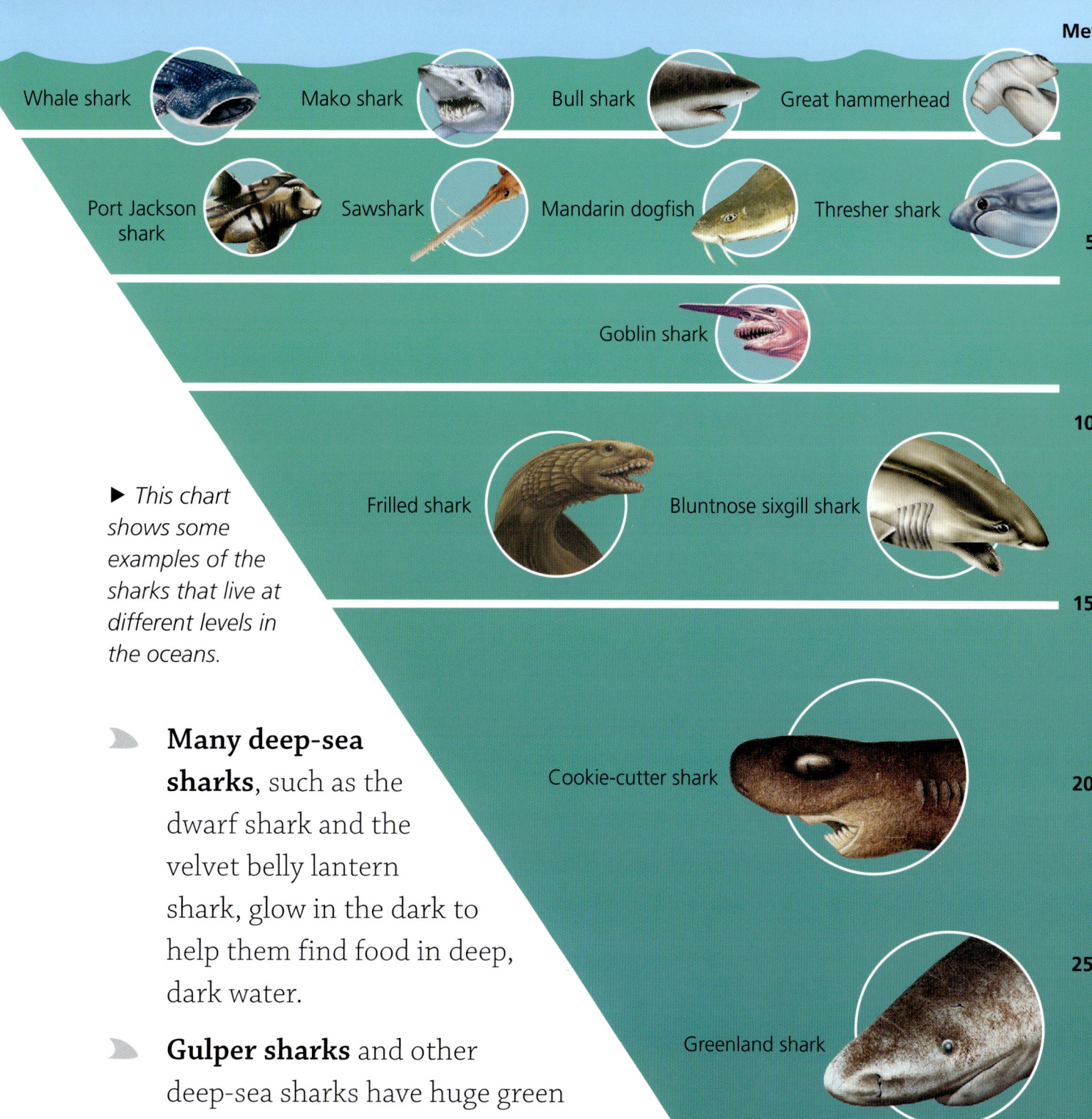

▶ This chart shows some examples of the sharks that live at different levels in the oceans.

- **Many deep-sea sharks**, such as the dwarf shark and the velvet belly lantern shark, glow in the dark to help them find food in deep, dark water.

- **Gulper sharks** and other deep-sea sharks have huge green eyes to help them see in dark and gloomy waters.

- **Living on the deep-sea floor** are sixgill, sevengill and sleeper sharks. They eat the food that sinks down from the surface of the sea.

▶ A basking shark feeding near the surface off the coast of Scotland, with its huge mouth wide open. After the whale shark, this is the second largest fish in the world.

Where sharks live

Life on the bottom

- **Many sharks live** near the sea bed. These sharks usually swim slowly, and spend time resting on the bottom or in sea caves.

- **Some of these sharks**, such as nurse sharks, swellsharks or catsharks, rest during the day and come out at night to hunt.

- **Angelsharks** have flat bodies that help them to lie close to the sea floor.

- **Their colours and patterns** give them good camouflage while they lie in wait for their prey.

- **Wobbegong sharks** look just like the rock, coral and seaweed on the sea bed, which enables them to make surprise attacks on fish and other sea creatures.

- **Sharks that hide** on the sea bed may take in water through a breathing hole (spiracle) behind their eyes to stop their gills becoming clogged up with sand or mud.

- **Sharks that live** on the bottom, such as nurse sharks, bamboo sharks and bullhead sharks, often have strong fins to help them clamber about on the sea bed or lift themselves up above the sea floor.

Where sharks live

- **Sawsharks use** their long, barbed snouts to dig up food from the sea bed.

- **Bottom-dwelling sharks** sometimes have sensitive feelers, called barbels, to help them locate food.

- **Leopard sharks** survive in very shallow water. They even follow the tide in and out to feed on shellfish and worms.

▼ *The two barbels on the snout of a nurse shark sense touch, water currents and chemicals in the water. They help the sharks to find prey hidden in the sand or mud on the sea bed.*

Tropics to poles

- **More species of sharks** live in warm or hot tropical oceans than in cold polar waters.

- **Most of the top shark hunters**, such as blue sharks or oceanic whitetip sharks, thrive in tropical oceans where the water is warmer than 21°C.

- **Other tropical species** that prefer to swim and hunt in warm waters include reef sharks, nurse sharks and whale sharks.

- **Temperate water sharks**, such as mako sharks, basking sharks and horn sharks, live in cooler waters, with temperatures ranging from 10–20°C.

- **The great white shark** lives in temperate waters, but also swims in tropical oceans and warm seas, such as the Mediterranean Sea.

◀ *Scalloped hammerhead sharks swim in warm temperate and tropical oceans all over the world. They migrate northwards in summer, but return to warmer tropical waters in the winter.*

DID YOU KNOW?
Scalloped hammerhead pups grow more slowly and reach smaller sizes in cooler waters than in warm tropical waters.

Where sharks live

- **Where water temperatures** are lower than 10°C, fewer sharks are able to survive and they move more slowly.

- **Cold water sharks** include the smoothhound shark, spiny dogfish, porbeagle shark and sleeper sharks.

- **The porbeagle shark** lives in waters with temperatures as low as 2°C, but is still able to chase fish at the surface of the sea.

- **The Greenland shark** is the only shark that survives under the polar ice in the North Atlantic Ocean.

- **Although the Greenland shark grows slowly**, it reaches a large size of over 6.5 m, and may live for 100 years or more.

▼ *Greenland sharks live in the cold waters of the North Atlantic Ocean – further north than almost any other shark.*

▶ The blue shark lives in open ocean all over the world, in both temperate and tropical waters. In tropical waters, it tends to swim to depths of up to 350 m to find cooler temperatures.

Where sharks live

Reef sharks

- **Many species of shark** live on or around coral reefs because of the warm waters, and the variety of food and places to shelter.

- **Reef sharks** often patrol along the edge of the reef, ready to catch day-hunting fish returning to the safety of the reef at night.

- **The names of some sharks**, such as grey reef sharks and blacktip reef sharks reflect their habitat.

- **Many reef sharks** are very curious. They will swim close to divers, or steal fish from the spears of fishermen hunting underwater.

- **Blacktip reef sharks** hunt for fish and small sea creatures in very shallow water on coral reefs. People may find these one-metre-long sharks brushing around their legs as they walk or swim on the reefs.

- **Whitetip reef sharks** rest during the day in caves or under rocks, and hunt for fish in packs at night. Their tough skin helps to protect them from the sharp coral.

- **Like many sharks**, reef sharks have dark backs and paler undersides. This helps to camouflage them from predators or prey, either looking down at the dark water below them, or up towards the lighter water at the sea's surface.

Where sharks live

- **The black fin tips** of the blacktip reef shark may help to break up its outline and improve its camouflage.

- **Reef sharks** do not usually make long migration journeys as they have a plentiful supply of food, and places to mate and rear their young all year round.

- **Grey reef sharks** use body language, such as arching their backs and pointing their front fins down, to warn rivals to keep away from their patch of coral reef.

▼ Caribbean reef sharks are the most common sharks on the reefs in the Caribbean Sea. They are large sharks, reaching lengths of 2–3 m.

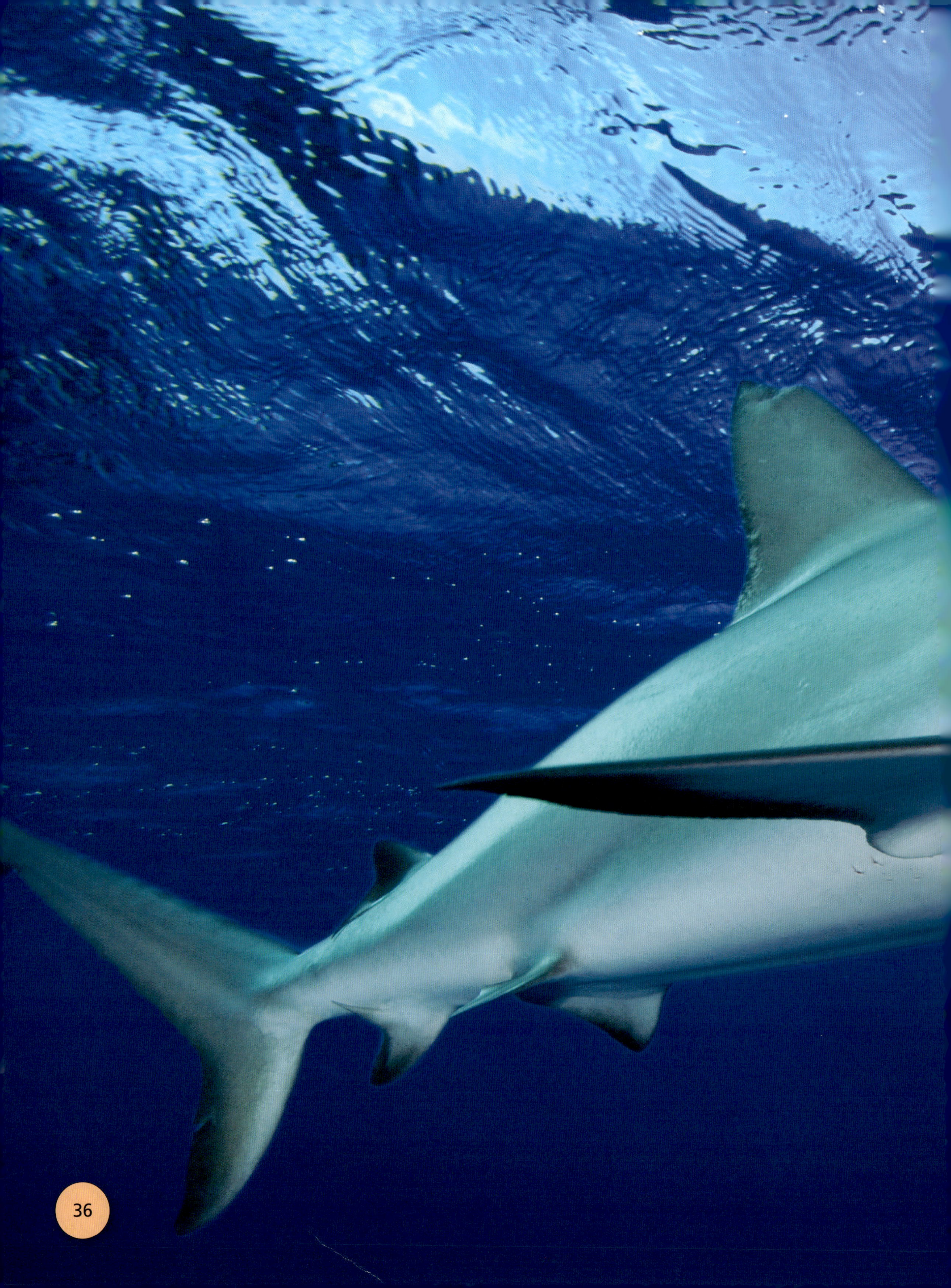

How sharks work

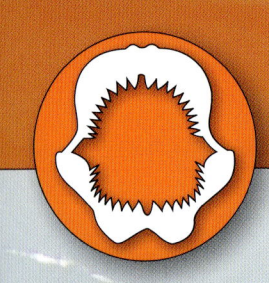

Shark shapes

- **All sharks have the same** basic body plan – a head with eyes, nostrils and a mouth, and a body with a tail and fins.

- **A typical shark** has a long, narrow, torpedo-shaped body. This helps it move quickly through the water.

- **Most sharks are built** for speed and are streamlined in shape. This means water can move past them easily with very little resistance or 'drag'.

- **The tip of a shark's nose** is called the snout. Most are pointed, like the tip of a bullet.

- **Some sharks have snouts** with unusual shapes. Sawsharks have very long, saw-like snouts and the goblin shark has a horn-shaped snout.

- **Frilled sharks live in the deep sea**. Their long, thin bodies are shaped more like those of eels than those of typical sharks.

How sharks work

- **Carpet sharks**, such as wobbegongs, have a flat body shape, which helps them to hide from predators and prey on the sea bed.

- **Angelsharks have wide**, spread-out fins that look like wings.

- **Hammerhead sharks** get their name because their heads are shaped like wide, flat hammers.

- **Engineers sometimes study sharks** to determine the best shapes for plane wings or boat hulls.

▲ The tasselled wobbegong's 'beard' provides extra camouflage.

◀ Tiger sharks drift slowly through the oceans but can suddenly shoot towards their prey with a surprising burst of speed.

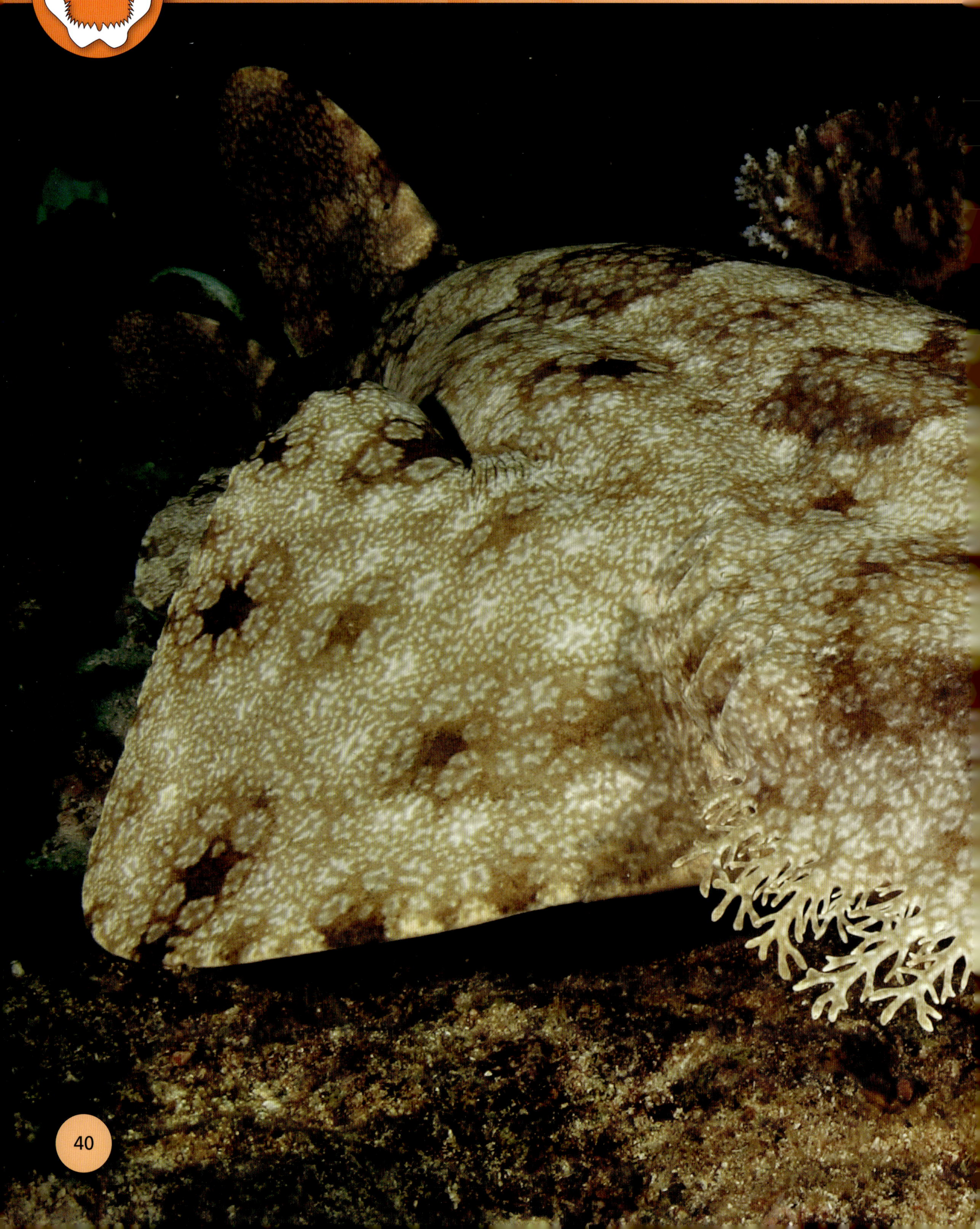

How sharks work

▼ The tasselled wobbegong has a flexible, flattened body. This helps it to wriggle into small spaces in coral reefs or inside caves in order to ambush its prey.

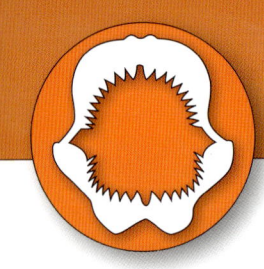

Shark fins

- **A typical shark has up to seven fins**, not including its tail. A shark's fins help it to balance, change direction in the water and also slow down.

- **Most sharks have five different types of fins**: dorsal, pectoral, pelvic, anal and caudal (tail) fins. Sharks usually have two dorsal fins, but some species only have one.

- **The large fin on the back** is called the first dorsal fin. It stops a shark's body swinging from side to side while swimming, and sometimes sticks out of the water.

- **Two large pectoral fins** near the front of the body help a shark to steer and stop it from sinking.

- **A shark's two pelvic fins** are underneath its body, near the tail. Like the pectoral fins, they also help to lift the shark up in the water and stop it sinking.

Upper lobe

Caudal fin (tail)

Lower lobe

▼ An epaulette shark can survive out of water for a few minutes.

DID YOU KNOW?
Without their fins, sharks wouldn't be able to stay the right way up – they would roll over in the water.

Pectoral fin

How sharks work

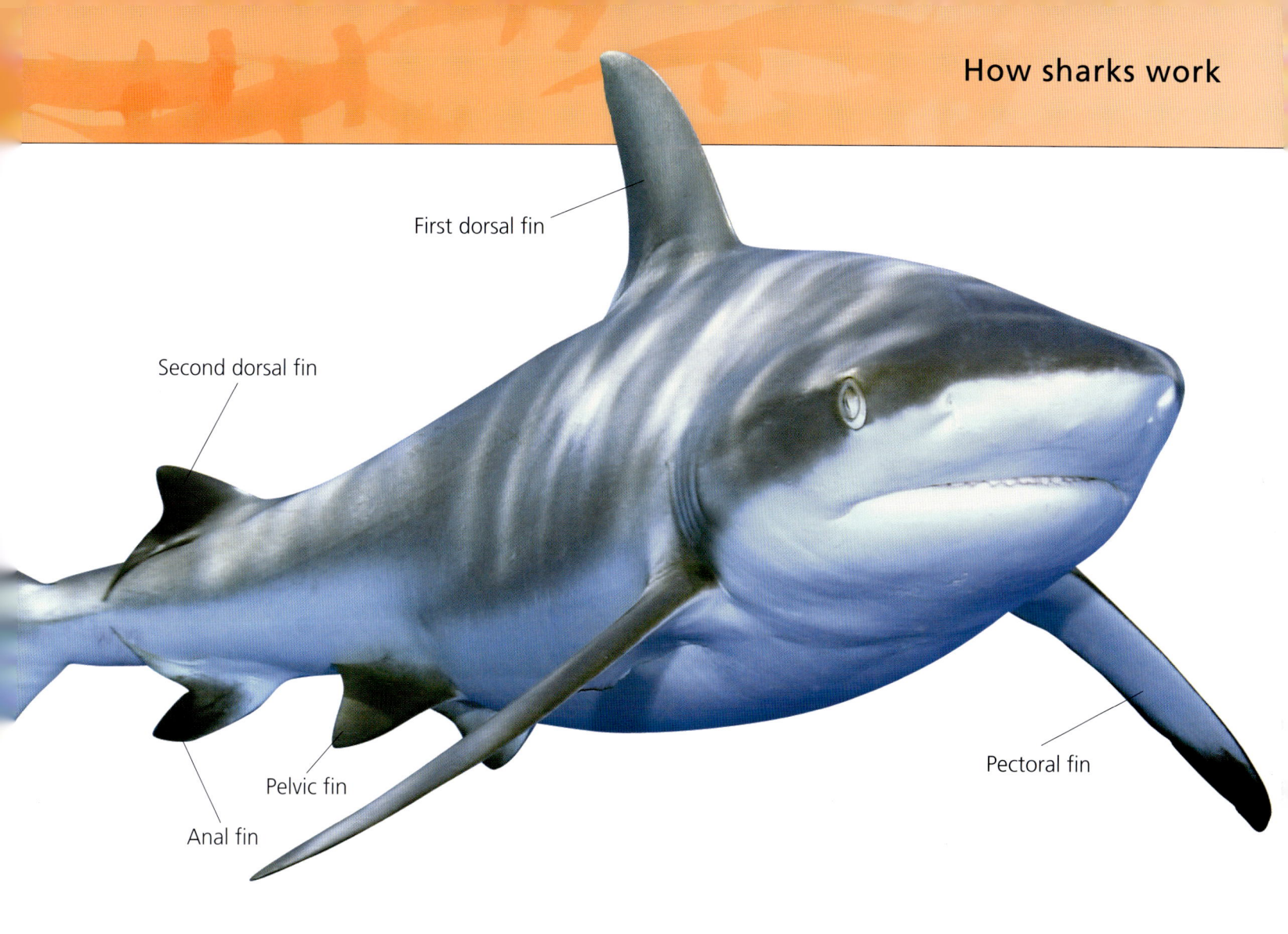

First dorsal fin
Second dorsal fin
Anal fin
Pelvic fin
Pectoral fin

▲ The grey reef shark has a typical shark shape with seven fins. The tail powers the body through water.

- **A shark has one anal fin**, which is under its body, nearer the tail than the pelvic fins. The anal fin helps to stop the shark from rolling sideways.

- **Megamouth sharks have soft**, rounded fins for swimming slowly in the deep ocean.

- **The wing-like fins** of angelsharks help them to accelerate quickly when they are chasing prey.

- **Epaulette sharks** use their pectoral fins like legs to 'crawl' along the sea bed.

- **A whale shark's pectoral fin** is up to 2 m in length.

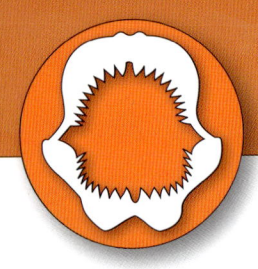

Shark tails

▼ *The upper lobe of the silky shark's tail is slightly longer than the lower lobe, which helps it to cruise through the open ocean.*

- **The tail is also known** as the caudal fin. The anal fin is just in front of the tail.

- **A shark's flattened tail** helps to push it through the water.

- **Sharks that live** at the bottom of the sea, such as the nurse shark, usually have large, flat tails, with a large upper lobe to the tail.

- **Sharks that swim** in the open ocean tend to have slimmer, more curved tails, but still have a larger upper lobe to the tail.

- **The two tail lobes** are an equal size in the fastest sharks, such as the mako shark.

- **This makes the tail** a curved shape and produces a powerful thrust, propelling the shark forwards at high speed.

- **The keel**, or ridge, on the tail of some sharks, such as the porbeagle, mako or great white, provides stability while swimming and probably helps them to turn more easily in the water.

How sharks work

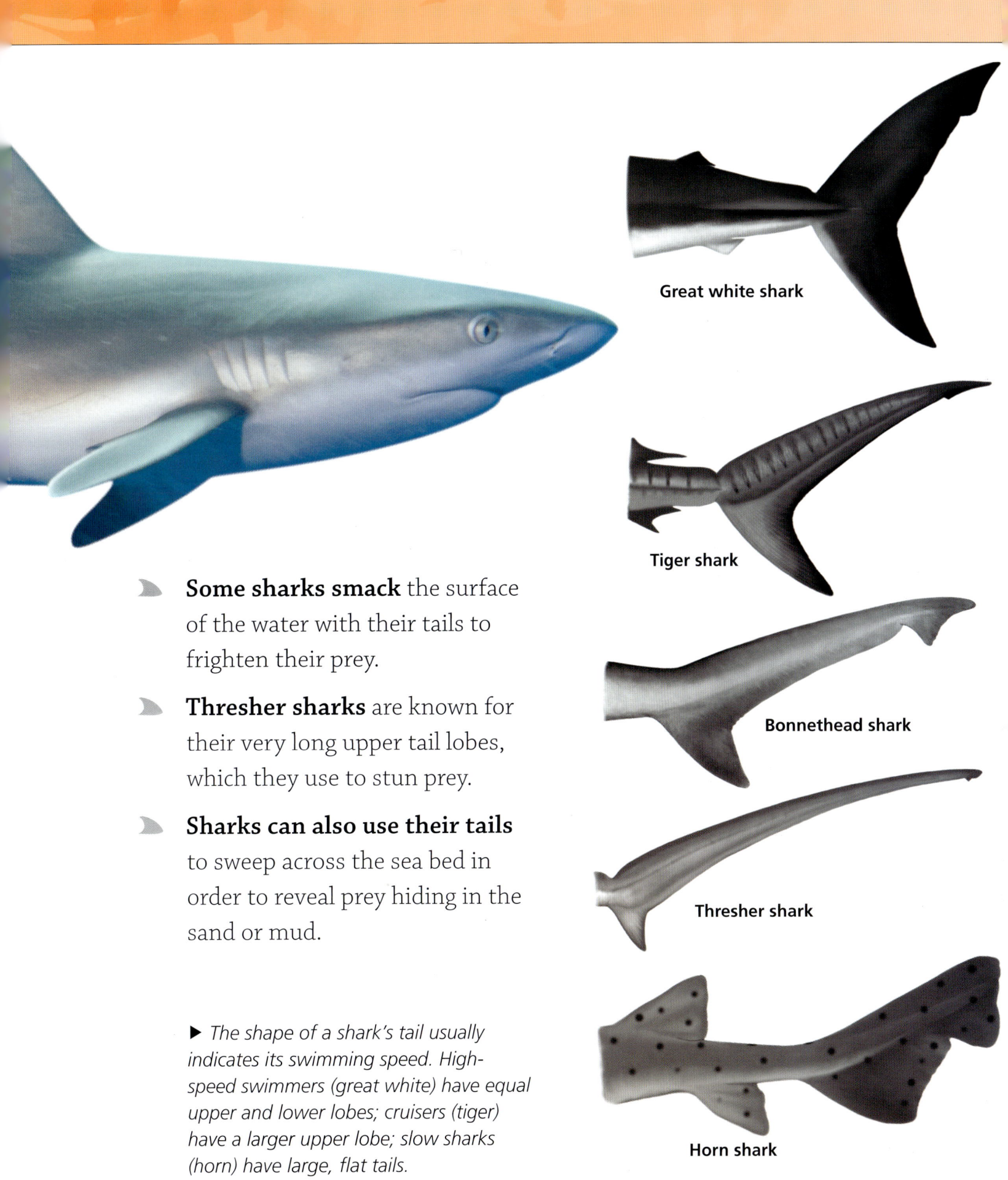

Great white shark

Tiger shark

Bonnethead shark

Thresher shark

Horn shark

▸ **Some sharks smack** the surface of the water with their tails to frighten their prey.

▸ **Thresher sharks** are known for their very long upper tail lobes, which they use to stun prey.

▸ **Sharks can also use their tails** to sweep across the sea bed in order to reveal prey hiding in the sand or mud.

▶ The shape of a shark's tail usually indicates its swimming speed. High-speed swimmers (great white) have equal upper and lower lobes; cruisers (tiger) have a larger upper lobe; slow sharks (horn) have large, flat tails.

45

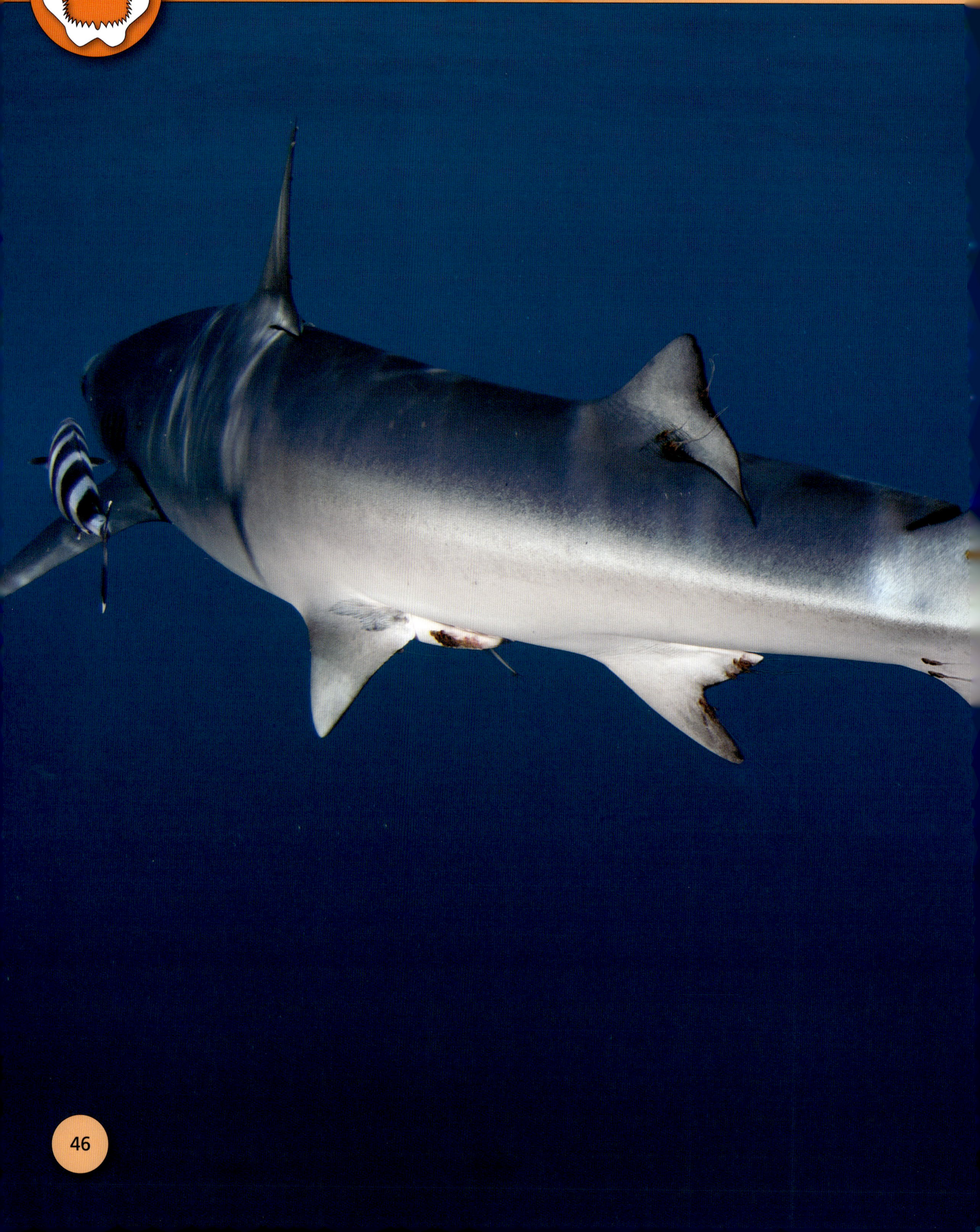

How sharks work

▲ The large upper lobe of a blue shark's tail provides power for slow cruising speeds, but this sleek, streamlined shark is also able to move rapidly when hunting.

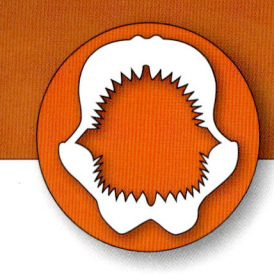

Sandpaper skin

- **Unlike other fish**, sharks don't have scales. Instead their skin is covered with tiny, hard points called denticles.

- **The word denticle** means 'little tooth'. Denticles range from microscopic in size to about 5 mm across.

- **Denticles give protection** from enemies and help sharks slide easily through the water.

- **If you were to touch a shark's skin**, it would feel very rough. Some swimmers have been badly scratched just from brushing against a shark.

- **The denticles** on the side of a shark's body are the sharpest to ensure fast movement through the water.

- **Many sharks release** a slimy substance from their skin to make their bodies move faster through water.

- **A shark's denticles** overlap like tiles on a roof, which allows the shark's skin to bend.

- **Denticles** are very different from the scales of bony fish, such as salmon. They have the same composition as teeth and are on little stalks.

- **A shark's denticles** eventually fall out and are replaced, just like their teeth.

- **The bramble shark** has large, thorn-like denticles, whereas the silky shark has tiny denticles and a smoother skin than most other sharks.

DID YOU KNOW?
Large sharks have very thick skin – thicker than a human finger. The whale shark's skin is about 10 cm deep.

How sharks work

Bramble shark

Silky shark

Whale shark

▲ A shark's denticles channel the water flowing across its body so as to reduce the energy needed for swimming. They also help sharks to swim quietly, enabling them to sneak up on their prey.

49

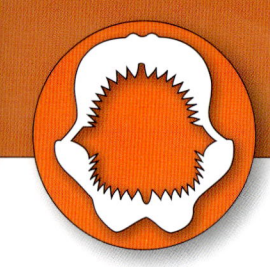

A look inside

- **Sharks are vertebrates** – they have a skeleton with a backbone. Many animals, including all fish, reptiles, birds and mammals, are vertebrates.

- **Shark skeletons** are not made of bone. Instead they are made of a strong, flexible substance called cartilage.

- **A thick layer of muscle** just underneath the skin helps a shark to move its body from side to side as it swims through the water.

- **Most of the vital organs** are in a cavity in the middle of the body. A shark has many of the same organs as other animals.

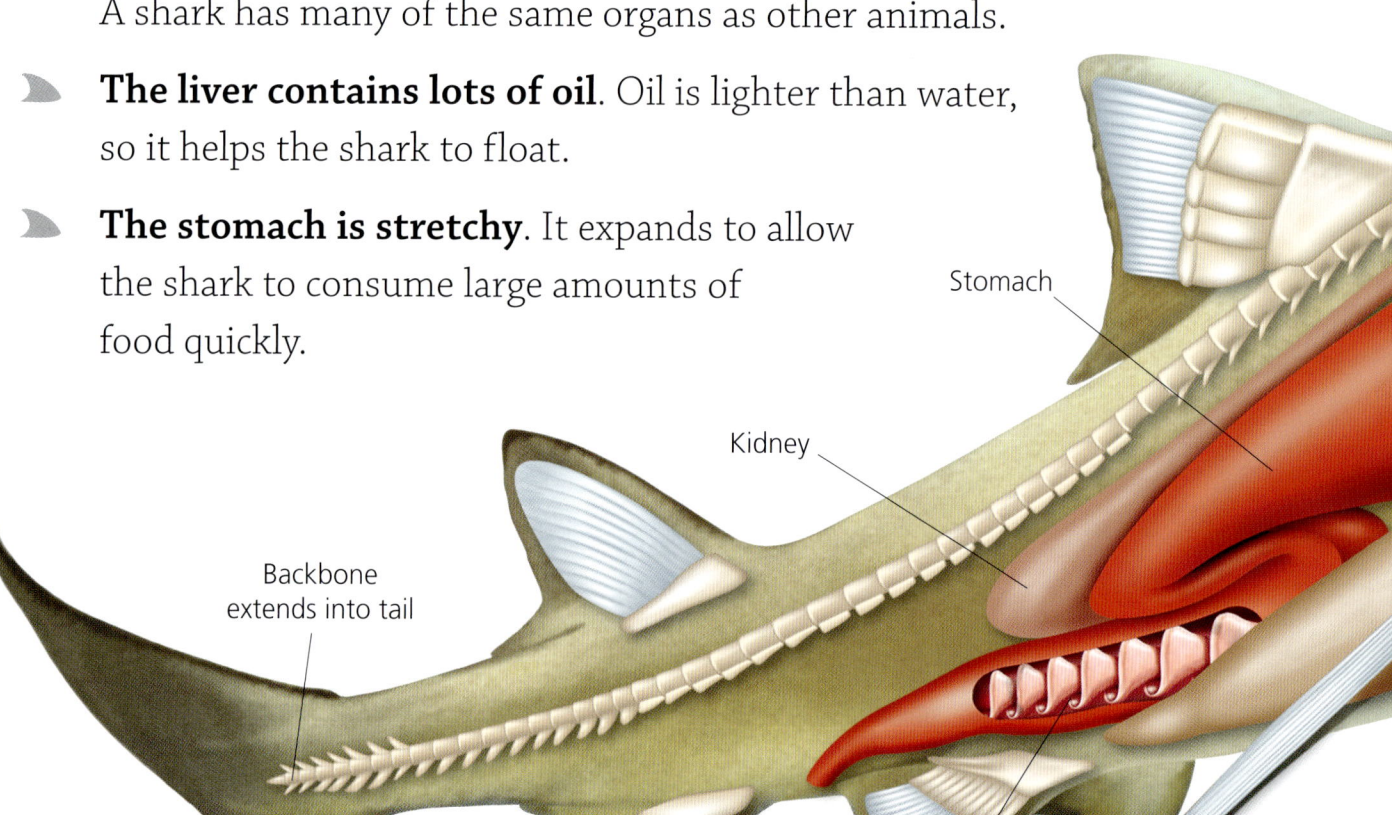

- **The liver contains lots of oil**. Oil is lighter than water, so it helps the shark to float.

- **The stomach is stretchy**. It expands to allow the shark to consume large amounts of food quickly.

Stomach

Kidney

Backbone extends into tail

Intestines have a spiral valve to help absorb food

How sharks work

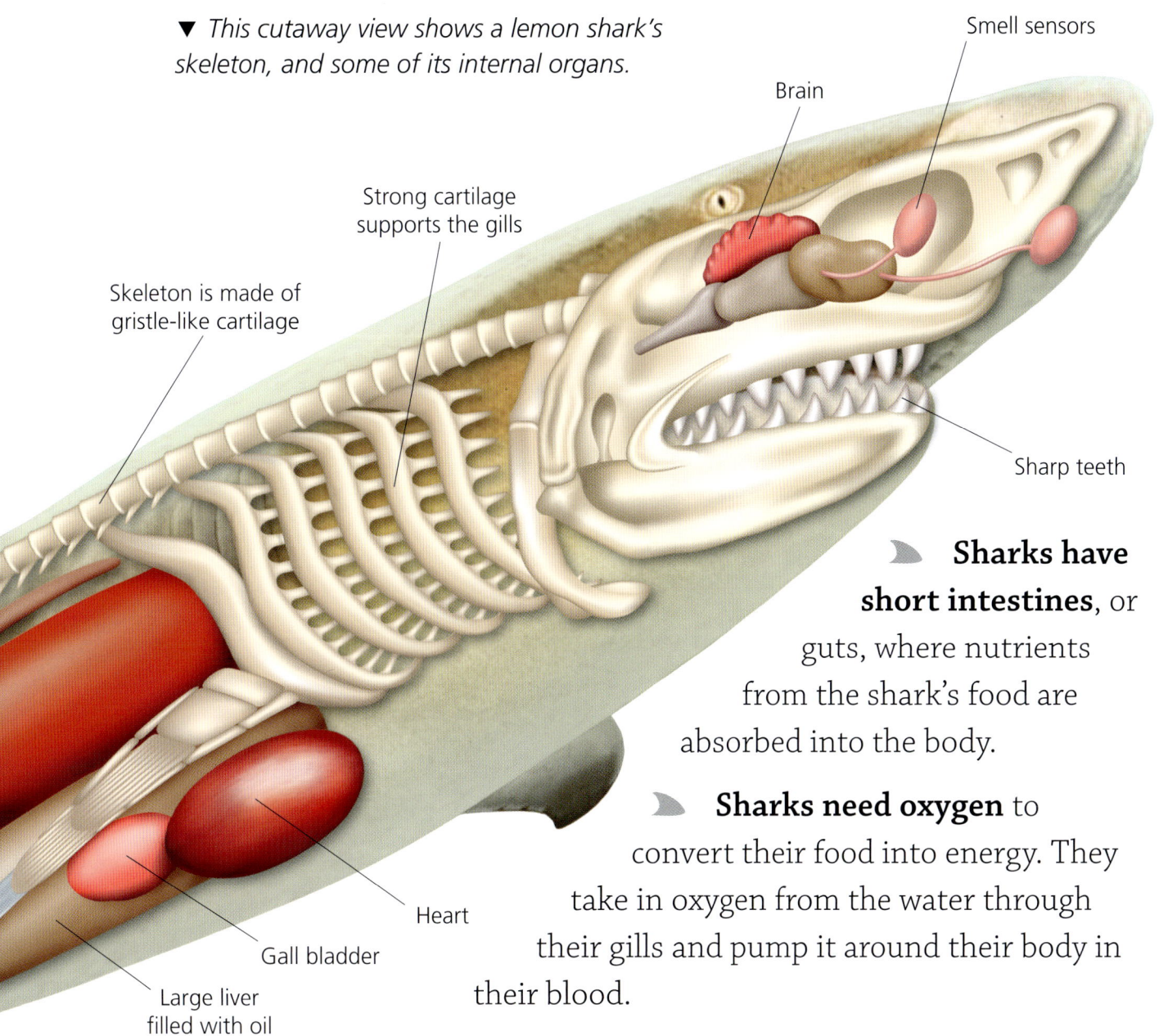

▼ *This cutaway view shows a lemon shark's skeleton, and some of its internal organs.*

Smell sensors
Brain
Strong cartilage supports the gills
Skeleton is made of gristle-like cartilage
Sharp teeth
Heart
Gall bladder
Large liver filled with oil

▶ **Sharks have short intestines**, or guts, where nutrients from the shark's food are absorbed into the body.

▶ **Sharks need oxygen** to convert their food into energy. They take in oxygen from the water through their gills and pump it around their body in their blood.

▶ **Most sharks are cold-blooded**, which means their blood is the same temperature as the water around them.

▶ **A few species**, such as great white, salmon shark and mako shark, are warm-blooded – they can heat their blood to be warmer than their surroundings. This helps them to swim faster and allows them to move into cooler water to hunt.

51

52

How sharks work

◀ A scary view inside the mouth of a tiger shark, showing the arches of cartilage that support the gills. Large teeth with sharp, serrated edges line the jaws.

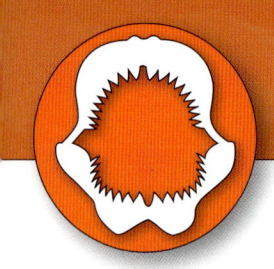

Flexible skeleton

- **Cartilage is the substance** shark skeletons are made of. It is tough, rubbery, and usually white or pale blue in colour.

- **Most other fish have bones** instead of cartilage. They are called bony fish, while sharks, rays and skates are all known as cartilaginous fish.

- **Sharks have simpler skeletons** than bony fish. For instance, a shark's skull is made of only ten pieces of cartilage, whereas a bony fish has over 60 bones in its skull.

- **Cartilage is lighter than bone**, so sharks' bodies are strong and lightweight.

- **Because cartilage is flexible**, sharks can twist and turn easily in the water.

- **Human skeletons** are mostly made of bone, but some parts are cartilage, such as the flexible tip of your nose.

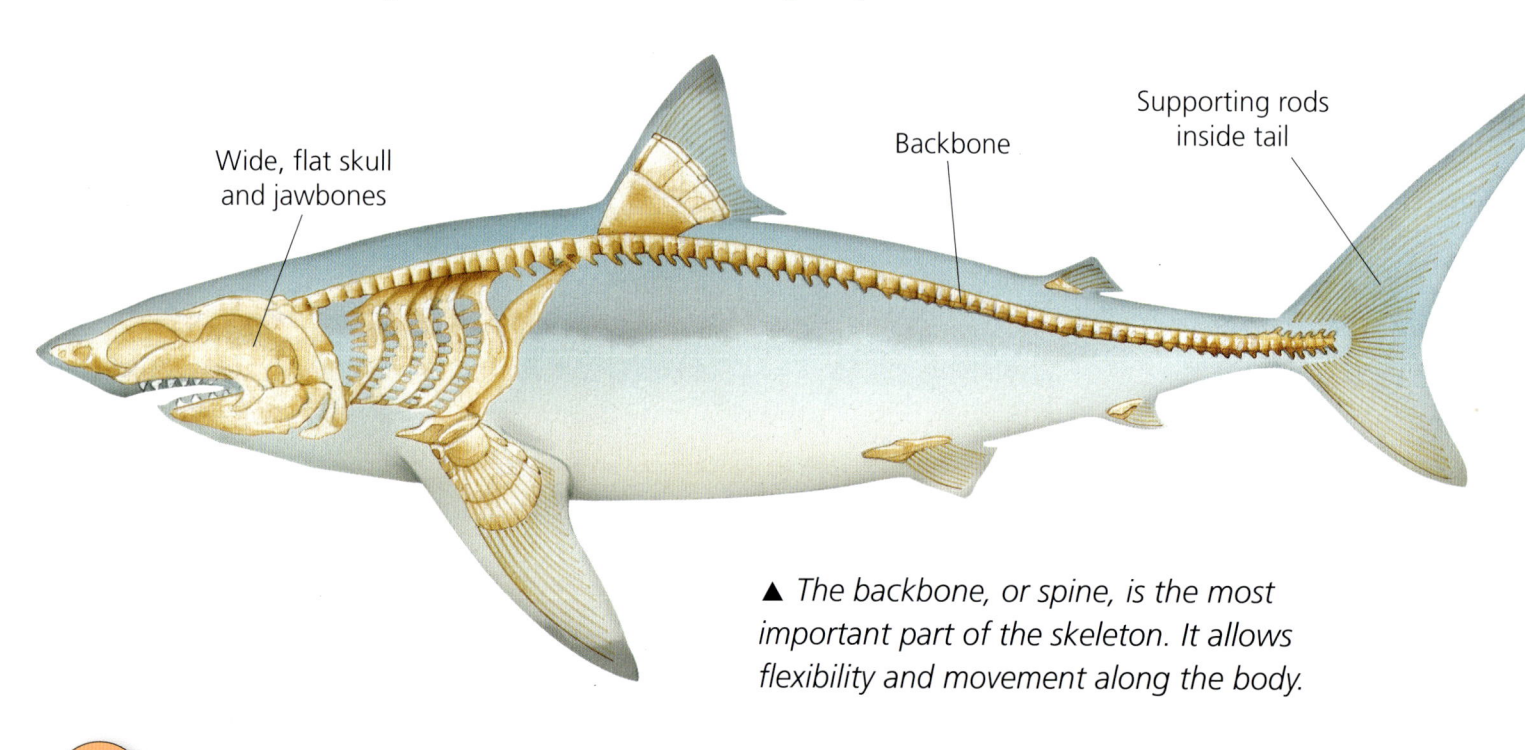

Wide, flat skull and jawbones

Backbone

Supporting rods inside tail

▲ *The backbone, or spine, is the most important part of the skeleton. It allows flexibility and movement along the body.*

How sharks work

- **The spine and skull** are harder than the rest of the skeleton. They need to be stronger to support the shark's body and protect its brain.

- **Shark fins and tails** contain hundreds of stiff, thin rods of cartilage, which give them their shape.

- **The cartilage in a shark's skeleton** keeps growing throughout its life.

- **A shark's delicate gills** are supported by arches of cartilage. The jaws probably developed from the first gill arch and are not attached to the shark's skull.

- **A shark's spine** is made up of a string of hourglass-shaped vertebrae under an arch that protects the spinal cord.

▲ Inside the hammer-shaped head of this great hammerhead shark is a wide, flattened skull made of cartilage.

DID YOU KNOW?
Some shark species are so flexible, they can bend right around and touch their tails with their snouts.

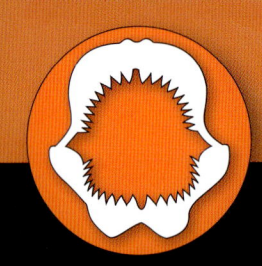

Teeth and jaws

- **A hunting species**, such as the great white or the tiger shark, has several rows of teeth.

- **A shark's gums** are like a conveyor belt. The rows of teeth constantly move slowly forwards. Gradually the front row wears out and a new row replaces them.

- **Only the two front rows of teeth** are used for biting. The rest are lining up to replace them.

- **In a lifetime**, some sharks will get through 30,000 teeth.

▼ *Port Jackson sharks have small, sharp, pointed teeth at the front of their jaws and large flattened teeth at the back, for crushing sea urchins, starfish and shellfish.*

How sharks work

▶ The tiger shark has large, saw-edged, hooked teeth in both jaws. It has a varied diet, from fish, sea snakes, sea turtles and seabirds, to jellyfish, rotting meat and rubbish.

- **You can sometimes find** shark teeth washed up on beaches.

- **A shark's teeth are as sharp as razors**. Each tooth has serrated edges with tiny, sharp points, like a saw. This allows them to cut through meat easily.

- **The biggest teeth** belong to the great white shark. Its teeth can grow to more than 6 cm in length.

- **Some species**, such as smooth-hound sharks, don't have sharp biting teeth. Instead they have hard, flat plates in their mouths for grinding up crabs and shellfish.

- **The outside of a shark's teeth** is made up of fluoride – an ingredient in most toothpastes as it prevents tooth decay. This means that sharks don't get holes in their teeth.

- **A shark's jaws are loosely attached** to its skull. They can sometimes slide forwards to allow the shark to open its mouth very wide and take big bites out of its prey.

DID YOU KNOW?
The horn shark has a blunt snout and huge nostrils, like a pig. One of its nicknames is 'pig fish'.

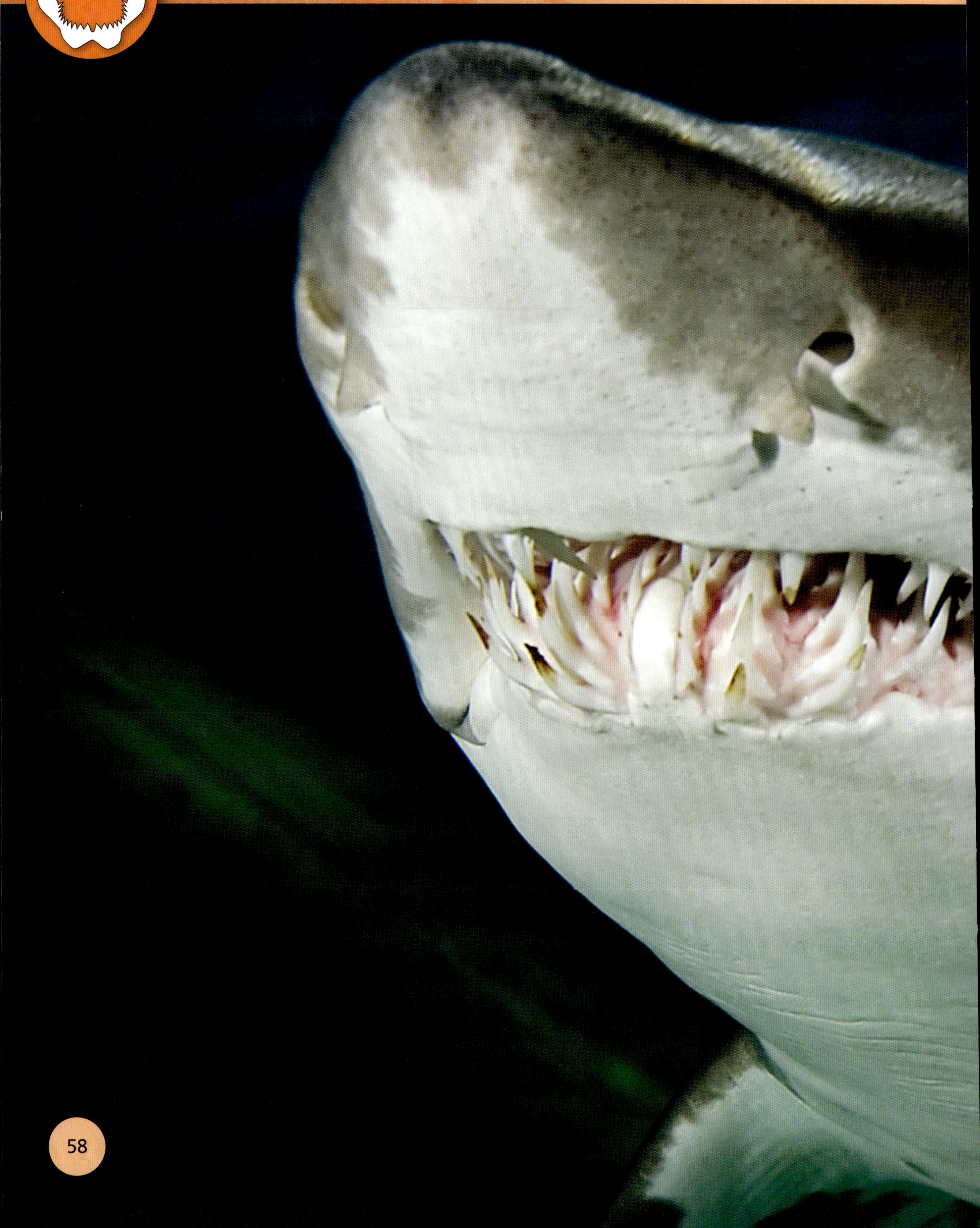

How sharks work

◀ The sand tiger shark has up to 100 slender, pointed teeth in its mouth. It is also called the raggedtooth shark, because the teeth are jumbled and criss-crossing.

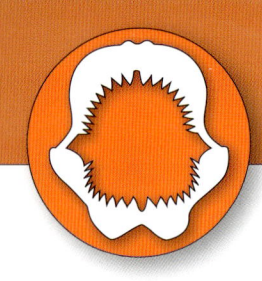

Breathing underwater

- **Like all animals**, sharks need to take in oxygen to survive. They breathe by taking in oxygen from the water through the gills in their throats.

- **Most sharks have five pairs of gills**. Each gill is made up of a set of hair-like filaments full of blood vessels.

- **Each filament is further divided** into tiny, leaf-like branches, called lamellae. This makes a big surface area for absorbing as much oxygen as possible.

- **A few primitive sharks**, such as frilled sharks and cow sharks, have six or seven pairs of gills.

▼ When a tawny nurse shark rests on the sea bed, it lifts the floor of its muscular mouth to pump water over its gills. This means it can keep breathing, even though it is not moving.

How sharks work

▼ A shark's gills are made of fine blood vessels. They have extremely thin walls to allow oxygen to pass quickly from the water to the blood.

Cartilaginous arches support the gills

Heart

Blood vessels

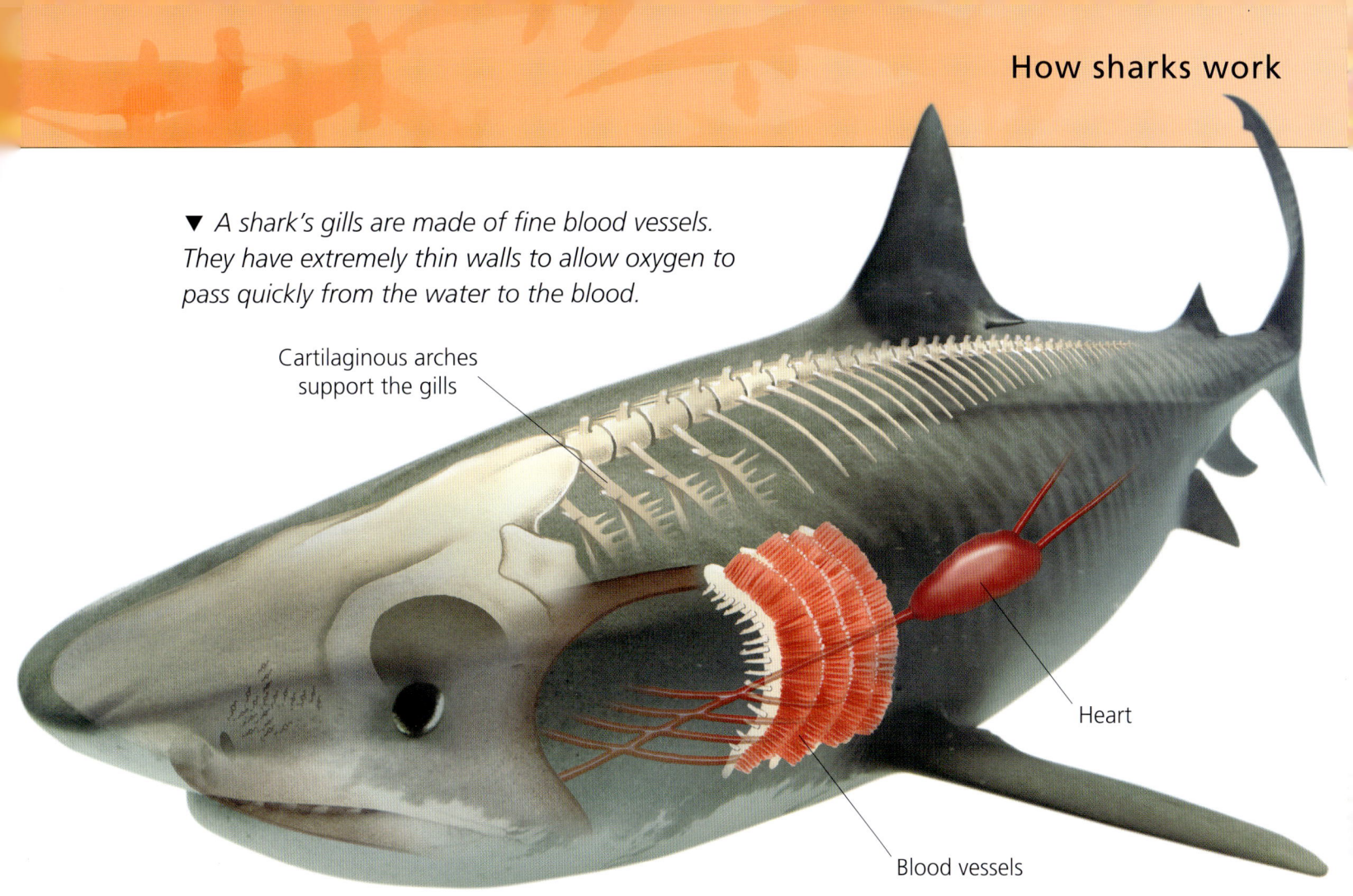

- **Many shark species have extra breathing holes** called spiracles just behind their eyes, which also take in oxygen from the water.

- **As a shark swims**, water flows into its spiracles or mouth and past the gills, where oxygen is absorbed from the water and into the bloodstream.

- **The water flows out again** through the gill slits – the lines on the sides of a shark's neck.

- **Some fast species**, such as the mako shark, have to swim continuously so that water keeps flowing over their gills. If they stop swimming they suffocate.

- **Slow-moving species**, such as the Port Jackson shark, are able to pump water across their gills using the muscles in their mouth and neck, so they can stop for a rest and still keep breathing.

- **Some sharks**, such as the basking shark and the whale shark, use their giant gills to catch food as well as to breathe.

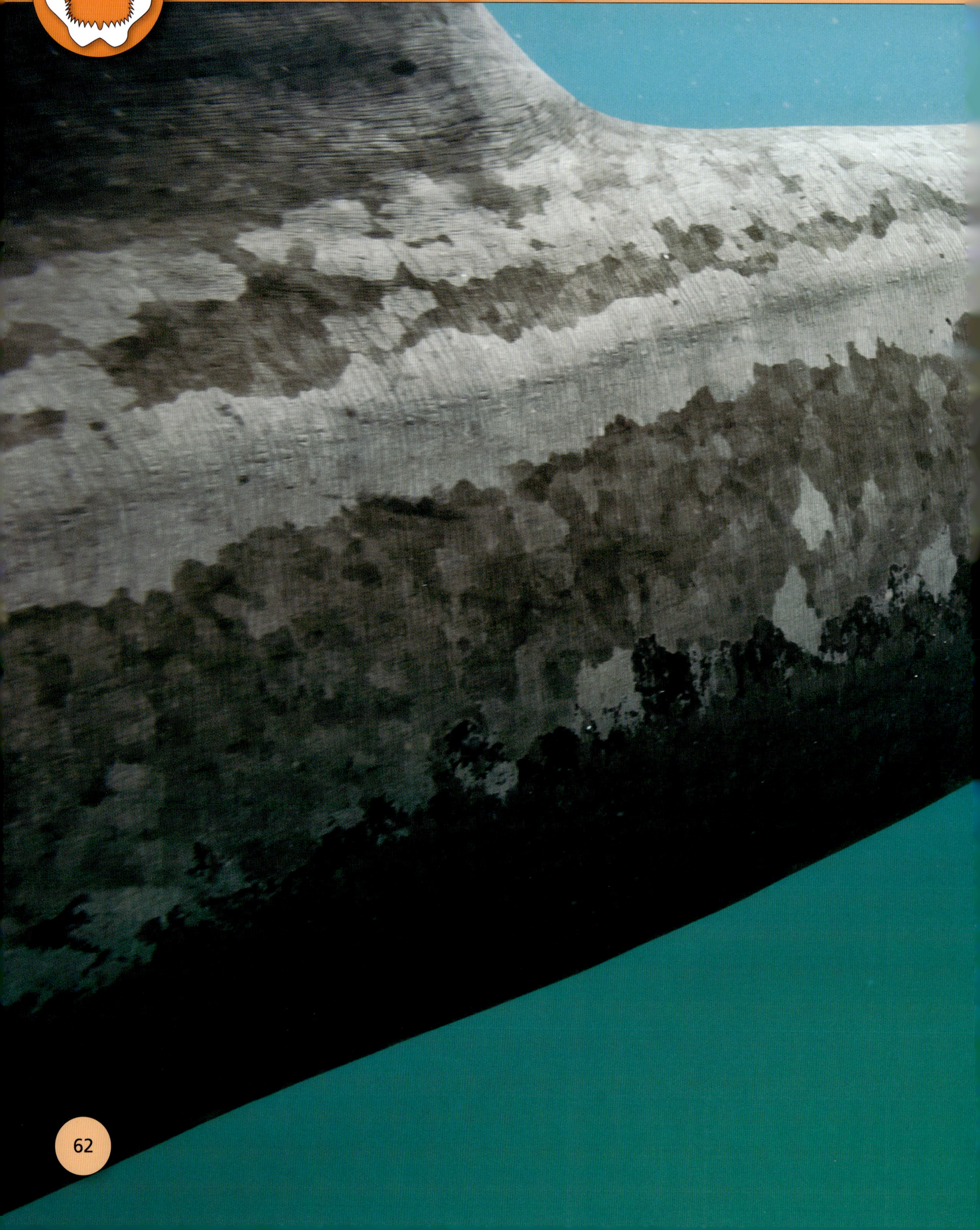

How sharks work

▲ The dark bristles, called gill rakers, inside the huge gill slits of a basking shark filter plankton from the water. The old gill rakers fall off in the winter and new ones grow in the spring.

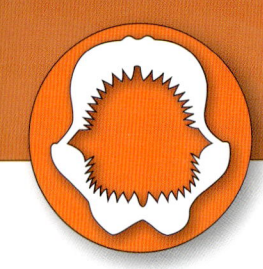

Heart and blood

- **A shark's heart pumps blood** around its body, delivering oxygen and food nutrients and taking away waste.

- **Blood goes from the heart** to the shark's gills to pick up oxygen, and then travels around the body before returning to the heart.

- **The heart** is just behind the shark's lower jaw.

- **It is made of a thick blood vessel** folded back on itself and divided into four chambers.

- **One-way valves** in each chamber keep the blood flowing in the same direction and prevent it from flowing backwards.

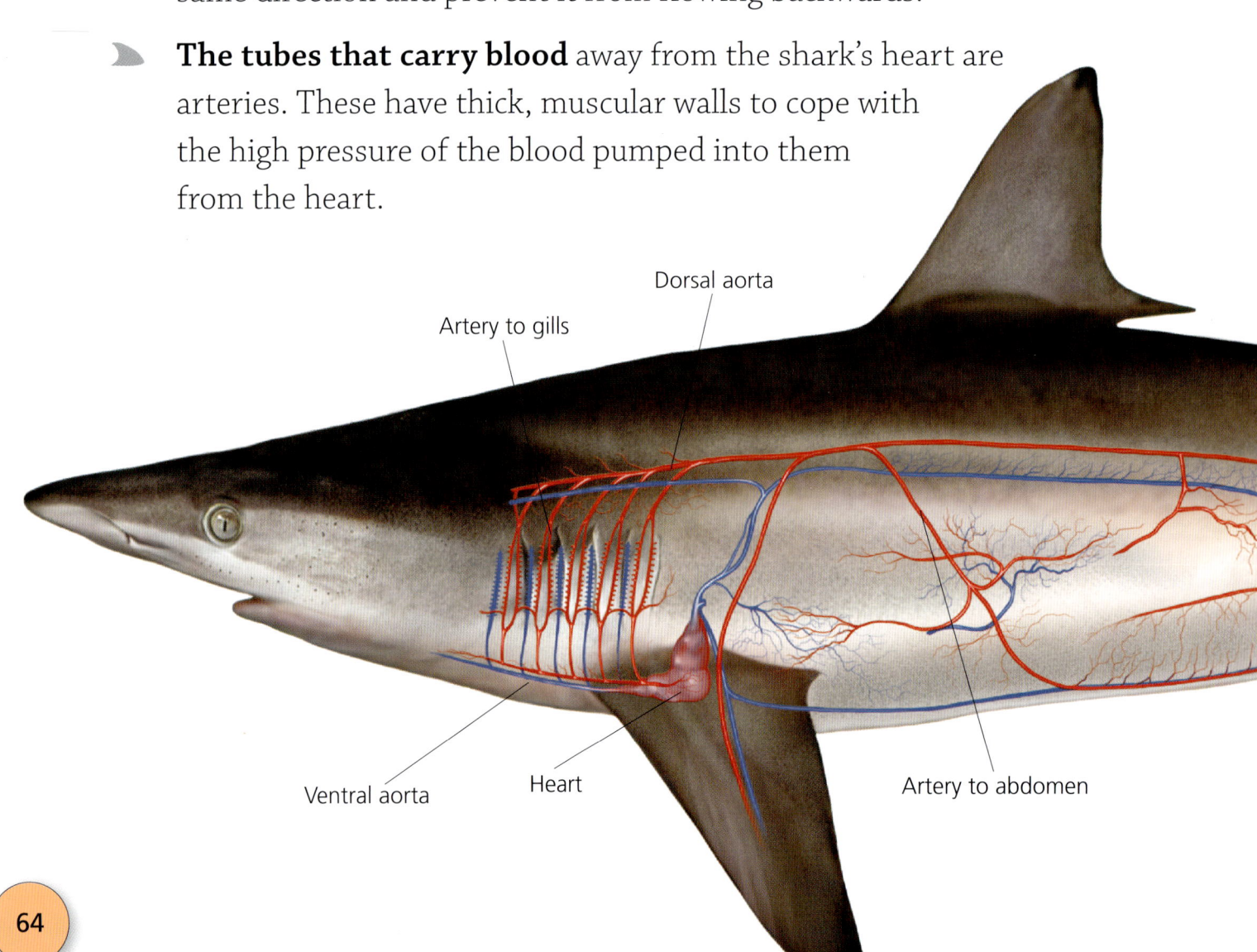

- **The tubes that carry blood** away from the shark's heart are arteries. These have thick, muscular walls to cope with the high pressure of the blood pumped into them from the heart.

Dorsal aorta
Artery to gills
Ventral aorta
Heart
Artery to abdomen

How sharks work

> **The tubes that carry blood** back to the shark's heart are veins. Vein walls are thin and floppy since the blood is at a low pressure.

> **When the heart relaxes between beats**, it sucks blood in from the veins to refill the heart.

> **Some sharks**, such as the great white, mako shark and salmon shark, have a network of veins and arteries that work like a radiator to collect the heat in the blood and send it back into the body.

> **These sharks keep their body warmer** than the surrounding water. Most sharks, however, cannot control their body heat and are a similar temperature to the water around them.

DID YOU KNOW?
A salmon shark's core body temperature can be over 20°C warmer than the surrounding water.

Artery to tail
Vein from tail

▲ *Cutaway view of part of a silky shark's blood system, including the many blood vessels around the gills.*

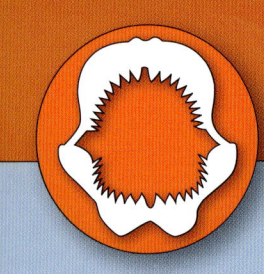

Muscles for moving

- **A shark's body is packed with muscle** – about twice as much muscle as the human body.

- **These muscles are arranged** in tight, overlapping bands that form a zigzag pattern under the shark's skin.

- **Sharks have three main types of muscle**: skeletal muscle that moves the skeleton, muscle that moves blood, food and waste through the shark's insides, and cardiac muscle that makes the heart work.

- **The cardiac muscle** works automatically all the time, throughout the whole of a shark's life.

- **Sharks have two types of muscle** for moving their skeleton – red muscle and white muscle.

DID YOU KNOW?
About 85 percent of a shark's body weight is made up of its muscles.

How sharks work

- **Over 90 percent is white muscle**, which is used for making short, rapid bursts of speed.

- **About 10 percent is red muscle**, which has a good blood supply and can work for long periods without getting tired.

- **White muscle works faster** than red muscle but gets tired quickly, so it has to stop working while it recovers.

- **Two giant bands of skeletal muscle** run along the length of a shark's body, on either side of the spine.

- **These muscles alternately shorten and lengthen** to make the shark's tail bend from side to side.

▼ *A great white shark has such powerful muscles that it sometimes leaps right out of the water when catching its prey. This is called breaching.*

68

How sharks work

▼ When great white sharks leap clear of the water, they often cartwheel through the air. Sometimes they grab their prey, such as this seal, in their powerful jaws. At other times, the prey escapes and then the chase is on.

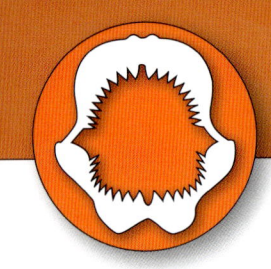

Digesting food

- **A shark's digestive system** consists of a long tube, with the mouth at one end and an exit hole, called the cloaca, at the other.

- **The cloaca is located** between a shark's pelvic fins, near its tail.

- **Digesting a meal** takes a long time in most sharks. Sandbar sharks and blue sharks take about three days to digest a meal.

- **Warm-blooded sharks**, such as the great white and mako shark, digest a meal more quickly, in about one or two days. Their warm bodies speed up the digestive process.

- **The process of digestion** begins in a shark's stomach, where strong acids and juices break the food down into a soupy paste.

- **Sharks may cough up inedible items**. Many sharks, such as lemon, mako and tiger sharks, can even turn their stomach inside out and push it out of their mouths to rinse out unwanted contents.

Cloaca

How sharks work

> **DID YOU KNOW?**
> Some sharks have spiral-shaped droppings because of the shape of the valves inside their intestines, or guts.

- **A shark can shoot its stomach** out of its mouth and swallow it back inside its body again in just a few seconds.

- **Inside a shark's short gut** is a special valve structure, which slows down the movement of food. This gives more time for food to be digested efficiently and allows more nutrients to be absorbed.

- **There are three main valve shapes**: a spiral valve (catsharks), a ring valve with many thin plates (great white), and a scroll valve, like a loose scroll of paper (lemon and hammerhead sharks).

- **Many parasites**, such as tapeworms, live hidden away in the twists and turns of the valve in a shark's intestines. Each parasite is specialized to feed on that particular stage of the digested food.

▲ Cutaway view of silky shark's digestive system, showing the spiral valve inside its intestine.

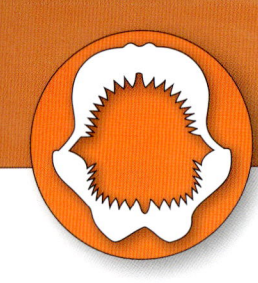

Eyes and vision

- **Most sharks have big eyes**, good eyesight and can see in colour.

- **Sharks need to be able to see well** in the dark as there is limited light underwater.

- **Some species have a special eyelid** called the nictitating membrane. This closes over the eye when the shark is about to bite, to protect it from damage.

- **White sharks and whale sharks** don't have nictitating membranes. Instead, they swivel their eyes back into their eye sockets to protect them. This means they can't see their prey as they bite.

- **Many sharks have a layer of shiny plates** called the *tapetum lucidum* (Latin for 'bright carpet') at the back of their eyes. It collects and reflects light, helping them to see, even in the gloomy darkness.

▼ *A tiger shark draws its nictitating membrane over its eye. The membrane can cover the eye completely.*

Nictitating membrane

How sharks work

Slit-shaped pupil

▲ *Some species, such as blacktip reef sharks, have cat-like, slit-shaped pupils.*

- **The *tapetum lucidum*** makes shark eyes appear to glow in the dark.

- **Deepwater and nocturnal sharks** have huge, glowing, green eyes to capture as much light as possible in the darkness.

- **Some sharks have a third eye**, called a pineal eye, under the skin in their foreheads. It can't see as well as a normal eye, but it can sense daylight.

- **The shy-eye shark gets its name** because when it is caught, it covers its eyes with its tail to shield them from the light.

- **River sharks** have very tiny eyes because they live in muddy water, where it is hard to see. They rely on their other senses to find their way and locate food.

74

How sharks work

◀ A close-up of the huge eye of the great lanternshark. This shark lives in the darkness of the deep ocean at depths of up to 4500 m.

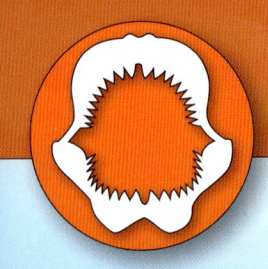

Sensing smells

- **As a shark swims**, water constantly flows into the nostrils on its snout. It then travels over the scent-detecting cells inside the nostrils. A shark uses its nostrils purely for detecting scents in the water.

- **About two thirds of a shark's brain** processes all the information about smells in its surrounding environment.

- **Sharks can smell blood in water**, even if it's diluted to one part in ten million. That's like one pinhead-sized drop of blood in a bathtub of water.

- **Swimmers have been known** to attract sharks just by having a tiny scratch on their skin.

- **Sharks use their sense of smell** to detect prey, but probably also to detect mates and to help them find their way on long migration journeys.

- **Some sharks** can detect smells in the air. Oceanic whitetip sharks sometimes point their noses up through the water's surface to see if there is any smelly food nearby, such as a rotting whale carcass.

How sharks work

- **The biggest parts of a shark's brain** are the olfactory lobes – the area used for processing smells.

- **The great white has the biggest** olfactory lobes of all sharks, which means it probably has the best sense of smell.

- **A shark homes in on a scent** by zigzagging its snout from side to side and then moving towards the side where the smell is strongest.

- **The sense of smell** is the most important sense for many sharks.

◀ The nostrils of hammerhead sharks are at the tips of their 'hammers', so they smell in stereo, which helps these sharks to track down the source of a smell.

DID YOU KNOW?
Great white sharks can smell tiny amounts of blood in water up to 5 km away!

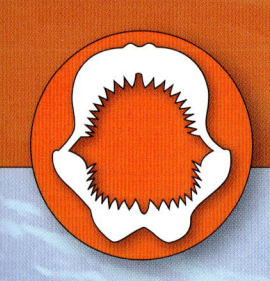

Hearing sounds

- **Sharks have ears**, but they're very hard to spot. The openings are tiny holes, just behind the eyes. People sometimes confuse the spiracles, which are used for breathing, for ears.

- **In the sea**, sound travels in the form of vibrations rippling through the water. Sharks hear by sensing these vibrations.

- **Inside the ear** is a set of looping, fluid-filled tubes called the labyrinth. Inside the labyrinth are microscopic hairs. Vibrations travel through the fluid, moving the hairs, which send signals to the shark's brain.

- **Sharks hear low sounds best**, such as the noise made by an injured animal underwater.

- **Sharks can detect these sounds** from more than 198 m away.

▼ Sharks can also detect the sounds of air bubbles coming from scuba-diving tanks, so this blue shark can hear the diver breathing!

How sharks work

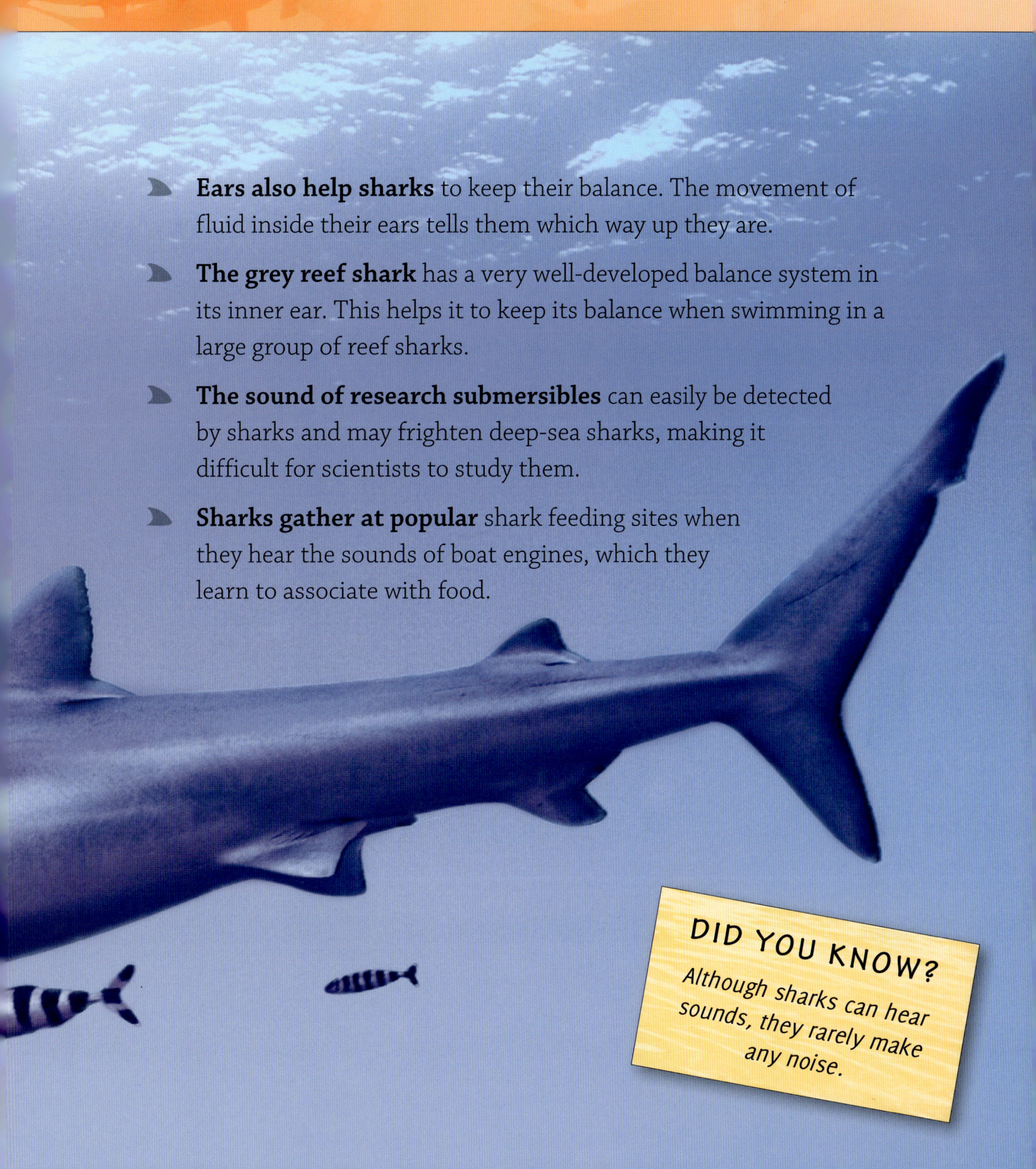

- **Ears also help sharks** to keep their balance. The movement of fluid inside their ears tells them which way up they are.

- **The grey reef shark** has a very well-developed balance system in its inner ear. This helps it to keep its balance when swimming in a large group of reef sharks.

- **The sound of research submersibles** can easily be detected by sharks and may frighten deep-sea sharks, making it difficult for scientists to study them.

- **Sharks gather at popular** shark feeding sites when they hear the sounds of boat engines, which they learn to associate with food.

DID YOU KNOW?
Although sharks can hear sounds, they rarely make any noise.

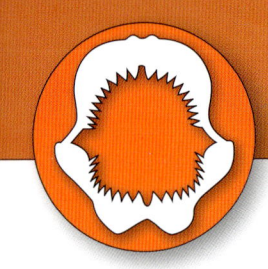

Touch and taste

- **Like us**, sharks can feel things that touch their skin. They have millions of nerve endings that can feel pressure, temperature and pain.

- **They also have an extra sense organ** called the lateral line. This is a long tube running down each side of a shark's body, under its skin. All fish, not just sharks, have lateral lines.

- **As a shark swims**, ripples in the water pass into the lateral line through tiny holes in the skin. Hairs inside the lateral line sense the ripples, and send signals to the brain.

- **The shark's brain interprets** the signals from its lateral line as possible prey, predators or other sharks.

- **The lateral line also helps a shark** to keep its balance and avoid bumping into objects in its surroundings.

- **As it is most effective for picking up vibrations** close to the shark's body, the lateral line helps sharks to find their way in murky or dark water, when their other senses are not much use.

DID YOU KNOW?
A shark's lateral line can pick up the movements of prey in the water from distances of 100 m or more.

Lateral line

How sharks work

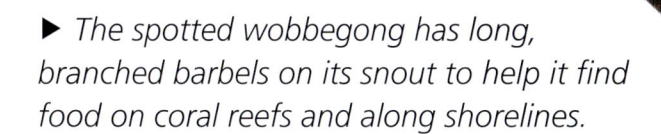

▶ The spotted wobbegong has long, branched barbels on its snout to help it find food on coral reefs and along shorelines.

- **Sharks taste the animals or objects** they bite with the tastebuds inside their mouths. They can also taste chemicals dissolved in the water. This helps them to find prey and avoid pollution.

- **Sharks use their sense of taste** to help them decide whether to swallow or spit out the object or piece of food. Great white sharks tend to spit out human flesh. They prefer the taste of fatty blubber from their usual prey, such as seals.

- **Some species have fleshy whiskers** on their snouts called barbels, which help them to sense the location of food on the sea bed.

- **Sharks with barbels** include nurse sharks, bamboo sharks, sawsharks and wobbegongs.

▲ The lateral line runs down the side of the entire length of a shark's body.

81

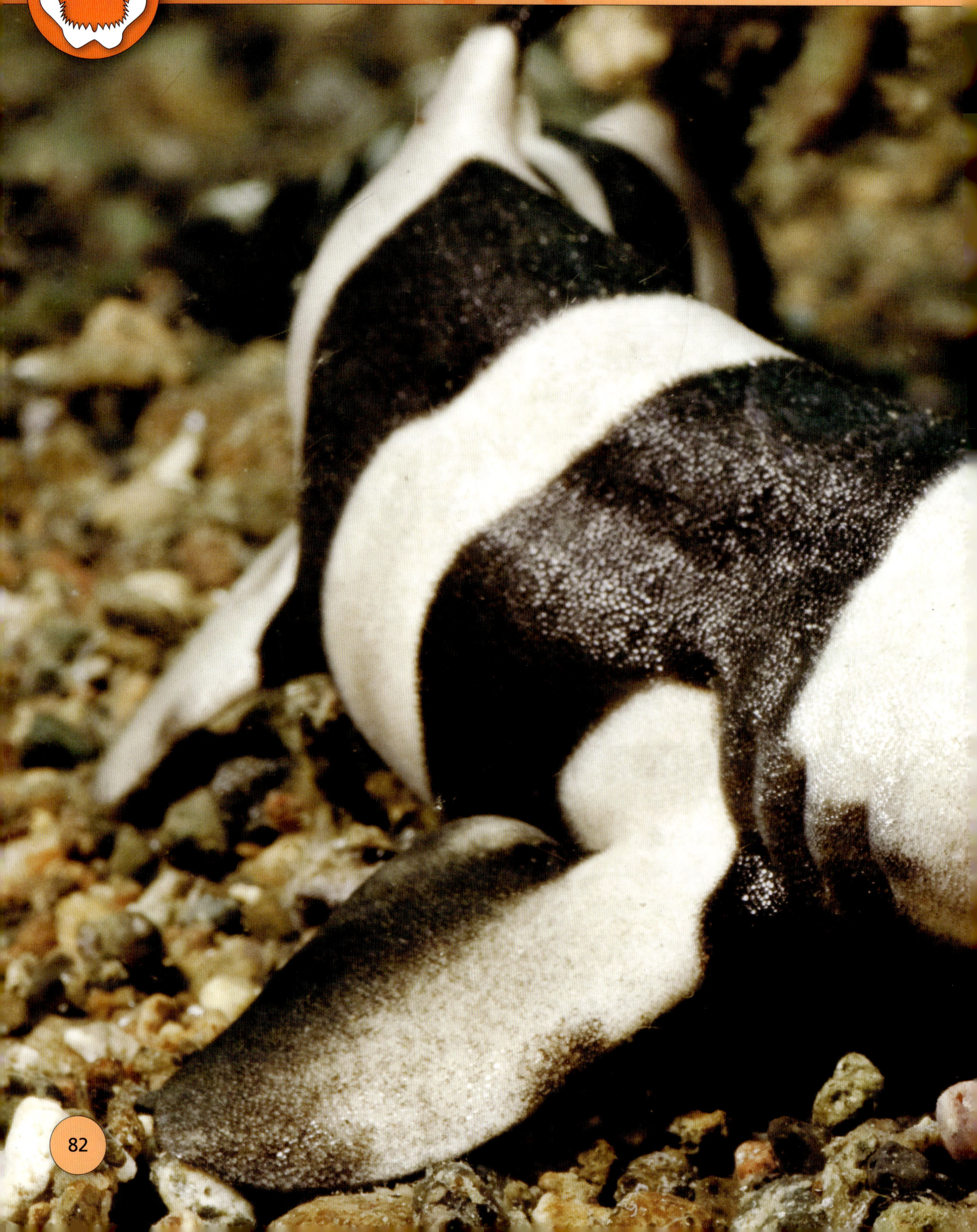

How sharks work

▼ A young brown-banded bamboo shark, showing the sensory barbels around its mouth. These sharks live on coral reefs and can survive out of water for up to half a day.

83

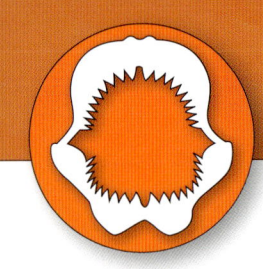

The sixth sense

- **A shark has six senses**. Besides vision, hearing, touch, taste and smell, it can sense the tiny amounts of electricity given off by other animals.

- **To detect electricity**, a shark has tiny holes in the skin around its head and snout. They are called the ampullae of Lorenzini.

- **The ampullae of Lorenzini** are named after Stefano Lorenzini (born *c.*1652). He was an Italian scientist who studied the anatomy of sharks.

- ***Ampullae* are a type of Roman bottle**. The ampullae of Lorenzini have a narrow-necked bottle shape.

- **Each ampulla contains a jelly-like** substance, which collects electrical signals.

▶ The dots on this tiger shark's snout are the ampullae of Lorenzini.

DID YOU KNOW?
Some other animals, such as the duck-billed platypus, can detect electricity too.

How sharks work

- **All animals give off tiny amounts** of electricity when their muscles move. Electricity doesn't travel well through air, but it does through water.

- **The ampullae of Lorenzini** can sense animals within a range of about one metre.

- **Some sharks use their electrical sense** to find prey that is buried in the sea bed.

- **A fierce hunting species**, such as the tiger shark, has up to 1500 ampullae of Lorenzini.

- **Slow-moving sharks** that live on the sea bed have only a few hundred ampullae of Lorenzini.

- **Sharks sometimes bite on** sea bed cables because these objects produce electric signals.

▼ Sharks, such as this great white, are sometimes attracted to the metal cages protecting underwater photographers because the metal gives off electricity.

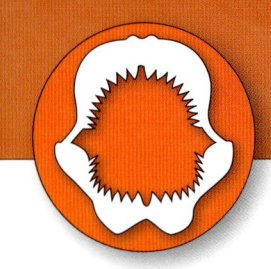

Smart sharks

- **Most shark species** have big brains for their body size and are probably smarter than many bony fish.

- **Almost all of the brain** is used for processing information from the senses. The parts used for learning and thinking are small.

- **In relation to their body size**, hammerhead sharks have the biggest brains.

- **Scalloped hammerheads** are one of the smartest sharks. They are fast, fierce hunters.

- **Hammerheads spend time in groups** and scientists think they have simple social systems.

- **In captivity**, some sharks have learned to do simple tasks in exchange for rewards.

- **Captive lemon sharks have been taught** to ring bells, press targets, swim through mazes and recover rings in order to receive rewards of food.

- **Sharks are curious** and inquisitive animals. They are able to solve problems, as well as to learn and remember things. All these qualities are signs of intelligence.

- **Some species are brighter than others**. Fast hunters such as great whites are the most intelligent. Slow-moving bottom-feeders such as carpet sharks are less smart.

DID YOU KNOW?
Captive lemon sharks learn how to perform scientific tests 80 times faster than cats or rabbits.

How sharks work

▼ *A scientist releasing a young lemon shark during a study of how lemon sharks avoid predators in the wild. Studying the behaviour of young sharks helps scientists to understand more about how sharks learn to survive.*

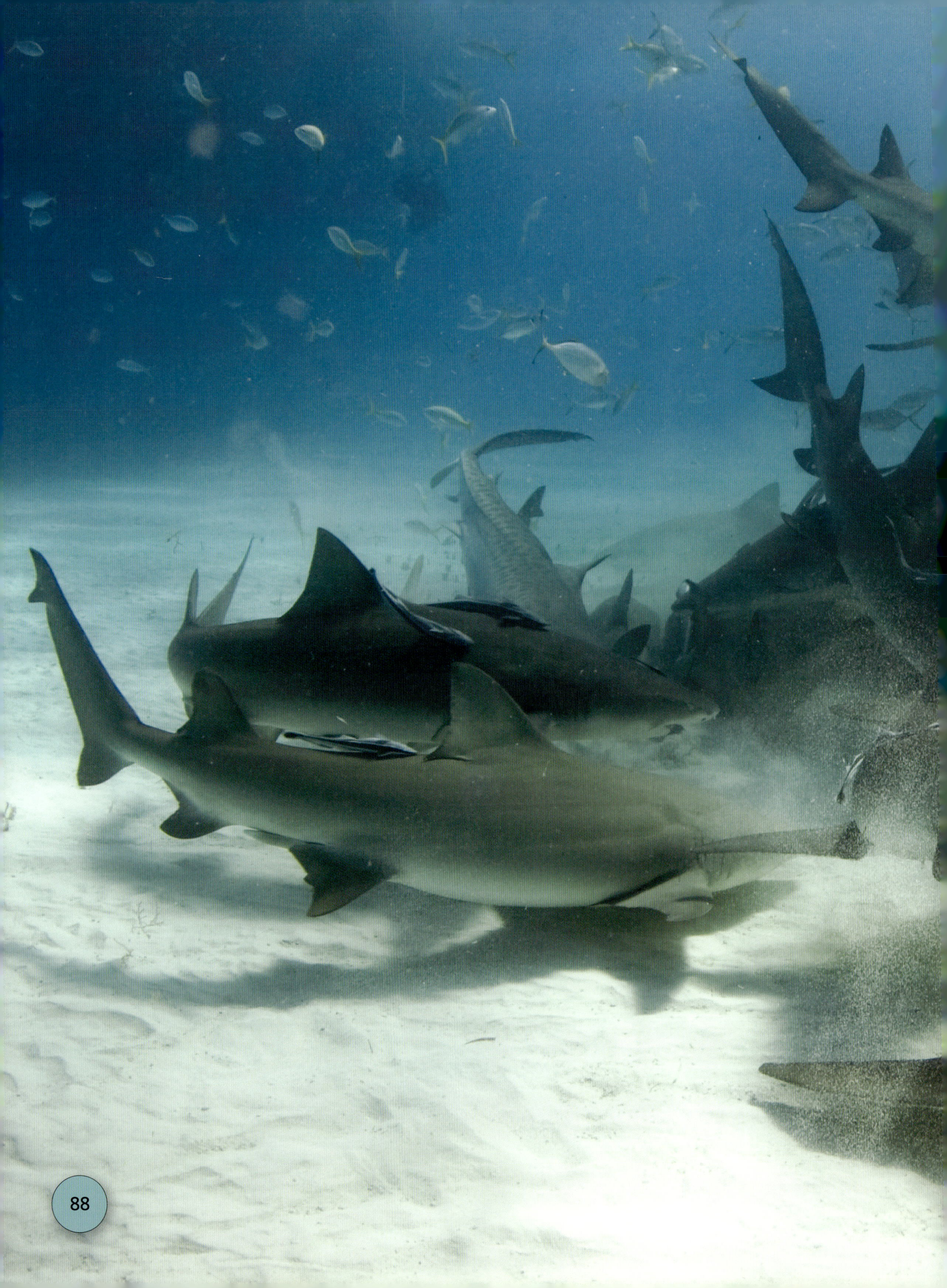

Life in the water

On the move

- **Most sharks don't have a fixed home.** They are constantly swimming, looking for food or a mate.

- **Sharks don't build nests**, dig burrows or make any other kind of shelter.

- **Some species appear to have** a territory, or special area of their own, that they patrol and guard.

Life in the water

- **Whitetip reef sharks** stay in the same area for several months, or even years, although they don't defend it like a true territory.

- **Some sharks**, such as horn sharks, pick a special nursery area in which to lay their eggs.

- **Underwater sea caves** are used by some species as a place to rest during the day.

- **Certain species of sharks** have preferences about where they live. The Galapagos shark is only found around groups of small, tropical oceanic islands.

- **Some sharks** have a daily routine, spending the day in deep waters, but moving to shallow waters near the shore to feed at night.

- **Blacktip reef sharks** seem to prefer their own space. As they swim up and down the edge of a coral reef, individuals will move their jaws or open their mouths to tell other blacktip reef sharks to keep their distance.

- **Some sharks need to keep moving** all the time in order to breathe. These sharks sleep with their eyes open, allowing parts of their brain to rest while they continue swimming.

◄ *Whitetip reef sharks rest during the day on the sea bed, and inside underwater caves or rock crevices. At night, they hunt for fish and octopuses among the coral.*

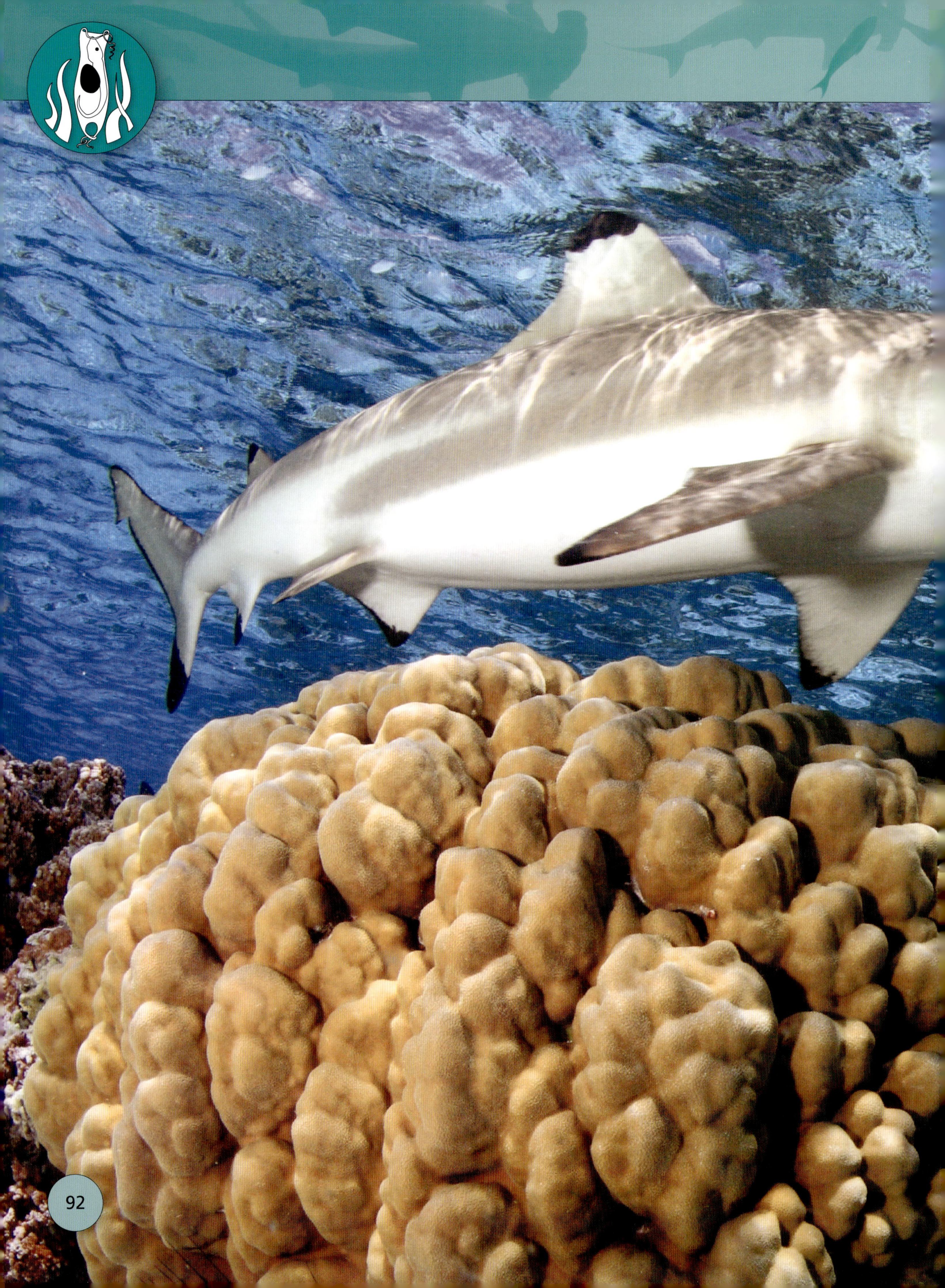

Life in the water

▲ A blacktip reef shark swimming in its usual habitat – very shallow water above a coral reef. This shark is a powerful swimmer and an athletic hunter of small fish and invertebrates.

Swimming skills

- **To propel itself through water**, a shark moves its tail from side to side.

- **The pectoral and pelvic fins** help sharks to steer and swim up and down.

- **Sharks normally swim** with a regular rhythm. They don't dart around like most bony fish do.

- **Many species swim** in a figure-of-eight pattern if they feel threatened.

- **Sharks swim silently** through the water and sneak up on prey.

- **Some types**, such as sand tiger sharks, swallow air to help them float better.

- **Some sharks are so flexible** they can bend their bodies into a horseshoe shape to completely change direction.

- **To slow down**, sharks change the angle of their pectoral fins and push against the water. The fins work rather like brakes.

- **A shark's oily liver helps** it to float, because oil is lighter than water. The basking shark's giant liver makes up about one quarter of its body weight and helps it to float at the surface of the sea, where it feeds.

Life in the water

▶ **Many sharks don't need to float** in the water because they spend a lot of time on the sea bed. Some bullhead sharks spend as much time using their fins to 'walk' on the sea bed as they do swimming.

▼ With its slim, streamlined body and long, wing-like pectoral fins, the blue shark is well suited to both cruising near the surface or diving to deeper waters.

DID YOU KNOW?
If sharks don't keep swimming, they gradually sink onto the sea bed.

Fast sharks

- **Large sharks swim at an average speed** of about 2.4 km/h, but the most active hunters can speed along much faster when they need to catch prey.

- **It is difficult for scientists** to measure the speed of sharks accurately in the wild because they don't swim in a straight line over a measured course, like a human swimmer.

- **The fastest shark** is the shortfin mako, which can reach speeds of over 50 km/h and possibly over 75 km/h.

- **The mako has a streamlined body** and a pointed snout to cut through the water easily, as well as powerful swimming muscles.

- **The mako needs to swim fast** to catch its speedy prey, such as swordfish and sailfish, which are two of the world's fastest fish.

- **The top speed of the great white shark** is at least 40 km/h, but it may swim as fast as 56 km/h in short bursts of speed.

- **The mako and the great white** are able to swim so fast because they are warm-blooded, which makes their muscles more efficient than most other sharks.

- **The blue shark** is like an underwater glider plane, with long front fins and a flat belly. It can reach speeds of up to 40 km/h, gliding down to the ocean depths and then swimming back to the surface again.

Life in the water

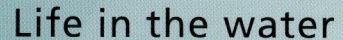

▲ The shortfin mako is the world's fastest, most active and most muscular shark. It is able to jump over 5 m above the water's surface and also makes very long journeys across oceans.

DID YOU KNOW?
The great white shark can swim seven times faster than the best Olympic swimmers!

▸ **Compared with a submarine**, a blue shark needs six times less driving power. This is partly due to its denticles, which reduce the drag of the water by as much as 8 percent.

98

Life in the water

▲ The skin of a blue shark is smooth to the touch, as it is covered with small overlapping denticles. Its smooth skin, together with its streamlined shape, helps it to move quickly.

Long-distance travel

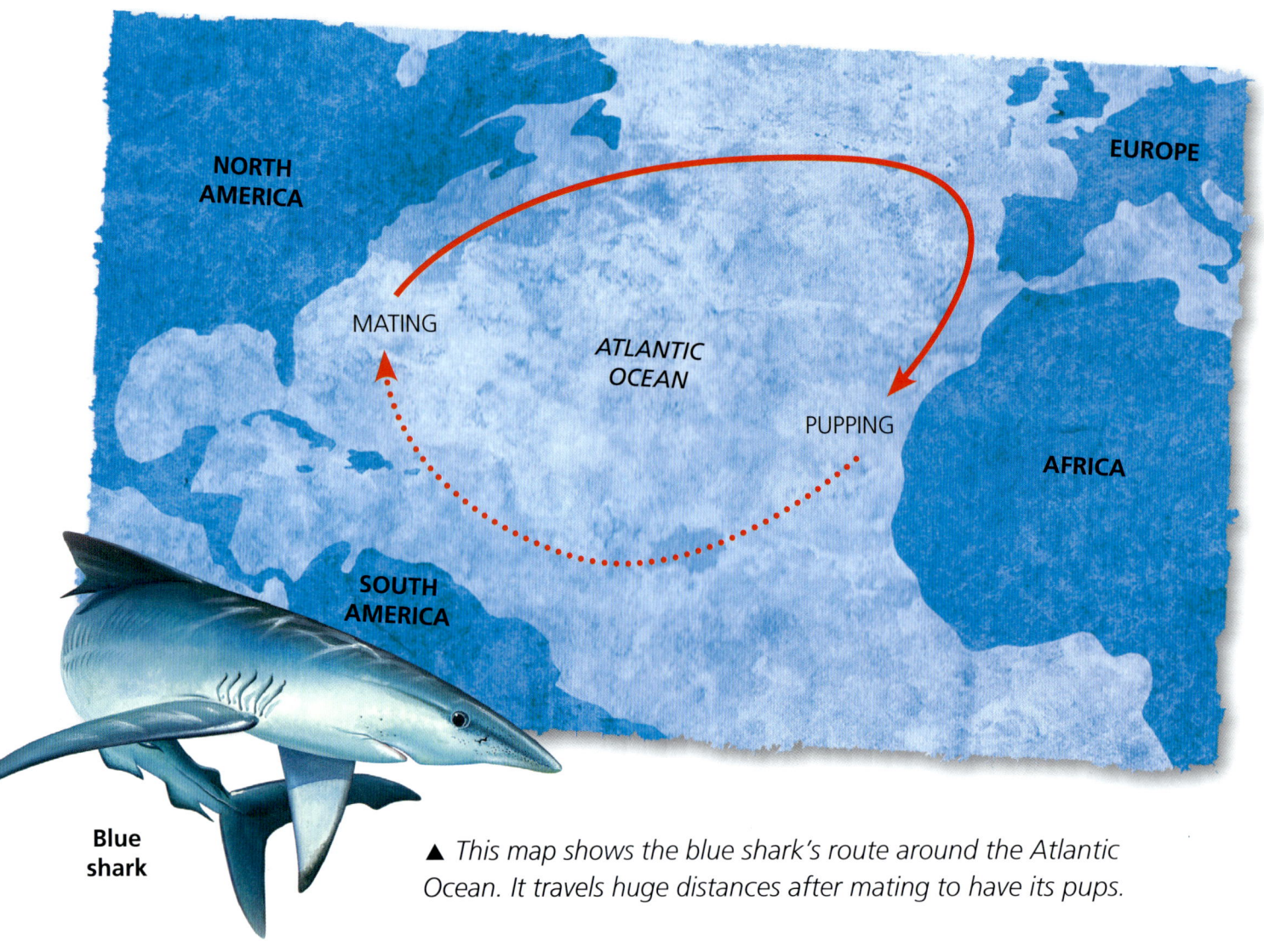

▲ *This map shows the blue shark's route around the Atlantic Ocean. It travels huge distances after mating to have its pups.*

▶ **Many shark species travel long distances** over the course of their lives. As all the seas and oceans are connected, it is easy for them to cover huge distances.

▶ **Dogfish sharks** that have been tagged and released back into the sea have been located more than 8000 km away from where they were first caught.

▶ **Migrating means moving around**, usually from season to season, according to a regular pattern.

Life in the water

- **The longest migrations** are made by blue sharks. They swim around the Atlantic Ocean in a huge circle and can cover more than 15,000 km in just one year.

- **Sharks sometimes mate** in one place, then swim far away to another area to lay their eggs or have their pups.

- **They also migrate to find food**, following shoals of fish as they move around the oceans.

- **Scientists think sharks** may use their ampullae of Lorenzini to detect the Earth's magnetic field, helping them to navigate and find their way over long distances.

- **Many species** spend the day in deep water, but swim up to the surface at night. This is called vertical migration.

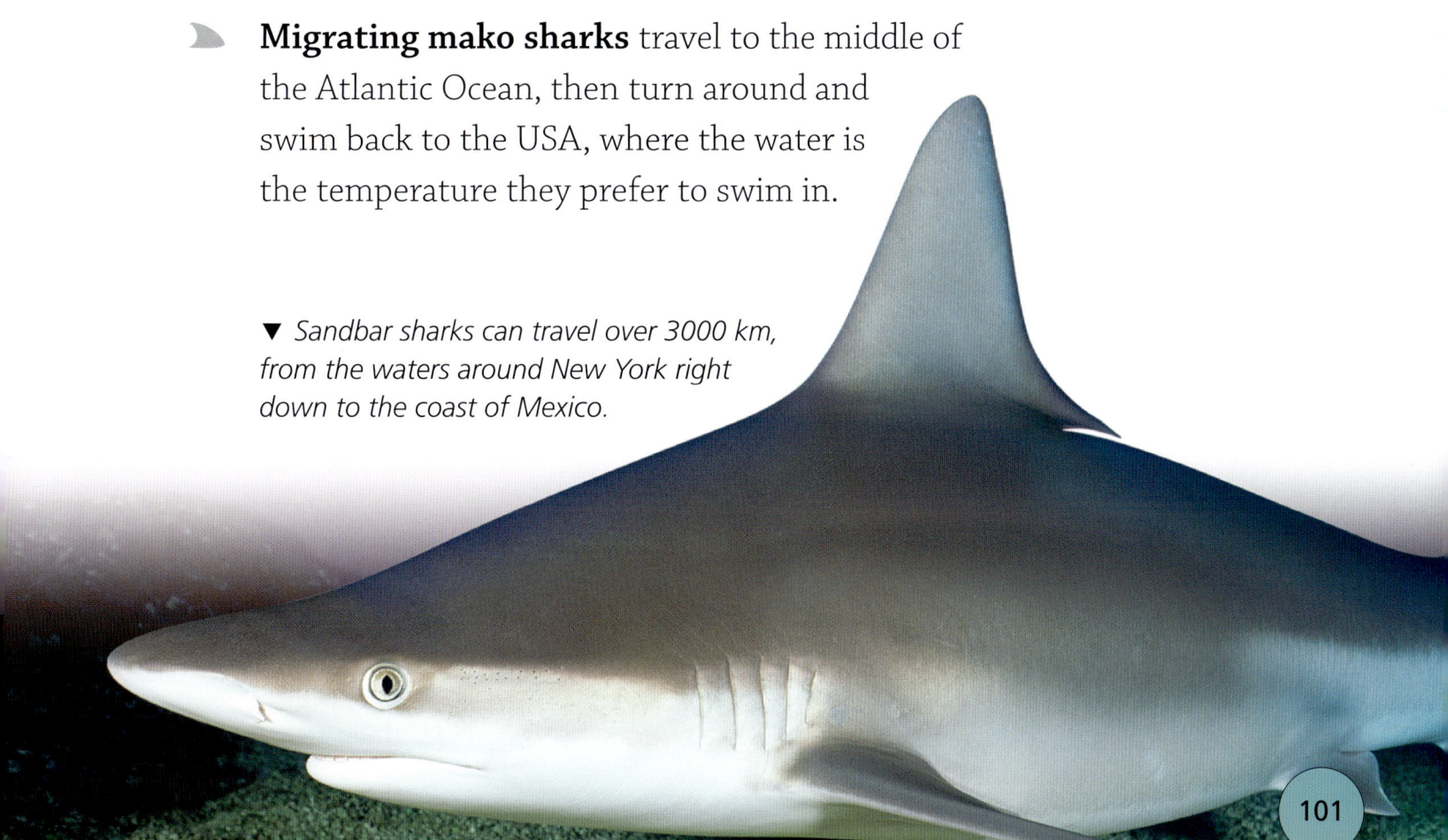

- **Migrating mako sharks** travel to the middle of the Atlantic Ocean, then turn around and swim back to the USA, where the water is the temperature they prefer to swim in.

▼ *Sandbar sharks can travel over 3000 km, from the waters around New York right down to the coast of Mexico.*

Food and feeding

- **Large, fast, hunting sharks**, such as great whites and bull sharks, feed on large fish (including other sharks), as well as seals, turtles, octopuses, squid, seabirds and other sea creatures.

- **Smaller sharks**, such as dogfish sharks, hunt smaller fish, octopuses and squid.

DID YOU KNOW?
In general, sharks prefer the taste of prey such as fish, seals and turtles to the taste of humans.

Life in the water

- **Slow-moving species**, such as nurse sharks, angelsharks and carpet sharks, crunch up crabs, shrimps and shellfish that they find on the sea bed.

- **Filter-feeders feed on plankton** – tiny floating animals and plants – which they filter from the water.

- **There are hardly any animal species** in the sea that aren't part of the diet of one shark species or another.

- **Tiger sharks** will eat anything they can find, even objects that aren't food, such as tin cans.

- **Most sharks don't eat every day**. Some large hunters can go without food for months.

- **Some sharks prefer to eat** just a few types of food. Giant hammerhead sharks like to eat stingrays and the sicklefin weasel shark prefers a diet of octopus.

- **Big sharks often feed** on smaller sharks. Sometimes, they are cannibals, eating sharks of their own species. Tiger sharks are cannibals.

- **A big shark can eat** more than half its own body weight in one meal.

◀ When small fish are in danger from sharks, they often cluster together in a tight sphere called a bait ball. These bronze whaler sharks have disturbed the cluster to make the fish easier to catch.

103

▶ Strangely, the biggest sharks eat the smallest food. A basking shark swims along with its massive mouth open, and tiny floating sea creatures are trapped on its gills, ready to be swallowed.

Life in the water

105

Going hunting

- **Most sharks are nocturnal** – they hunt at night – or crepuscular – they hunt at dusk.

- **Sharks use several senses** to track down and home in on prey. They locate it from a distance by smell, and use their electric sense, sight and hearing to close in on it. Sharks can also feel ripples in the water made by the movement of other animals.

- **Before attacking**, some sharks 'bump' their prey with their snouts, probably to see if it's edible.

- **When it is about to bite**, a shark raises its snout and thrusts its jaws forwards, so that its teeth stick out.

- **Some species shake their prey** from side to side to help rip it apart. Sharks don't usually chew – they tear their prey into chunks or just swallow it whole.

- **Sometimes lots of sharks are attracted** to a source of food, and they all rush to eat it at the same time. This is known as a feeding frenzy.

Life in the water

▼ *A school of lemon sharks stir up clouds of white sand as they compete for their share of food.*

DID YOU KNOW?
Sharks have very strong jaws. Some can bite other animals in half – even those with tough shells, such as turtles.

⬤ **Most hunters prefer prey** that's weak or helpless because it's easier to catch. Sharks are good at smelling blood – it tells them when an animal is injured.

⬤ **Many species give their prey** a fatal bite, then move away while it bleeds to death. They return later to feed on the body.

⬤ **A great white shark usually attacks** from behind or below so its prey does not see it coming. It moves so fast, it may leap right out of the water with its victim in its jaws.

⬤ **Cookie-cutter sharks** scoop out chunks of flesh from much larger living animals, such as whales or tuna fish.

Pack hunters

- **Some sharks work together** to catch prey. They catch more food by working as a team.

- **Tiny pygmy sharks** hunt together so they can catch and kill fish much bigger than themselves.

- **Blacktip reef sharks** co-operate to drive fish into shallow water and onto the beach. Then they wriggle onto the beach, grab the fish and slide back into the sea.

- **A group of sharks** will often herd fish into a tight ball by swimming towards them from different directions. The sharks then grab the fish from the outside of the ball.

- **Sharks that herd fish** like this include silky, dusky, bronze whaler, whitetip reef and sandtiger sharks.

- **Thresher sharks work in pairs**, using their long tails to push fish into swirling balls of bite-sized mouthfuls.

- **Two or three great white sharks** may sometimes hunt together and share each other's catches.

- **When many young seabirds** or seals enter the water for the first time, groups of sharks, such as tiger sharks, gather to eat as much as they can.

- **Whitetip reef sharks** hunt in groups on coral reefs, working together to find and capture prey.

▶ *Spiny dogfish sometimes gather in huge groups and swim along the sea bed, forcing prey to swim away. Any animal that cannot escape is eaten by the sharks.*

Life in the water

110

Life in the water

◀ Whitetip reef sharks swim fairly slowly, so they prefer to hunt at night. They use their keen senses of smell and hearing to find prey hiding in holes and caves on coral reefs.

Filter-feeding

- **The biggest shark species of all** – whale sharks, basking sharks and megamouths – eat plankton, which is the smallest prey. These sharks are called filter-feeders.

- **Plankton is made up of** small sea creatures such as shrimps, baby crabs and squid, little fish and tiny, free-floating plants. It drifts along with the currents.

- **Filter-feeding sharks** have gill rakers. These are comb-like bristles in their throats that sieve plankton out of the water.

- **Gill rakers are coated** in mucus to help plankton stick to them.

- **Filter-feeders swallow** the plankton they have collected, while water they have sieved escapes from their gills.

- **These sharks have massive mouths**, so they can suck in as much water as possible.

- **To collect a kilogram** of plankton, a shark has to filter one million litres of water.

- **In one hour**, a whale shark filters around 2 million litres of water, and collects 2 kg of food.

Life in the water

- **Whale sharks sometimes suck** in shoals of little fish, such as sardines, that are also busy feeding on plankton.

- **The blue whale**, the world's biggest animal, is also a filter-feeder.

▼ *Whale sharks open their big mouths wide to take in lots of water. Then they filter plankton from the water as it flows over their comb-like gills and back out of the body.*

Scavenging food

- **Scavenging means feeding** on other hunters' leftovers, or on animals that are dying or already dead.

- **Almost all sharks** will scavenge if they cannot find other food.

- **Some species**, such as the Greenland shark and the smooth dogfish, get a lot of their food by scavenging.

- **In deep water**, sharks often feed on dead sea creatures that sink down from higher levels.

- **Sharks scavenge human food** too, especially waste food that's thrown overboard from ships.

- **Sometimes sharks eat fish** caught in fishing nets before the nets are pulled to the surface.

- **Great whites also scavenge**, especially on the bodies of dead whales.

Life in the water

- **Scavenging is a kind of natural recycling.** It keeps the oceans clean, and makes sure leftovers and dead animals are rapidly removed rather than left to slowly decompose in the water.

- **The tiger shark** is famous for its scavenging habits and will eat almost any dead meat, from fish, squid and sea snakes to seals, dolphins and whales.

- **Tiger sharks** will also eat the carcasses of land animals, such as chickens, dogs, horses and cows that are washed into the sea.

▼ It can take up to 100 years for a whale carcass to be eaten by scavengers. More than 30,000 different types of animal feed and live off the carcass at different stages.

DID YOU KNOW?
Old, rotting meat is bad for humans to eat, but many wild animals such as sharks can eat it safely.

▼ Tiger sharks eat almost anything, from turtles, dolphins and squid to cans, bottles and other human rubbish. Their wide-ranging diet enables them to survive food shortages that would threaten the survival of other sharks.

Life in the water

Lighting up

▼ *Each species of lanternshark, such as this velvet belly, has its own distinct pattern of glowing photophores.*

- **Some shark species can glow in the dark**. When animals give off light, it is known as bioluminescence, meaning 'living light'.

- **Glowing sharks** are often found in the deepest, darkest oceans.

- **Some deep-sea glowing species**, such as the velvet belly shark, may use their lights to illuminate their surroundings and help them see prey.

- **Lanternsharks have glowing dots** around and inside their mouths, which may attract small fish and lure them in.

- **Some sharks that live** at medium depths have glowing undersides. This makes them hard to see from below, as their light bellies match the light coming down from the sea's surface.

Life in the water

- **The cookie-cutter shark** is one of the brightest of all the 'glow-in-the-dark' sharks. Most of its body is hidden from below by its glowing belly. However, its neck does not glow, making it appear like a tiny fish and helping to attract prey close to its sharp teeth.

> **DID YOU KNOW?**
> The cookie-cutter shark's Latin name, Isistius, comes from the Egyptian goddess of light, Isis.

- **Sharks may use bioluminescence** to communicate. For example, green dogfish sharks feed in groups. Their light patterns may help them to find each other in murky water.

- **Glowing lights may help** sharks to find a mate of their own species in the darkness of the deep ocean.

- **Bioluminescence is made in tiny organs** in the skin called photophores. In a photophore, two chemicals are combined, creating a reaction that gives off light.

- **Other animals have bioluminescence** too, including deep-sea fish such as the anglerfish, as well as fireflies and some types of worms.

▶ *The viperfish has rows of photophores along its underside. These help to hide it from predators below.*

Staying safe

- **Smaller sharks make a tasty snack** for other animals, so they need to defend themselves against predators, such as dolphins and porpoises.

- **The biggest species** are rarely eaten by other sea creatures, but they can still be hunted by humans.

DID YOU KNOW?
An electric ray can produce an electric shock from its body to warn off potential predators.

Life in the water

- **Some sharks are good at hiding.** They slip between rocks or into caves to escape from predators.

- **When in danger**, some species swim in a jerky, random manner to confuse their attacker.

- **Thresher sharks** use their tails to fight off predators, as well as for attacking prey.

- **Shark skin acts like armour**, making it hard for predators to bite them.

- **Species with spines** can often put a predator off by giving it a sharp stab.

- **Rough sharks** have large spines on their back but they also have very rough skin, which scratches predators if they try to attack – their skin is rather like barbed wire.

- **Most species are scared of humans**. If they hear divers, they will usually swim away.

- **Saw sharks may use their saw-like snouts** to defend themselves against predators.

◀ A swellshark can puff up its body with air when it is in a small space in-between rocks. A predator can't pull the shark out because it is wedged in so tightly.

121

Spikes and spines

- **Many prehistoric sharks** had sharp spines in front of their dorsal fins. Scientists think they may have helped hold the fins up.

- **Today only a few species** have spines, spikes or sharp horns on their bodies. They are usually used for defence against attackers.

- **Spines are made** of modified, extra-large denticles.

- **Some dogfish sharks** and horn sharks have two sharp fin spines in front of their dorsal fins.

- **The spined pygmy shark** is the only species that has just one fin spine, which can inflict a painful wound. Other kinds have two spines, or none at all.

- **Smaller species are more likely to have spines**. They are most at risk of being eaten by other animals, so they need defences to deter their enemies.

- **Spiny dogfish coil themselves** right around their enemies to stab them with their spines.

Second dorsal fin spine

▶ The piked dogfish has a spine in front of each of the dorsal fins on its back. The spines inject a mild poison into an attacker.

Life in the water

▸ **The sharp spines of the** spiny dogfish and Port Jackson sharks inject poison into an attacker.

▸ **Velvet belly lanternsharks** have glowing spines, which are visible from above and the side. These 'light sabres' warn predators to keep away because these spiny sharks would be hard to swallow.

▸ **Stingrays** have poisonous stings in the middle of their tails.

First dorsal fin spine

▲ *Like other bullhead sharks, the Australian Port Jackson shark has a spine in front of each dorsal fin.*

In disguise

- **Many sharks can disguise themselves** to look like their surroundings. This is called camouflage.

- **Camouflage is a good way to hide** from enemies, but it can also be used to help sharks sneak up on their prey without being seen.

- **Many small species**, such as zebra sharks, epaulette sharks and wobbegongs, have brown or grey patterns to help them blend in with coral and seaweed.

- **The marbled catshark** is named after the camouflage patterns on its skin, which look like the patterns in marble rock.

- **Sharks are often darker** on their top half and paler underneath. This is called countershading. A shark with countershading viewed from below will blend with the brightly lit sea surface. Seen from above, it will blend with the murky depths.

- **Some wobbegong sharks** have barbels that look like seaweed around their mouths. Fish and other prey think the wobbegong is a harmless piece of seaweed and swim right into the shark's open mouth.

- **Angelsharks** have flat, smooth bodies. When they lie on the sandy seabed they become almost invisible.

- **The shovelnose shark** or guitarfish, a type of ray, disguises itself by burying its body in the sand or mud on the sea floor, with only its eyes sticking out.

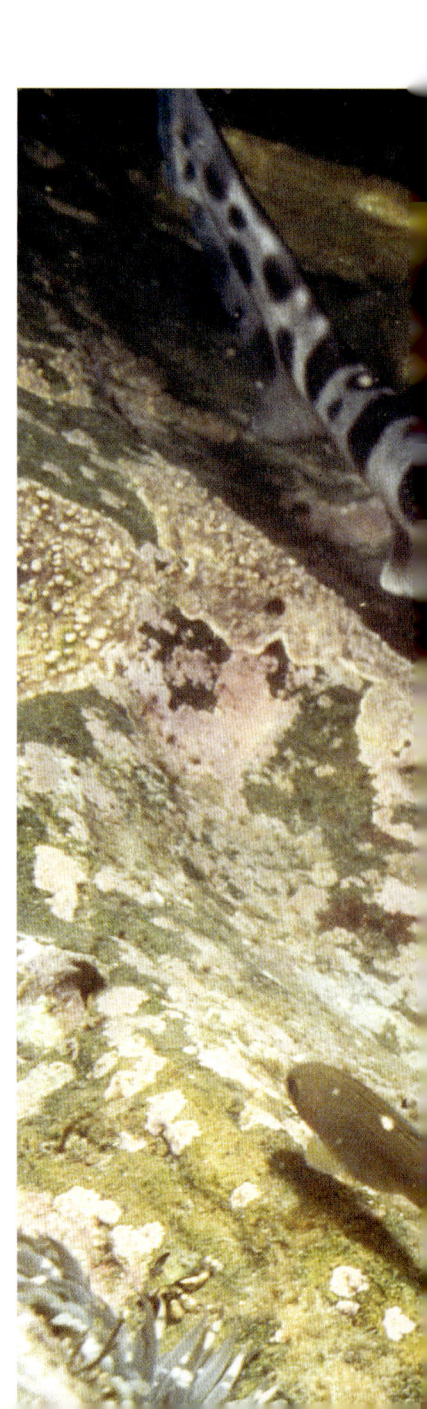

Life in the water

- **The cookie-cutter shark** uses patches of light on its skin to attract hunting fish, seals or whales to come close – then the cookie-cutter takes a bite out of them.

- **When leopard sharks are young**, they have spots for camouflage. As they get older and bigger, they don't need as much protection, so the spots fade.

▼ *The spots on a young leopard shark's body help to break up its body shape and make it hard to see against a rocky background.*

126

Life in the water

▼ A Pacific angelshark is almost invisible when it buries itself in sand on the sea bed. Even when it emerges from hiding, its spotted skin helps to hide it from predators.

Loners and groups

- **Many shark species**, such as bull sharks, are solitary. This means that they live alone.

- **Sharks don't live in families**. They meet up to mate, but do not stay together afterwards. Once born, young sharks do not live with their parents either.

- **Some sharks form groups** with other members of their species. Whitetip reef sharks often rest together in small groups of about ten individuals.

- **Sharks may form groups** because there is safety in numbers. A group is less likely to be attacked than a single shark.

- **Being in a group** may also help sharks to find a mate.

- **Some species**, such as lemon sharks, blue sharks and spiny dogfish, form single-sex groups of just males or females outside the breeding season. Scientists are not sure why.

- **Pygmy sharks, spiny dogfish**, silky sharks and some other species hunt together to catch prey.

- **Basking sharks** have been seen in groups of 50 or more, in places where there is lots of plankton floating on the sea for them to eat.

- **Great white sharks** sometimes travel in pairs or small groups.

- **Shark pups often stay together** in shallow water 'nurseries', well away from larger adult sharks, which might eat them.

▶ During the day, hammerhead sharks hunt together in schools. At night, they separate to hunt alone.

Life in the water

DID YOU KNOW?
Groups of nurse sharks sometimes relax by lying in a heap on the sea bed.

129

Sending messages

- **Animals don't have complicated languages** like humans – but they can still communicate.

- **Sharks can 'talk' using body language**. They make different postures, just as humans show their feelings using different expressions.

- **When a shark is aggressive** or frightened, it arches its back, raises its snout, and points its pectoral fins down.

- **Sharks also release special scents** called pheromones to send messages to other sharks. These can indicate if a shark is looking for a mate or feeling agitated.

- **When they live in a group**, the strongest sharks usually become the leaders. They will sometimes fight with the other sharks to show their dominance.

- **A few species can make sounds**. Swellsharks can make a barking noise, but experts are not sure if it is a way of communicating.

Life in the water

DID YOU KNOW?
Bioluminescence (lighting up) helps some species to communicate. It can enable a shark recognize another shark of the same species in the dark.

- **A threatened sand tiger shark** makes a sound rather like a gunshot when it slaps its tail loudly on the water's surface.

- **Great white sharks** warn rivals to keep away by showing their sharp teeth, splashing their tail at the surface, or even hitting a rival with their strong tail.

- **If a rival does not back off**, the great white will give it a small bite and hope that it swims away without the need for a proper fight, which may injure both sharks.

- **Part of the threat display** of the grey reef shark is to swim stiffly in a figure-of-eight loop.

◀ This shark is displaying aggression. Its raised snout, arched back and lowered fins mean it is ready to attack.

Male and female sharks

- **In most species of sharks**, the females are larger than the males. This may help them to produce large eggs, or look after the developing pups inside their bodies.

- **Female sharks may weigh** up to a quarter more than male sharks of the same species.

- **Male and female sharks** look similar on the outside. The main difference is that males have two claspers for delivering sperm to the females.

- **The claspers of a male shark** are folds of skin with grooves. They are formed from the inner sides of the pelvic fins, which are rolled around like a scroll.

- **Each clasper has a mechanism** for pumping the sperm through the channel in the middle of the scroll.

- **Claspers vary** in different species. They may be flat, round, smooth or covered with denticles (skin scales) shaped like hooks or spurs.

- **Inside a female shark** there are usually two ovaries, which make eggs, and two egg tubes, called oviducts.

- **Sperm from a male shark** fertilizes the eggs inside the oviducts of the female shark.

Life in the water

- **Sometimes, sperm from a male shark** is stored by a female shark for fertilization in the future, perhaps in a year or more.

- **After fertilization**, the eggs are covered with a tough, protective covering and move into the female's womb, or uterus, which has two chambers.

▼ *Male blacktip reef sharks are smaller than females. Males are 91–100 cm long, whereas females are 96–112 cm long.*

Male

Female

Meeting and mating

- **Like most animals**, sharks have to mate in order to reproduce and have offspring (babies).

- **During mating**, a male and female shark of the same species join together. Sperm cells from the male fertilize the egg cells inside the female. The eggs develop inside her body into young.

- **When they mate**, the male uses two body parts called claspers to deliver cells into an opening in the female's body, called the cloaca.

- **A small, flexible male shark**, such as a dogfish, wraps its body tightly around the female to get in the right position for mating.

- **Many species including nurse sharks** and blue sharks have special mating areas in shallow parts of the sea.

- **In other species**, such as whitetip reef sharks, females release chemicals called pheromones to help males locate them.

- **Males sometimes bite females** to show that they want to mate with them.

- **Females often have thicker skin** than males (up to three times as thick) so that being bitten during courtship doesn't harm them.

- **Sharks don't mate very often**. Most species only reproduce once every two years.

- **Lemon sharks mate while slowly swimming** along, with the back of their bodies touching, but their heads apart.

▶ *Male whitetip reef sharks sometimes spend time resting in shallow water during the day. If they smell a pheromone scent from a female, they will try to find her.*

Life in the water

136

Life in the water

◀ The scars on this female great white indicate where a male bit her to hold onto her during mating. Female sharks have thicker skin than males to protect them during mating.

137

Laying eggs

- **Many sharks have young** by laying eggs. Most bony fish also reproduce this way. Sharks that lay eggs are called oviparous sharks. They typically lay between ten and 20 eggs at a time.

- **Oviparous species** include bullhead, dogfish, horn, zebra and swellsharks.

- **A mother shark** doesn't guard her eggs. She lays them in a safe place, such as between two rocks or under a clump of seaweed, then leaves them to hatch.

- **The eggs are enclosed** in protective cases, which come in many shapes, including tubes, spirals and pillows.

- **When the female first lays her eggs**, the cases are soft and flexible, but they harden when they come into contact with the seawater.

- **Like a chicken egg**, a shark egg contains a yolk that feeds the baby as it grows.

- **Inside the egg**, the baby shark grows for between six and ten months before hatching.

▼ *The egg cases of bullhead, or horn, sharks are spiral shaped, like a screw or auger.*

Life in the water

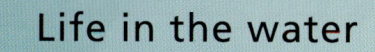

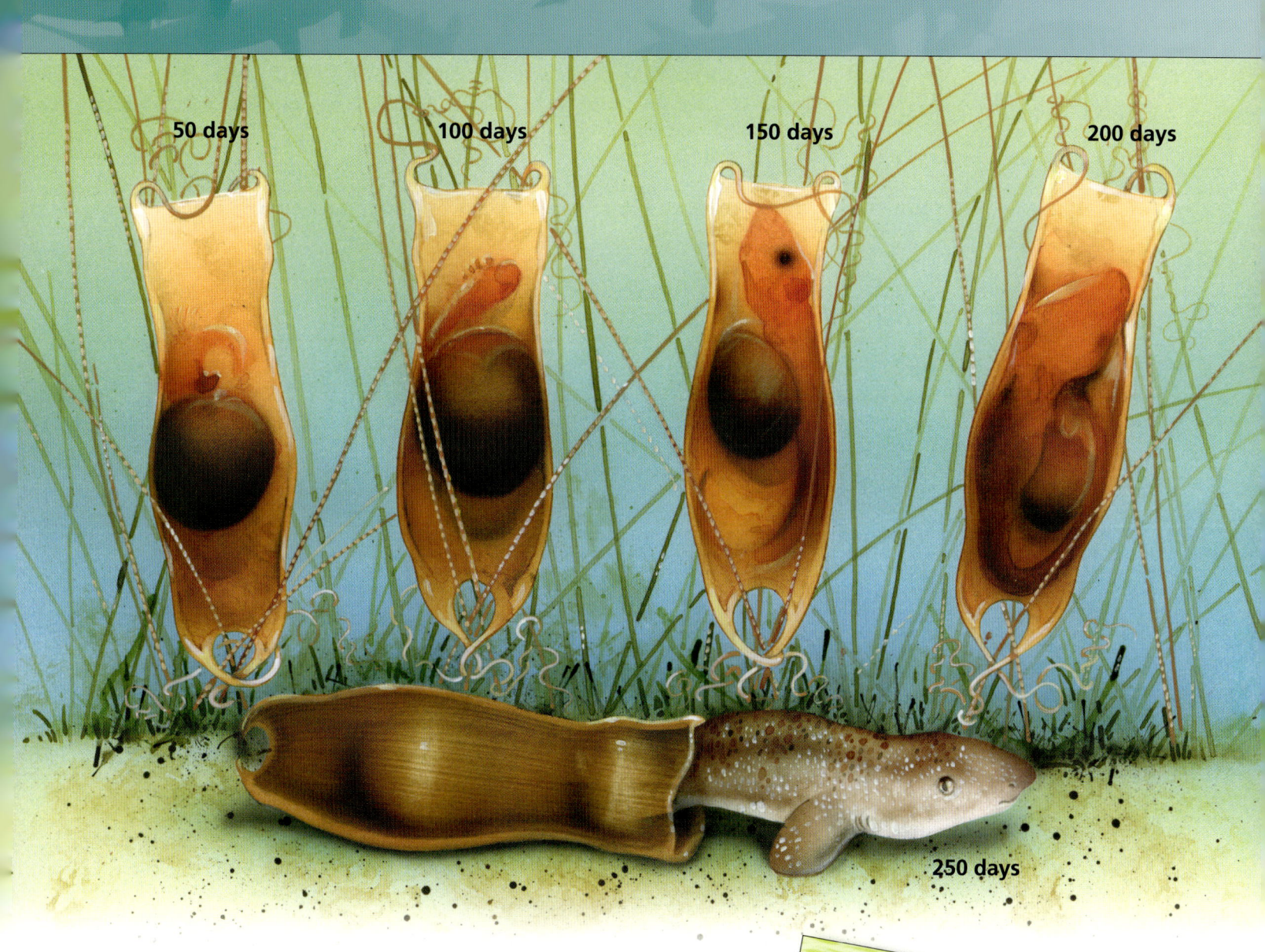

50 days **100 days** **150 days** **200 days**

250 days

▲ *A baby catshark develops slowly in its protective case. At 50 days it is smaller than the yolk, its store of food.*

- **You can sometimes find** empty shark egg cases washed up on beaches. They are known as mermaids' purses.

- **Female sharks** lay relatively large eggs compared to their body size. For instance, a female shark about 1.8 m long lays egg cases 5–10 cm long.

- **A huge female whale shark** lays eggs cases up to 30 cm long.

DID YOU KNOW?
Catshark eggs have sticky strings on them that wind around seaweed, holding the eggs securely in place.

▶ The empty egg case of a swellshark, with wiry strands still fixing it to coral. The baby shark uses large denticles along its back to break free of the egg case. The shark is about 15 cm long at this early stage of its life.

Life in the water

Giving birth

- **Not all sharks lay eggs.** Some give birth to live young. These sharks are known as viviparous or ovoviviparous.

- **In ovoviviparous species**, such as basking sharks, the young, called pups, grow inside eggs. They hatch out while inside the mother's body, before being born.

- **About 40 percent of all sharks** are ovoviviparous, including frilled sharks, sand sharks, thresher sharks, tiger sharks, nurse sharks and mako sharks.

- **In viviparous sharks**, such as hammerheads, the pups grow inside the mother's body, but not in eggs.

DID YOU KNOW?
Viviparous young are attached to their mothers by an umbilical cord, just like human babies.

▼ A newborn lemon shark swims away from its mother. Lemon shark pups are 60–65 cm long at birth.

Life in the water

- **Viviparous sharks develop** inside the mother's uterus, or womb, where they receive food through a structure called a placenta, which develops from the pup's yolk sac. The placenta is attached to the wall of the mother's uterus.

- **Mother sharks with pups** developing inside them like this are 'pregnant'. Most shark pregnancies last up to about one year.

- **Some shark pregnancies** are much longer. In the spiny dogfish, pregnancy lasts up to two years.

- **In sand tiger sharks** and several other species, the strongest pups eat the others while they are still inside the mother's body.

- **Most shark pups** are born tail-first, but some, such as sand tiger sharks, are born head-first.

- **Baby hammerhead sharks** are born head-first, but have their 'hammer-heads' folded back to avoid harming their mother.

Newborn sharks

- **Most shark pups** look like smaller versions of their parents. They often have a narrower body shape and stronger colours.

- **Some species**, such as sand tiger sharks, give birth to just two pups in a litter.

- **The pups** of some species are born with the yolk still attached. The yolk continues to nourish the shark as it grows.

- **Newborn sharks** are slimmer than their parents. Their long, thin shape makes them look more like water snakes.

- **Mako sharks** produce large, strong pups, which are ready to swim in the open ocean and begin hunting as soon as they are born.

- **Lemon sharks** hide among seaweed in shallow water for the first two years after they are born, before moving to deeper water.

- **Newborn dusky sharks** have a huge liver, which helps them to survive until they catch their first meal. The liver quickly reduces in size, from 20 percent of the pup's body weight at birth to only 6 percent after a few days.

Life in the water

▼ *The egg sac full of yolk is still attached to the body of this blue shark pup.*

◗ **Blue sharks give birth** to up to 135 pups at a time. The pups are about 51 cm long when they are born.

◗ **Some female sharks**, such as bonnethead sharks, zebra sharks, blacktip sharks and whitespotted bamboo sharks, are able to give birth to pups without mating with a male shark.

DID YOU KNOW?
Whale sharks are thought to be able to give birth to up to 300 pups at a time.

146

Life in the water

◀ A newly hatched brown-banded bamboo shark has stripes that camouflage it. The yolk sac it fed on inside the egg case is still attached, and provides food for a while longer.

Growing up

- **Sharks grow slowly.** It can take a pup up to 20 years to mature into an adult.

- **Blue sharks are among the fastest-growing.** A pup grows about 20 cm every year.

- **A Greenland shark** grows very slowly, only increasing in size by about 0.5 cm a year.

- **As pups are small**, predators try to eat them. The biggest danger comes from adult sharks. Pups may even be eaten by adults of their own species.

- **For every ten pups born**, only one or two will survive to be adults.

- **Many species of pups live** in 'nursery areas' – shallow parts of the sea close to the shore, where there are plenty of places to hide and smaller sea creatures to hunt.

- **Sharks are born** with a full set of teeth, so they can start to hunt straight away.

- **Adult sharks don't look after** their babies. Once the pup is born, or has hatched, it has to fend for itself.

Life in the water

▶ **A typical shark lives** for around 25–30 years, although some species, such as whale sharks and dogfish sharks, may live for 100 years or more.

▶ **When a shark dies**, scientists can tell how old it is by counting growth rings in its spine – like the rings inside tree trunks.

▼ Small lemon sharks are often eaten by larger sharks. This is why they spend the first few years of their lives living along sheltered shorelines, such as this mangrove swamp.

Friends and enemies

- **There are several types** of sea creature that have a close relationship with sharks. These include some fish species and parasites that feed on the skin, blood or insides of sharks.

- **Small, crab-like creatures** called copepods attach themselves to a shark's eyes, gills, snout or fins. They nibble the shark's skin or suck its blood.

- **Sea leeches bite sharks** on their undersides and suck their blood.

- **Many shark species have tapeworms** inside their guts. They feed on the shark's food.

- **Whale sharks sometimes** try to get rid of skin parasites, such as barnacles, by rubbing up against boats. The barnacles make the shark swim more slowly and may provide a route for an infection to get under the shark's skin.

- **Sometimes two species** can help each other. This kind of relationship between two animals is called symbiosis, which means 'living together'.

- **Many sharks visit 'cleaning stations'** where small fish and shrimps remove dead skin and parasites from their bodies – even from inside their mouth or gills.

- **Basking sharks** are sometimes covered with sea lamprey fish, which use their suckers to grip tightly to the shark's skin. These sharks may sometimes leap out of the water and crash back down again to try and dislodge the lampreys.

Life in the water

- **Remoras or 'shark suckers'** are fish that attach themselves to sharks using suction pads on their heads. They hitch a ride on the shark's body and feed on leftover scraps of food.

- **Sharks open their mouths** to let tiny cleaner wrasse fish nibble lice and dead skin from between their teeth.

DID YOU KNOW?
Giant manta rays may spend several hours at a 'cleaning station', whereas sharks zip through in just 5–10 seconds.

▼ A Greenland shark with a parasitic copepod attached to its eye (see page 184).

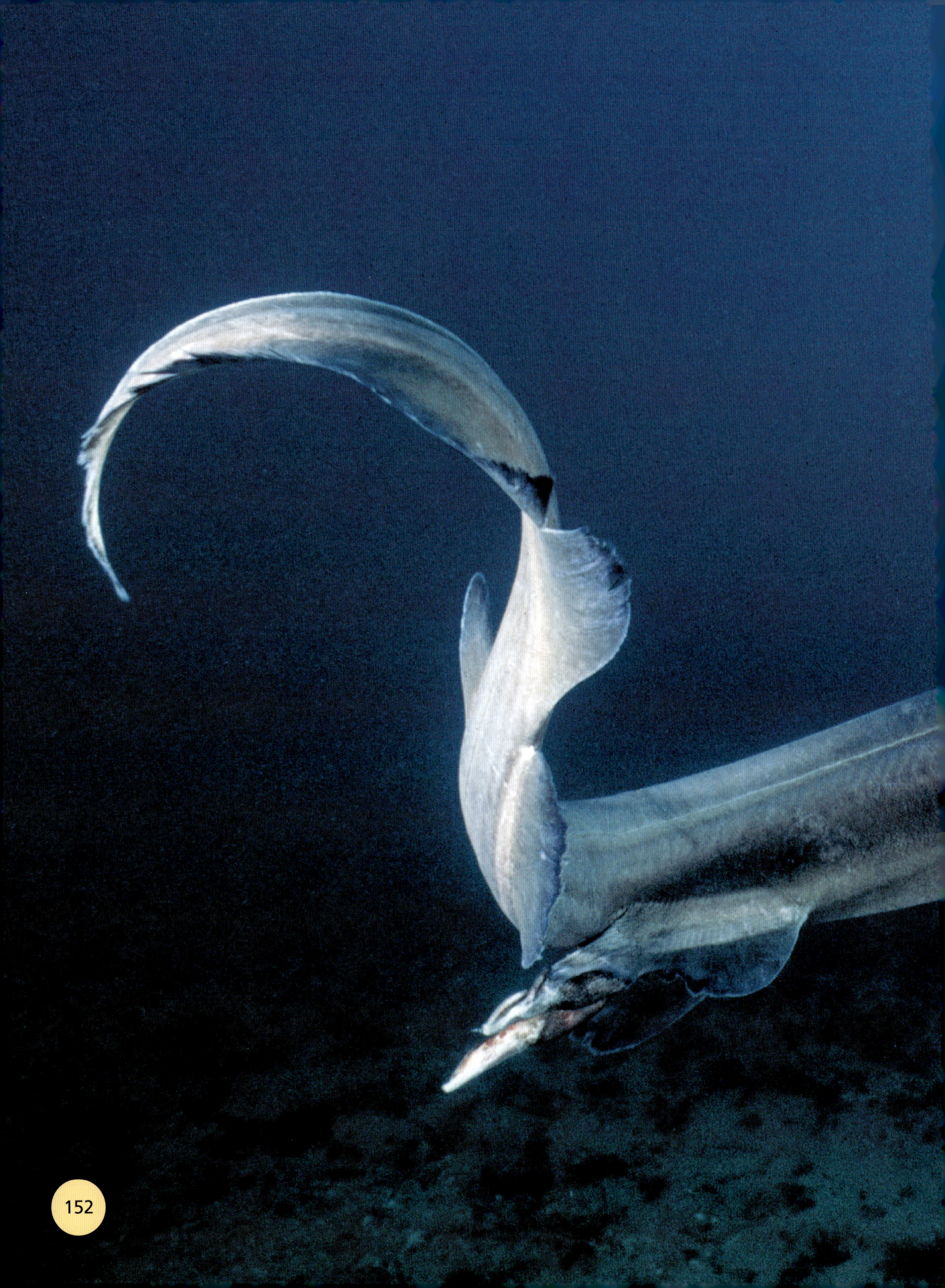

Shark families

Types of shark

- **There are more than 500 species** of shark and scientists divide them into eight large groups, called orders. They are then divided into about 34 smaller groups, or families.

- **Arranging species into groups**, or classifying them, helps scientists to study and identify them.

- **Scientists often disagree** about how to classify sharks, so there are several different ways to do it.

- **Shark orders and families** have long scientific names. For example, goblin sharks belong to the Mitsukurinidae family, in the Lamniformes order.

- **Some groups have common names too**. For example, species in the Lamniformes order are also known as mackerel sharks.

- **Each species** has its own scientific name, which is written in Latin. The first part identifies the genus to which the species belongs. The second part identifies the species within the genus.

Common name	Latin name	Meaning
Silky shark	Carcharhinus falciformis	Carcharhinus shows which group the shark belongs to. Falciformis means 'sickle shaped', and refers to the outline of the dorsal and pectoral fins.

▲ Each shark species is given a two-part Latin name.

- **Scientists decide which group** a shark belongs to by looking at features such as its body shape, markings, behaviour and DNA.

- **Sometimes, very different-looking sharks** can belong to the same group. Huge whale sharks and small, slender epaulette sharks are both in the same order.

Shark families

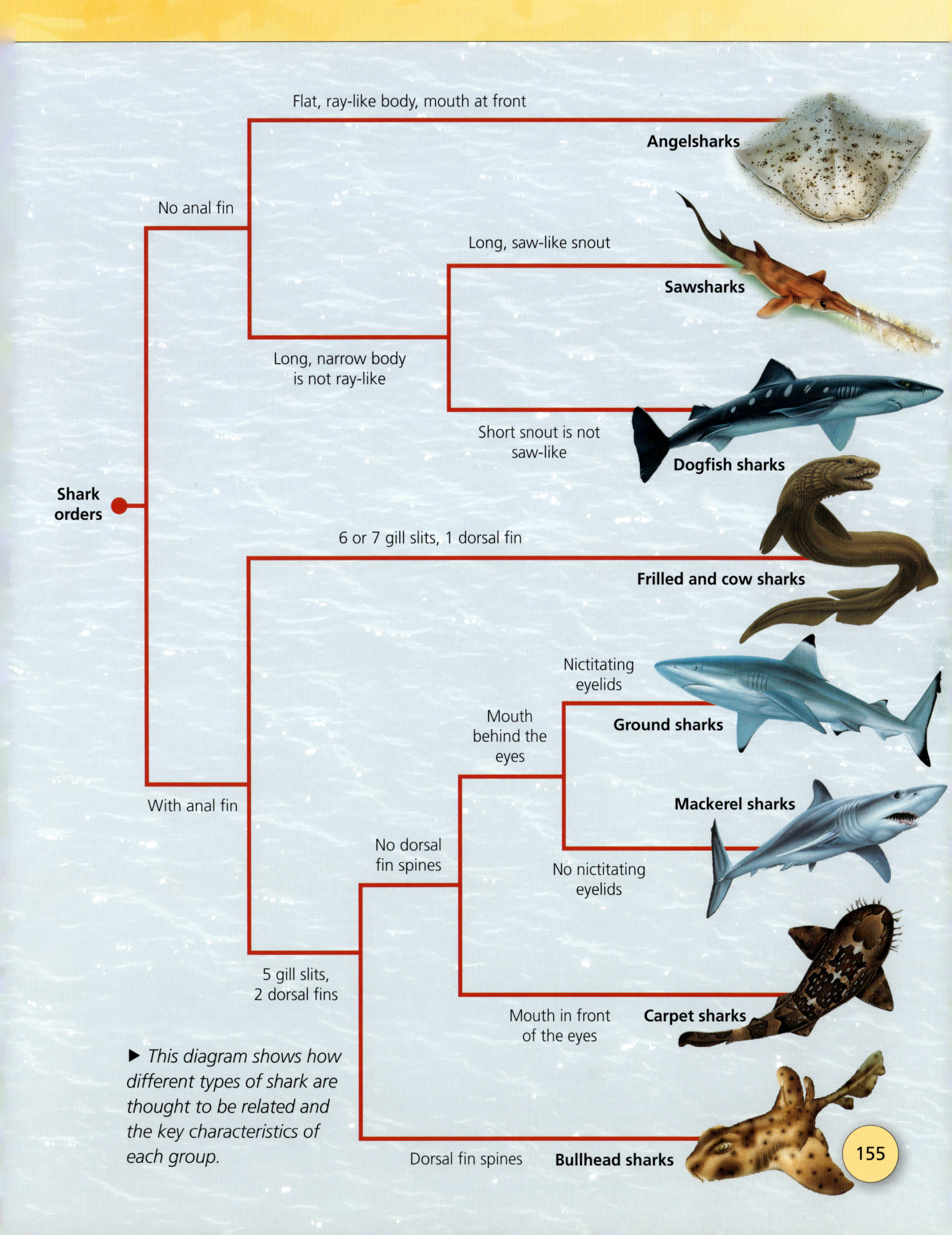

Flat, ray-like body, mouth at front — **Angelsharks**

No anal fin

Long, saw-like snout — **Sawsharks**

Long, narrow body is not ray-like

Short snout is not saw-like — **Dogfish sharks**

Shark orders

6 or 7 gill slits, 1 dorsal fin — **Frilled and cow sharks**

With anal fin

Nictitating eyelids / Mouth behind the eyes — **Ground sharks**

No dorsal fin spines

No nictitating eyelids — **Mackerel sharks**

5 gill slits, 2 dorsal fins

Mouth in front of the eyes — **Carpet sharks**

Dorsal fin spines — **Bullhead sharks**

▶ This diagram shows how different types of shark are thought to be related and the key characteristics of each group.

156

Shark families

▼ The lemon shark is in the requiem shark family, part of the largest order of sharks, the ground sharks. Its skin is yellow-brown to grey in colour, giving it good camouflage as it swims over the sandy sea floor of its habitat.

Frilled shark

- **The frilled shark** is the only species in its family.

- **A strange-looking shark**, it has big, frilly gill slits – the first pair reach around its head like a collar.

- **The long, thin body** reaches up to 2 m in length.

- **Frilled sharks** only have one dorsal fin, instead of two as most other sharks have.

- **Due to its snake-like appearance**, this shark is sometimes mistaken for an eel or a sea snake.

- **Frilled sharks** have unusual teeth with three sharp points on each tooth.

- **Found in the cold, deep water** of the Pacific and Atlantic oceans, frilled sharks feed on prey such as octopus and squid. Their jaws stretch wide to engulf their prey.

- **The frilled shark has six gill slits** behind its head on each side of its body. This is very unusual – most sharks have only five.

- **People used to think** that the frilled shark was extinct, as it was known only from ancient fossils. Living specimens were first discovered in the late 19th century.

- **The frilled shark's mouth** is at the front of its head, with the nostrils on top. Species that evolved more recently have their mouth and nostrils on the underside of the head.

One dorsal fin far back towards the tail

Shark families

Gills have frilly edges

▶ The frilled shark is extremely rare. Much more remains to be discovered about this unusual species.

Long, eel-like body

DID YOU KNOW?
The frilled shark's lateral line system is just an open groove, not buried in the skin as in other sharks.

Sixgill and sevengill sharks

- **There are four species** of cow shark in the Hexanchidae family. They are the bluntnose sixgill shark, the bigeye sixgill shark, the sharpnose sevengill shark and the broadnose sevengill shark.

- **Cow sharks are stocky sharks** with six or seven pairs of gill slits.

- **The first pair of gill slits** is not connected across the throat, as they are in frilled sharks.

- **Cow sharks** have an obvious notch at the end of their tail fin.

- **The bluntnose sixgill shark** is the biggest member of the family, with a heavy, powerful body reaching up to 5 m in length.

- **The bluntnose sixgill** lives in the deep sea and has a slow, sluggish lifestyle, but is a strong swimmer. It is capable of sudden bursts of speed to catch prey, such as fish, squid, crabs and shellfish. Large individuals may even eat seals.

- **The bigeye sixgill shark** has huge eyes, with large, round pupils to take in as much light as possible. This helps it to see in deep, dark water.

Shark families

◀ The powerful bluntnose sixgill shark has rows of large, comb-shaped teeth in its lower jaw. Its lateral line is clearly visible as a pale line along the side of its body.

DID YOU KNOW?
Female bluntnose sixgill sharks give birth to up to 108 pups at one time!

- **The broadnose sevengill shark** has rows of large comb-shaped teeth, which it uses to feed on ratfish, small sharks, seals and mackerel.

- **The broadnose sevengill** is a strong swimmer and a powerful predator. It attacks its prey at high speed, often moving to the surface of the sea to hunt at night.

162

Shark families

◀ The broadnose sevengill shark has many small black spots on its body. It often lives in groups, and these powerful sharks may work together to hunt large prey such as seals.

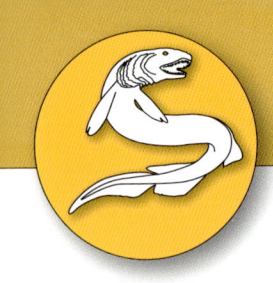

Prickly and bramble sharks

- **Prickly and bramble sharks** have large mouths and throats, which they may use to suck in prey, such as fish, octopus and squid, as these sharks swim slowly along close to the sea bed.

- **They have very small spiracles**, which are located well behind their eyes.

- **Prickly and bramble sharks** have much rougher skin than other sharks.

- **The bramble shark** has large, thorn-like spikes scattered unevenly over its body. The spikes are made of extra-large, extra-sharp denticles.

Shark families

- **Although they are large**, at about 3 m in length, bramble sharks are rarely seen. This is because they live in deep water.

- **The bramble shark** lives in the Atlantic Ocean, the Mediterranean Sea and the Pacific Ocean at depths of up to 900 m.

- **The female bramble shark** gives birth to 25–26 pups at a time.

- **The prickly shark** is a relative of the bramble shark. It looks similar, but has smaller spikes. It grows to around 4 m in length.

- **The prickly shark** lives in the Pacific Ocean at depths of up to 1100 m.

- **The largest recorded number** of prickly shark pups born at one time was 114!

▼ A bramble shark has the prickliest, roughest skin of any shark. Its whole body is scattered with sharp, thorny spikes.

166

Dogfish sharks

Dogfish sharks

- **The dogfish shark order** (Squaliformes), consists of about 130 species in six families: dogfish sharks, gulper sharks, lanternsharks, sleeper sharks, roughsharks and kitefin sharks.

- **These sharks usually have spines** in front of their dorsal fins and they have no anal fin.

- **They may have been named** 'dogfish' because many types move in large groups or packs, like wild dogs.

- **Another theory is that** dogfish sharks may have been given their name because they are the most common sharks. In the past, any common type of plant or animal was given the name 'dog' – dog rose, for example.

- **Spiny dogfish** can cause problems for fishermen. They tear up fishing nets to eat the fish and steal lobsters from lobster pots.

- **Millions of dogfish sharks** are caught every year for their meat, fins, oil and skin.

- **Female dogfish sharks** give birth to pups. They may have anything from one to over 50 pups in one litter.

- **The spiny dogfish** has the longest known gestation period of any shark. Females can be pregnant for up to two years.

- **The smalleye pygmy shark** is one of the smallest sharks. It measures less than 10 cm in length at birth.

- **Another small shark** in this group, the cookie-cutter shark, takes bites out of large victims, including whales.

Dogfish sharks

▼ A group of dogfish sharks on the prowl. They sometimes form schools of hundreds or even thousands of individuals.

DID YOU KNOW?
In America, spiny dogfish used to be caught, dried and burned as a fuel.

Mandarin dogfish

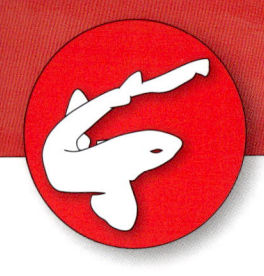

- **The mandarin dogfish** is named after its long barbels, which look like the long moustaches grown by Chinese officials.

- **The barbels** developed from nose flaps. They are sensitive to touch, water currents and chemicals in the water.

- **This shark** probably uses its sensory barbels to find prey, such as fish and crabs.

- **The two dorsal fins** on the shark's back each have a long, stout spine in front of them. The fins have pale or white edges.

Dogfish sharks

▼ *The mandarin dogfish has a stout, wide body, a very long tail, and large pectoral fins with rounded tips.*

- **The mandarin shark** has low, blade-like cutting teeth in both jaws. The teeth fit tightly together when the jaws close.

- **Mandarin sharks** live in the west of the Pacific Ocean, in the waters around Japan, New Zealand and Australia.

- **They usually swim** at depths of 150–450 m but may venture even deeper, to depths of over 600 m.

- **Male mandarin dogfish** grow to about 86 cm long. Females are slightly larger, reaching lengths of 92–108 cm.

- **Female mandarin dogfish** give birth to pups. Between ten and 22 pups are born at one time.

Spurdog sharks

- **Spurdog sharks have spines** in front of their dorsal fins, which they use to defend themselves.

- **The spines** of the spiny dogfish cause painful wounds as they have mild venom (poison) at the base.

- **The spiny dogfish** is also called the piked dogfish, spurdog, horned dog, spring dogfish and white-spotted dogfish.

- **In Europe**, spiny dogfish is used for 'fish and chips', and is sometimes called rock salmon or rock cod.

- **Female spiny dogfish** have between two and 32 pups at a time. The pups are about 27 cm long when they are born, but will grow to a length of about 137 cm.

- **Spiny dogfish** live in packs of hundreds or even thousands of individuals. They are slow swimmers, but go on long seasonal migrations as the water temperature changes.

- **Spiny dogfish live a long time**, up to an age of about 70–100 years. The age of younger fish can be measured from annual growth rings on the fin spines. The spines wear down in older fish.

- **The Cyrano spurdog** has an extremely long, broad snout. It is named after a French author, Cyrano de Bergerac, who had a remarkably long nose.

- **The shortspine spurdog** has a sensory barbel on its snout.

Dogfish sharks

▶ **The blacktail spurdog** is named after the black patch on its tail. It also has black tips to its dorsal fins.

▶ **The fatspine spurdog** has very stout spines on its dorsal fins.

▼ The spiny dogfish often has white spots along its sides. This fierce predator can catch prey much larger than itself.

▶ The strong spine in front of the dorsal fin of this spiny dogfish is clearly visible. This slender dogfish has a long, pointed snout and is usually less than one metre long.

Dogfish sharks

Gulper sharks

- **There are about 17 species** of gulper shark, which mainly live in deep water, from about 200–1500 m deep.

- **These sharks** have cylindrical bodies, and huge green or yellowish eyes to help them see in deep, dark waters.

- **The two fins on their back** have venomous, grooved spines for defence.

- **Deania species**, such as the birdbeak dogfish, have a very long snout and rough skin; Centrophorus species, such as the leafscale gulper shark, have a shorter, thicker snout and smoother skin.

- **The birdbeak dogfish** is also called the brier shark and the shovel-nosed shark. The first dorsal fin is quite long and low.

- **The denticles** (tiny scales on the skin) of the birdbeak dogfish are tall and topped with pitchfork-shaped crowns.

- **The denticles of the leafscale gulper shark** are shaped like leaves in adults, but are more like bristles in young sharks.

Dogfish sharks

- **Oil from the large livers** of gulper sharks is used to make cosmetics, medicines and machine oil.

- **Gulper sharks** only have one pup at a time. The pup is 30–42 cm long at birth but reaches up to 110 cm when fully grown.

- **Gulper sharks** have blade-like teeth. There are 33–40 rows in the top jaw and 30 rows in the lower jaw.

▲ The gulper shark is an endangered species because too many of these sharks have been caught by people for their meat and liver oil.

DID YOU KNOW?
The Seychelles gulper shark lives only around the Seychelles Islands in the western Indian Ocean.

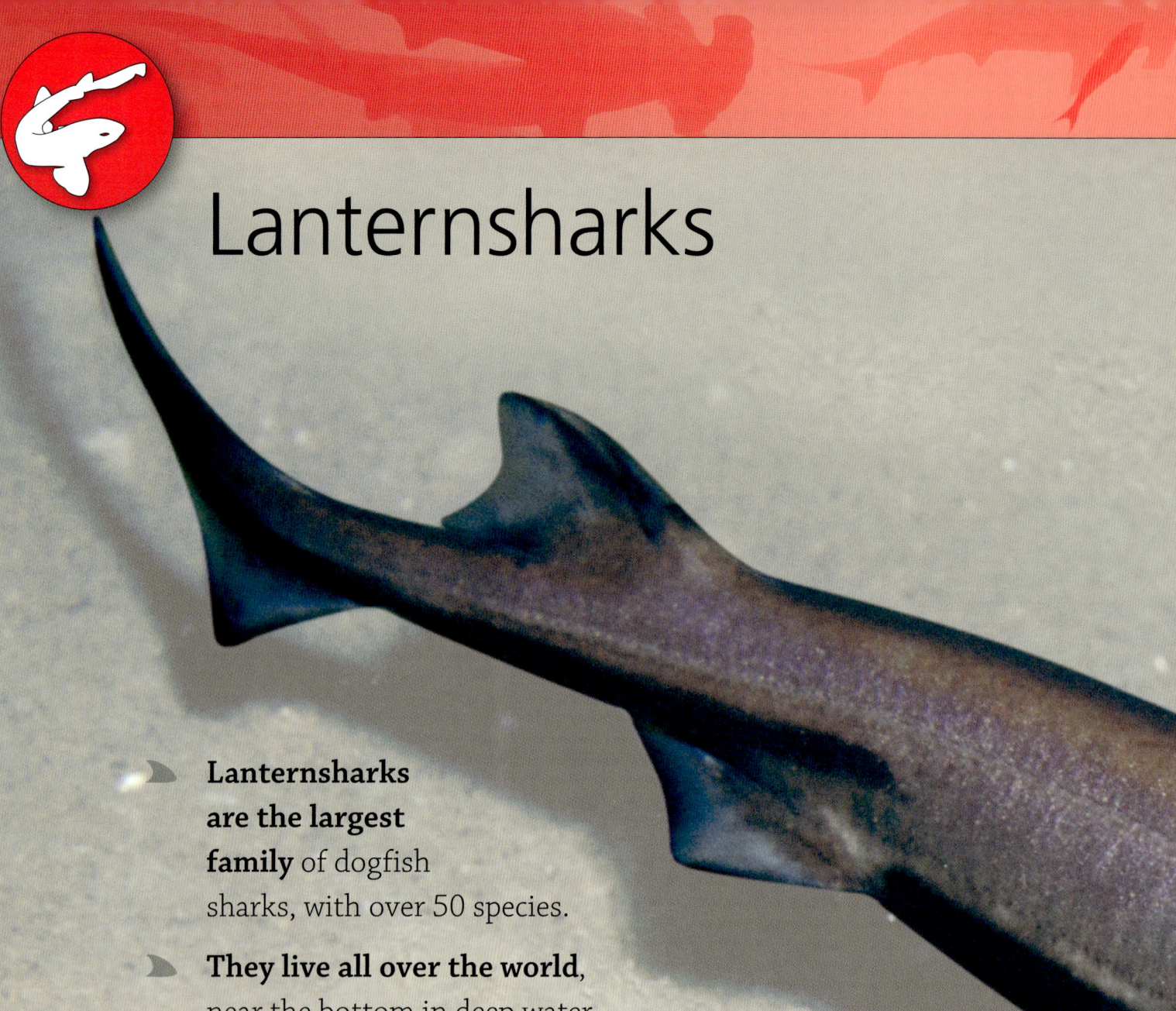

Lanternsharks

- **Lanternsharks are the largest family** of dogfish sharks, with over 50 species.

- **They live all over the world**, near the bottom in deep water, from 200–1500 m deep.

- **Two species in this family** may be the smallest known shark species. They are the dwarf lanternshark and the pygmy lanternshark, both of which grow to a maximum length of 21 cm.

- **The giant lanternshark** is four times longer than these tiny sharks. It grows up to 86 cm long.

- **Lanternsharks are named** after their ability to glow in the dark. They produce light from glowing spots called photophores on their bellies, sides and fins.

Dogfish sharks

- **There can be** as many as 500,000 photophores on just one shark.

- **Lanternsharks use hormones** to switch their light spots on and off. The hormones stimulate pigment (colour) cells to cover or uncover the light spots.

- **The light spots may help** to camouflage these sharks against lighter surface waters, or allow them to signal to other lanternsharks.

- **The rough skin of the granular dogfish** is covered in denticles with sharp, hooked points, whereas the bareskin dogfish has a fragile, almost naked, skin with only a few, widely spaced denticles.

- **The lined lanternshark** has lines of dots and dashes along the top of its silvery-brown body, like Morse code.

- **The viper dogfish** has huge, curved, fang-like teeth to catch large fish, which it then swallows whole.

◀ *The photophores (glowing spots) form distinct black marks on the abdomen, sides or tail of some lanternsharks.*

180

Dogfish sharks

◀ The velvet belly lanternshark is named after its black belly. It has rows of glowing spots on its head, just in front of the very short gill openings. This small shark is only about 30–40 cm long.

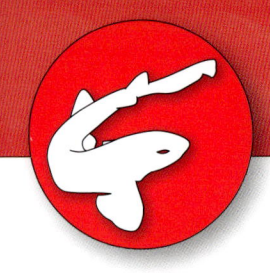

Sleeper sharks

- **There are about 18 species** of sleeper shark, living in most oceans, from the tropics to Arctic and Antarctic waters.

- **Sleeper sharks** range in size from relatively small (40–69 cm) to giant lengths of over 7 m.

- **They are named** after their slow, sluggish swimming habits.

- **The southern sleeper shark** is the largest Antarctic fish and one of the largest sharks. It usually grows to lengths of about 4 m, but can grow as big as a Greenland shark.

- **Female sleeper sharks** give birth to between four and 60 pups at a time.

- **Sleeper sharks feed on fish**, rays, octopuses, jellyfish, starfish, seabirds, seals and dead whales.

- **The Pacific sleeper shark** swims at depths from the surface to more than 2000 m underwater!

- **The large mouth of the Pacific sleeper shark** works like a vacuum cleaner to suck prey inside. Its powerful teeth help to cut up pieces of prey that cannot be swallowed.

- **The Pacific sleeper shark** feeds on giant Pacific octopus as well as fish, but is mainly a scavenger, feeding on dead bodies in the deep sea.

Dogfish sharks

- **Like the cookie-cutter shark**, the Portuguese dogfish bites chunks out of live whales, seals and bony fish.

- **The frog shark** has a smooth skin, with flat denticles. Its upper teeth are like spears for catching fish and small animals living on the sea bed.

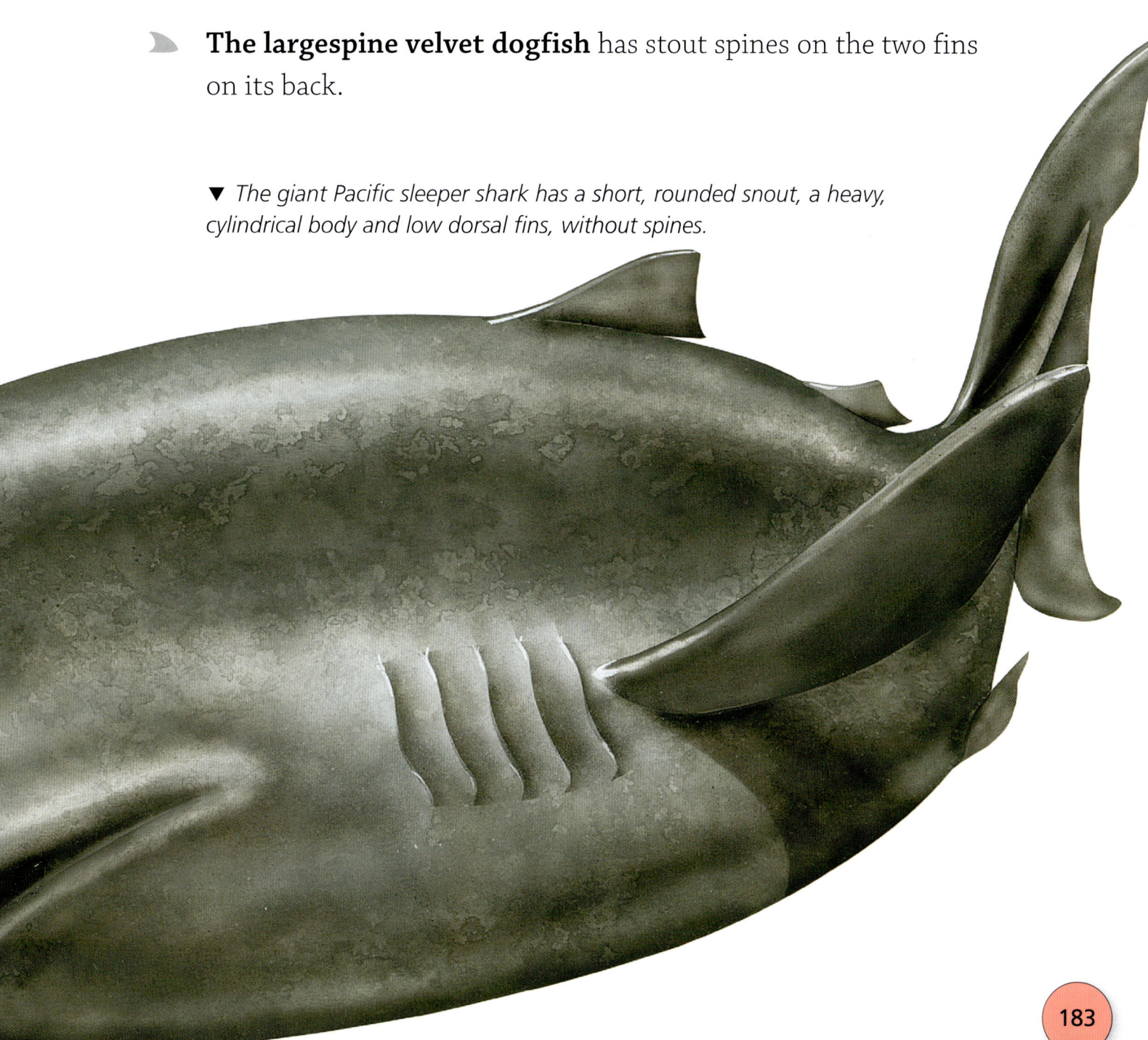

- **The largespine velvet dogfish** has stout spines on the two fins on its back.

▼ The giant Pacific sleeper shark has a short, rounded snout, a heavy, cylindrical body and low dorsal fins, without spines.

Greenland shark

- **Although closely related to dogfish**, Greenland sharks are much bigger – they can grow up to 6.5 m or more in length.

- **Greenland sharks** prefer cold water. They live in the north Atlantic, around Greenland, Iceland and Canada, and can stand temperatures as low as 2°C.

- **The Greenland shark** is a type of sluggish sleeper shark, which is related to another gigantic shark, the Pacific sleeper shark.

- **Alternative names for the Greenland shark** include ground shark, gurry shark, grey shark and sleeper shark. The Inuit name for this shark is *Eqalussuaq*.

- **Luminescent copepods** (tiny sea creatures) live in the eyes of the Greenland shark. They make the eyes glow in the dark, which may help lure prey towards the shark. They also damage the shark's eyes by eating the tissue of the cornea (the transparent covering at the front of the eye).

- **Greenland sharks eat fish**, squid, seals and sea lions, as well as scavenging on the dead bodies of whales. They are attracted by the smell of rotting meat in the water.

Dogfish sharks

▲ One of the largest of all sharks, Greenland sharks are often characters in Inuit legends.

DID YOU KNOW?
Greenland sharks may live for 100 or 150 years, or even longer.

- **In summer**, Greenland sharks swim to the surface to find food, but they spend the rest of their time at depths of around 1500 m.

- **Female Greenland sharks** give birth to between seven and ten pups at a time.

- **Inuit people caught Greenland sharks** on lines through iceholes. They used the skin to make boots and the teeth for knife blades.

- **Fresh Greenland shark meat** is poisonous, but can be eaten safely if it is boiled several times.

▶ A massive Greenland shark swimming under the ice covering the Arctic Ocean in winter. This shark has a small, rounded snout and a heavy body shaped like a cylinder.

Dogfish sharks

Roughsharks

- **The five species of roughshark** are small sharks with two high fins on the back, which look like triangular sails. One species is even called the sailfin roughshark.

- **Roughsharks are named** after their rough, tough skin, which is covered in large, prickly denticles, set very close together.

- **The fins** on a roughshark's back have sharp spines.

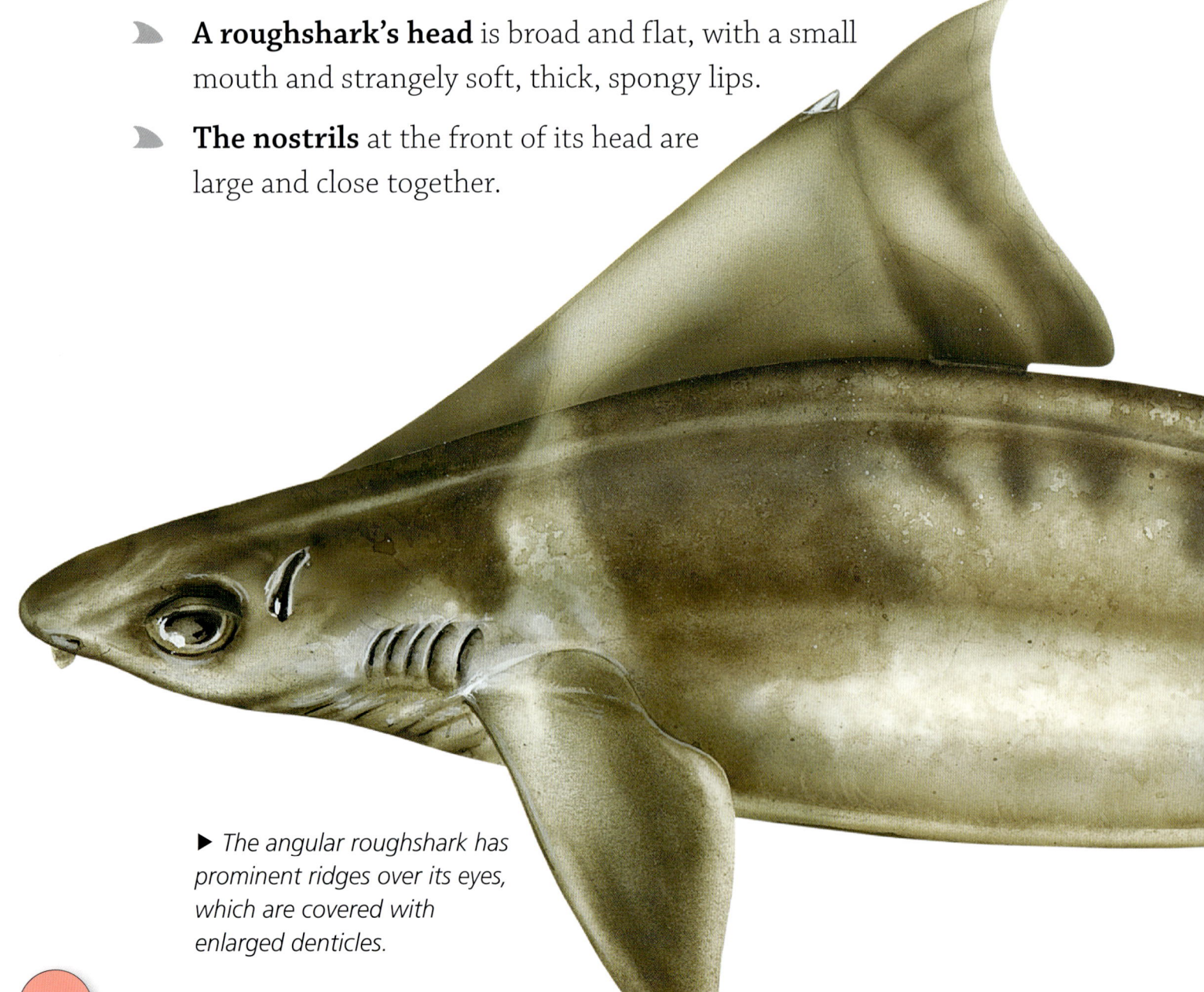

- **A roughshark's head** is broad and flat, with a small mouth and strangely soft, thick, spongy lips.

- **The nostrils** at the front of its head are large and close together.

▶ The angular roughshark has prominent ridges over its eyes, which are covered with enlarged denticles.

Dogfish sharks

- **The spiracles** are right behind the eyes. The angular roughshark has large spiracles, which are almost as tall as the length of its eyes.

- **The teeth in the top jaw** are like spears and arranged in a triangular pad.

- **In the bottom jaw** of a roughshark, there are between nine and 18 rows of teeth squashed tightly together to form a saw-like cutting edge.

- **Roughsharks live in deep water** and probably feed on fish, worms, shellfish and other small creatures living on the sea floor.

- **Female roughsharks** give birth to between seven and 23 pups at a time. The pups are about 25 cm long when they are born.

DID YOU KNOW?
One shark expert described prickly dogfish as 'the unloveliest of sharks' because they're so ugly.

Kitefin shark

- **The kitefin shark is a medium-sized shark** that grows to an average length of one metre. The longest recorded so far is 1.5–1.8 m.

- **The kitefin shark** lives in warm areas of the Atlantic, Pacific and Indian Oceans.

- **This shark lives in deep water**, usually on or near the bottom. It usually lives at depths of more than 200 m below the surface.

- **The kitefin shark** has a large liver full of oil. As oil is lighter than water, the liver works like a float to stop the shark from sinking, so it can hover above the sea bed looking for food.

- **Hunting on its own**, the kitefin shark catches deep-water fish and may take bites out of living prey.

Dogfish sharks

◀ *An aggressive predator, the kitefin shark attacks and kills prey using its powerful jaws and sharp teeth.*

DID YOU KNOW?
The kitefin shark has been seen at depths of nearly 3000 m below the ocean's surface.

- **The kitefin shark has thick,** fringed lips, and its lower teeth have jagged cutting edges.

- **The fins on the back of this shark** do not have spines and the back edges of most of its fins are see-through.

- **Female kitefin sharks** give birth to between three and 16 pups at a time. The pups are about as long as a child's arm when they are born.

- **Fishing for its meat** or oily liver threatens the survival of kitefin sharks in the future.

Pygmy sharks

- **Pygmy sharks** belong to the kitefin shark group.

- **These sharks are all small**, reaching lengths of about 15–30 cm. Sharks this small are harmless to humans.

- **Male smalleye pygmy sharks** and spined pygmy sharks measure only 15 cm when fully grown. They are two of the smallest living sharks.

- **Pygmy sharks** have luminous (glowing) undersides.

- **A glow-in-the-dark belly** may help to attract prey looking upwards for the bright light of the surface water, and also confuse predators in deeper, darker water.

- **The pygmy shark** has large, knife-like lower teeth that it uses to feed on squid, shrimps and fish.

- **The symmetrical tail** of the pygmy shark is paddle-shaped, and it has very small fins on its back. The first of these back fins is set well back on the body.

Dogfish sharks

- **Female pygmy sharks** give birth to about eight pups at a time.

- **The spined pygmy shark** was first discovered in 1908, off the coast of Japan.

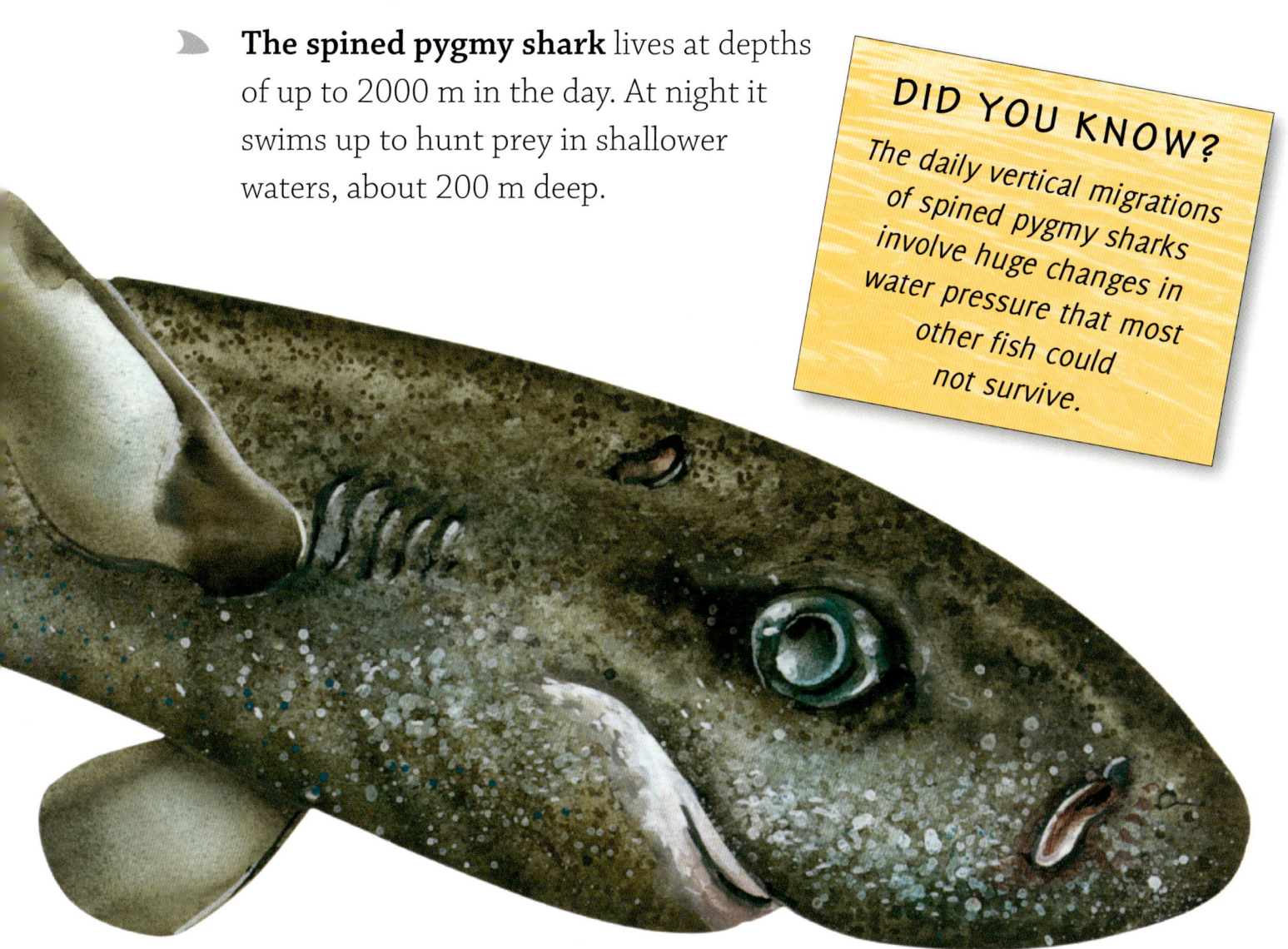

- **The spined pygmy shark** lives at depths of up to 2000 m in the day. At night it swims up to hunt prey in shallower waters, about 200 m deep.

DID YOU KNOW?
The daily vertical migrations of spined pygmy sharks involve huge changes in water pressure that most other fish could not survive.

▲ The pygmy shark has large eyes to help it see in the darkness of the deep sea.

Cookie-cutter sharks

- **Found around the world**, cookie-cutter sharks are strange, deep-water sharks.

- **There are two species** – the cookie-cutter and the large-tooth cookie-cutter.

- **The large-tooth** is the smaller of the two, but it has bigger teeth. Its teeth are bigger in relation to its body size than those of any other shark.

- **Cookie-cutters are brown** in colour and have greenish eyes. They are about 50 cm in length.

- **To feed**, a cookie-cutter attaches itself to its prey by sucking with its mouth. Then it swivels its sharp teeth around in a circle until it has cut out a lump of flesh.

- **As cookie-cutters** don't need to catch their prey, they can feed on animals much larger than themselves.

- **Many sharks**, dolphins, porpoises and whales have permanent round scars from cookie-cutter shark bites.

▲ Cookie-cutters open their mouths wide to bite circular chunks out of their prey. They rarely kill their victims.

Dogfish sharks

◄ The cookie-cutter has around 35 teeth in its upper jaw and 30 in its lower jaw.

► **The luminous underside** of the cookie-cutter shark can glow bright green and may help to attract its victims.

► **Although they are relatively poor swimmers** cookie-cutter sharks probably migrate from deep water (2000–3000 m down) to mid-water levels or the surface at night.

DID YOU KNOW?
Cookie-cutters have been known to take bites out of submarines and undersea cables.

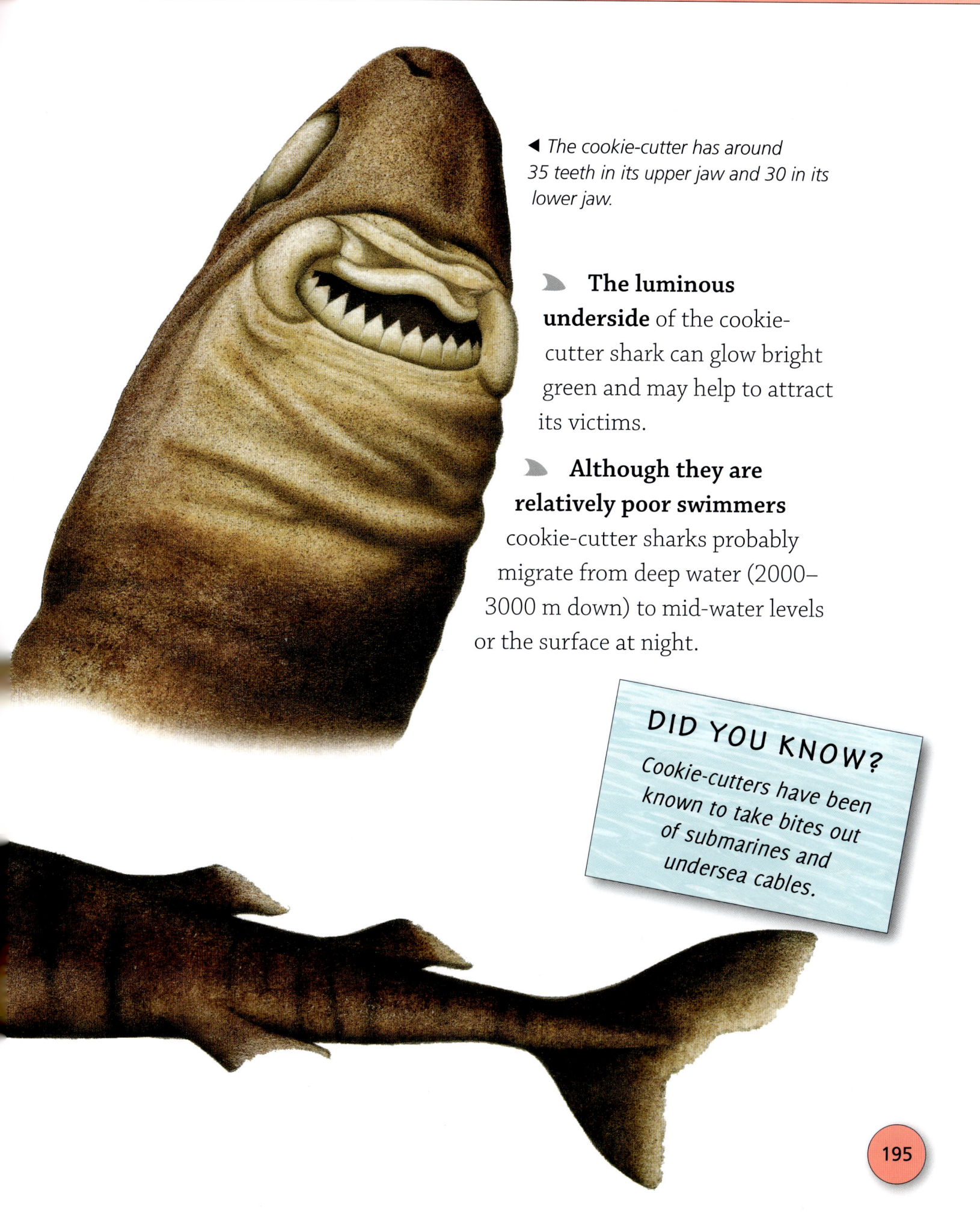

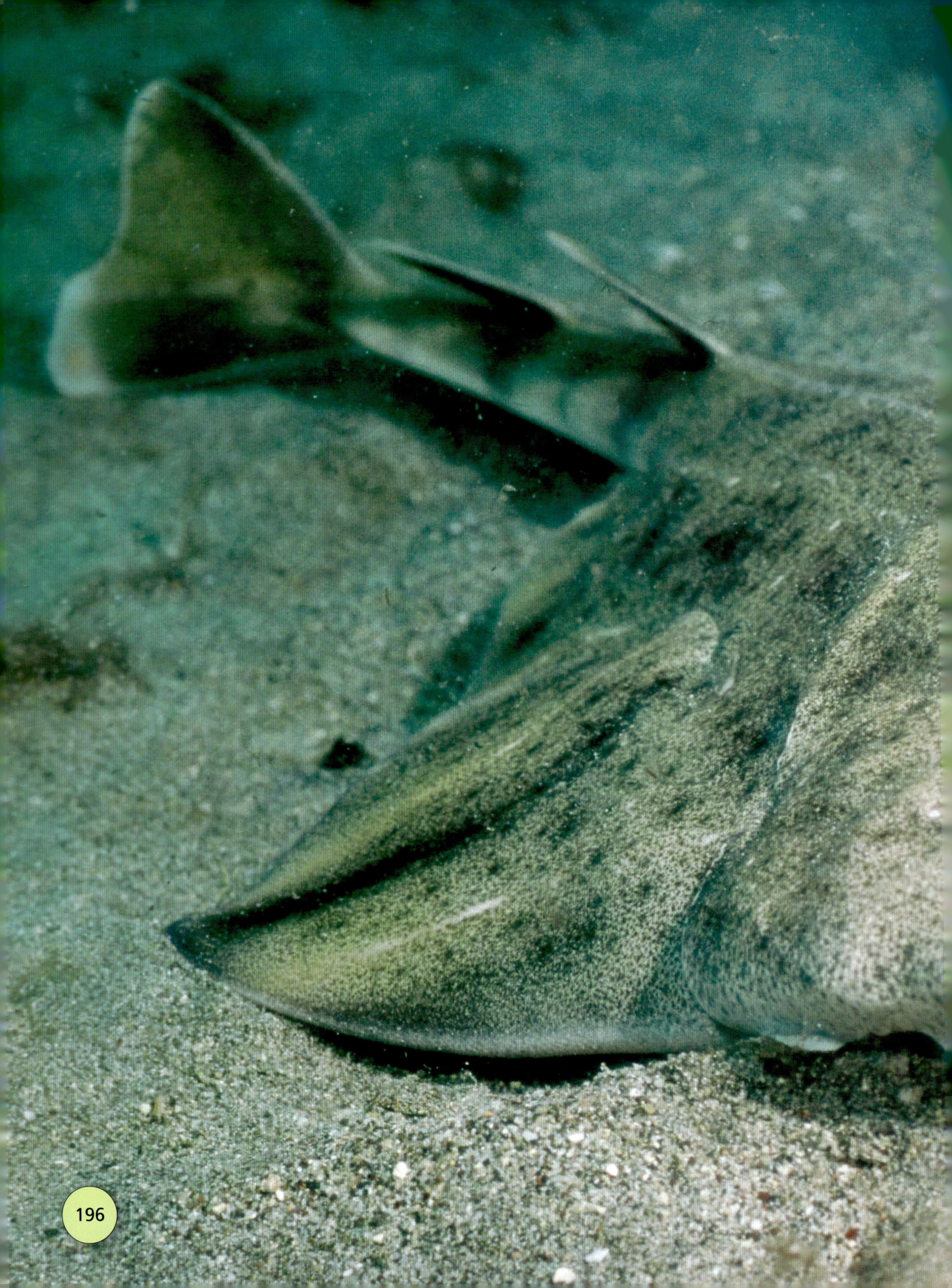

Angelsharks

Angelsharks

- **Angelsharks are named** after the wide, wing-like shape of their fins.

- **Monkfish is another name** for angelsharks. People used to think their fins looked like a monk's robes.

- **Like wobbegongs** and other bottom-dwelling sharks, angelsharks are camouflaged with spotted, speckled skin patterns.

- **These sharks** have flattened bodies. This allows them to stay close to the sea bed. Most are about 1.5 m in length.

- **By burying themselves** on the sea bed, angelsharks are hidden from passing fish and shellfish. They leap out to catch their prey with their small, sharp teeth.

▶ The angelshark has very rough skin on its back, and patches of small thorns on its snout and between its eyes.

Angelsharks

▶ This angelshark is well-camouflaged against a sandy sea bed.

◗ **These sharks can lie in wait** for over a week until their prey comes swimming past. One angelshark even managed to eat a cormorant – a type of large bird.

◗ **Angelsharks are harmless** to humans unless they are disturbed or provoked.

◗ **Female angelsharks** give birth to between one and 25 pups at a time.

◗ **Angelsharks draw in water** through their spiracles and pump it out over their gills to keep them from getting blocked with sand. Their gill openings are on the sides of their head, not underneath.

DID YOU KNOW?
Angelsharks are very large, reaching lengths of 2 m or more.

199

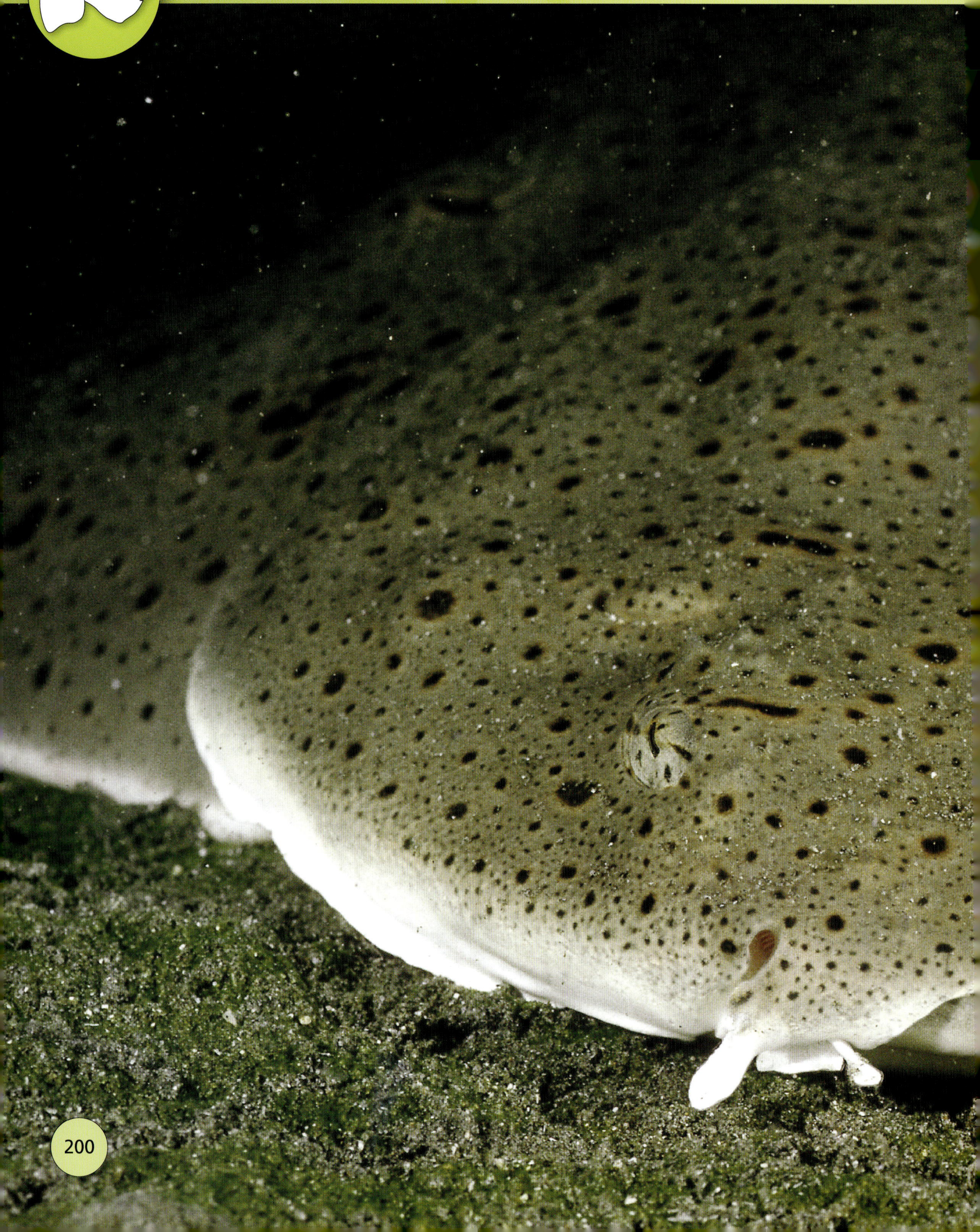

Angelsharks

▼ The Pacific angelshark has sensory barbels with broad tips near its nose, which it uses to taste and feel its surroundings. It has a wide, flat head that dips between its large eyes.

Types of angelshark

- **The angelshark** order contains at least 20 species, and more are being discovered and named by scientists.

- **The Japanese angelshark** is the biggest and reaches 2 m in length. It is hunted for food and was once also used to make shagreen (sharkskin sandpaper).

- **The sawback angelshark** is named after the large, thorn-like projections on its head and in a row along its back.

- **The Australian angelshark** has sensory barbels with fringed edges on the end of its wide, blunt snout.

- **The female Pacific angelshark** is pregnant for about the same time as a human. She gives birth to up to 13 pups at a time. About 20 percent of the young survive to become adults.

- **The sand devil is an angelfish** that lives in the western Atlantic Ocean. It is named after its aggressive behaviour when caught by people.

Angelsharks

- **Every three years**, angular angelshark females migrate to shallow waters near coasts to give birth to about five or six pups.

- **The ocellated angelshark** has six pairs of 'eye spots' on its side fins and the base of the tail. These may help to divert the attention of predators away from the shark's real eyes.

- **More than half of all angelshark species** are threatened with extinction because they are over-fished to provide food, oil, fishmeal and leather.

▼ *During the day, the Pacific angelshark lies buried in sand or mud, suddenly bursting from its hiding place to ambush its fish prey.*

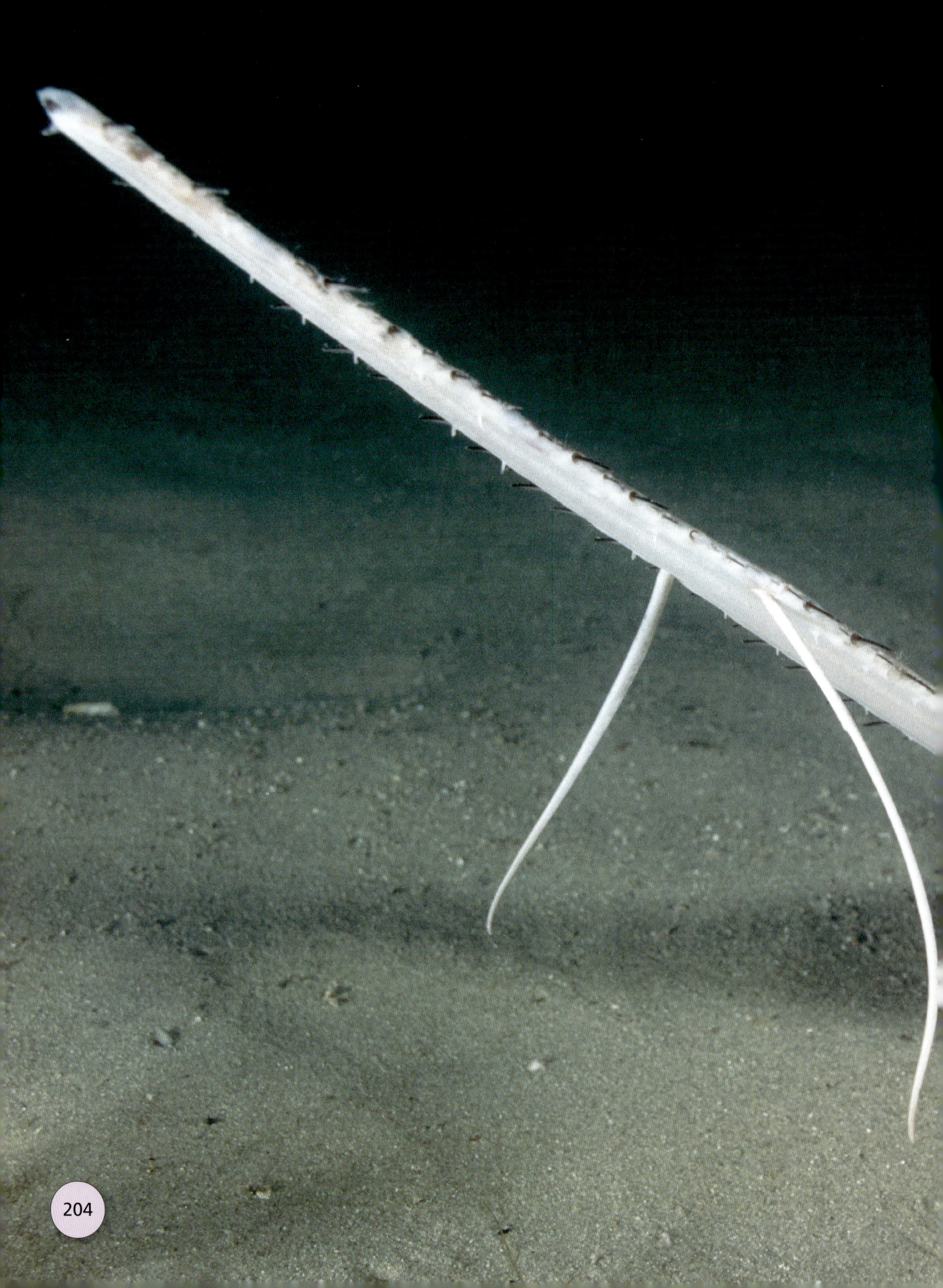

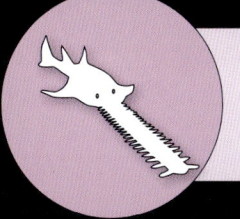

Sawsharks

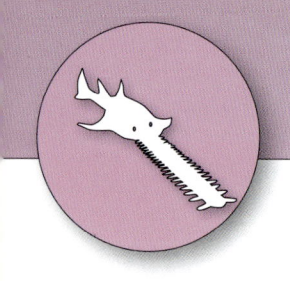

Sawsharks

- **Part of an order of eight shark species**, sawsharks have flat heads and long, saw-shaped snouts. They spend most of their time swimming or resting on the sea bed.

- **The snout** is called a rostrum. It is pointed and has teeth, called rostral teeth, of various sizes sticking out all the way around it.

- **At around 70–150 cm in length**, sawsharks are relatively small.

- **Sawsharks use their saws** for digging up prey such as shellfish from the sea bed. They slash and jab at their prey before eating it.

- **Two long barbels** halfway along the snout help the sawshark feel its way along the sea bed.

- **People eat sawsharks** in Japan and Australia.

- **Most sawsharks are grey**, but the Japanese sawshark is a muddy-brown colour.

- **Sawsharks also use their long saws** for defence or for competing with rivals during courtship.

- **Sixgill sawsharks** are the only sawsharks with six pairs of gill slits; other sawsharks have only five pairs. Sixgill sawsharks also have their barbels closer to their mouth than other sawsharks, but are otherwise very similar.

- **Female sawsharks give birth** to between seven and 17 pups at a time. The large rostral teeth lie flat against the pups' snouts until after they are born, so they don't injure their mother.

Sawsharks

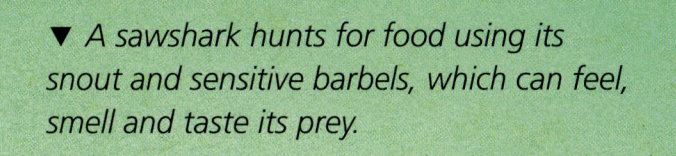

▼ A sawshark hunts for food using its snout and sensitive barbels, which can feel, smell and taste its prey.

DID YOU KNOW?
Sawsharks aren't usually seen near the shore. They prefer to live at depths of up to 400 m.

Snout

Rostral teeth

Barbel

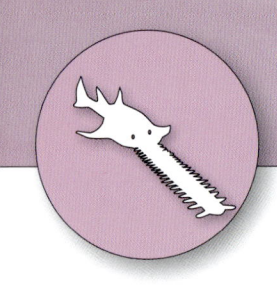

Longnose sawshark

- **The snout of a longnose sawshark** can make up one third of the total length of its body.

- **The long 'saw'** is not just a serious weapon. It is also able to sense vibrations and the electricity given off by other living things, including prey.

- **The long barbels** are sensitive to changes of pressure and chemical concentrations in the water.

- **The longnose sawshark** usually grows to about one metre in length, but it can reach maximum lengths of about 1.5 m.

▼ The barbels of the longnose sawshark are about half way along its remarkable snout. There are up to 21 rostral teeth along the sides of the long snout.

Sawsharks

- **The gill slits** are on the sides of the head and there are spiracles near the eyes.

- **Older longnose sawsharks** have tooth-like denticles on their side fins.

- **The longnose sawshark** occurs in groups, called schools, or gathers together with other longnose sawsharks to feed.

- **Living at depths of between 40 and 300 m**, longnose sawsharks prefer to hunt over sandy and muddy sea floors.

- **Female longnose sawsharks** give birth to between six and 19 pups at a time, after being pregnant for about one year.

- **Young longnose sawsharks** are 30–36 cm long when they are born and may survive for at least 15 years.

▶ The longnose sawshark lives in southern Australia, on or near sandy or gravelly sea beds. This is probably a young sawshark, since it has two or three smaller teeth in-between the large teeth on its snout.

Sawsharks

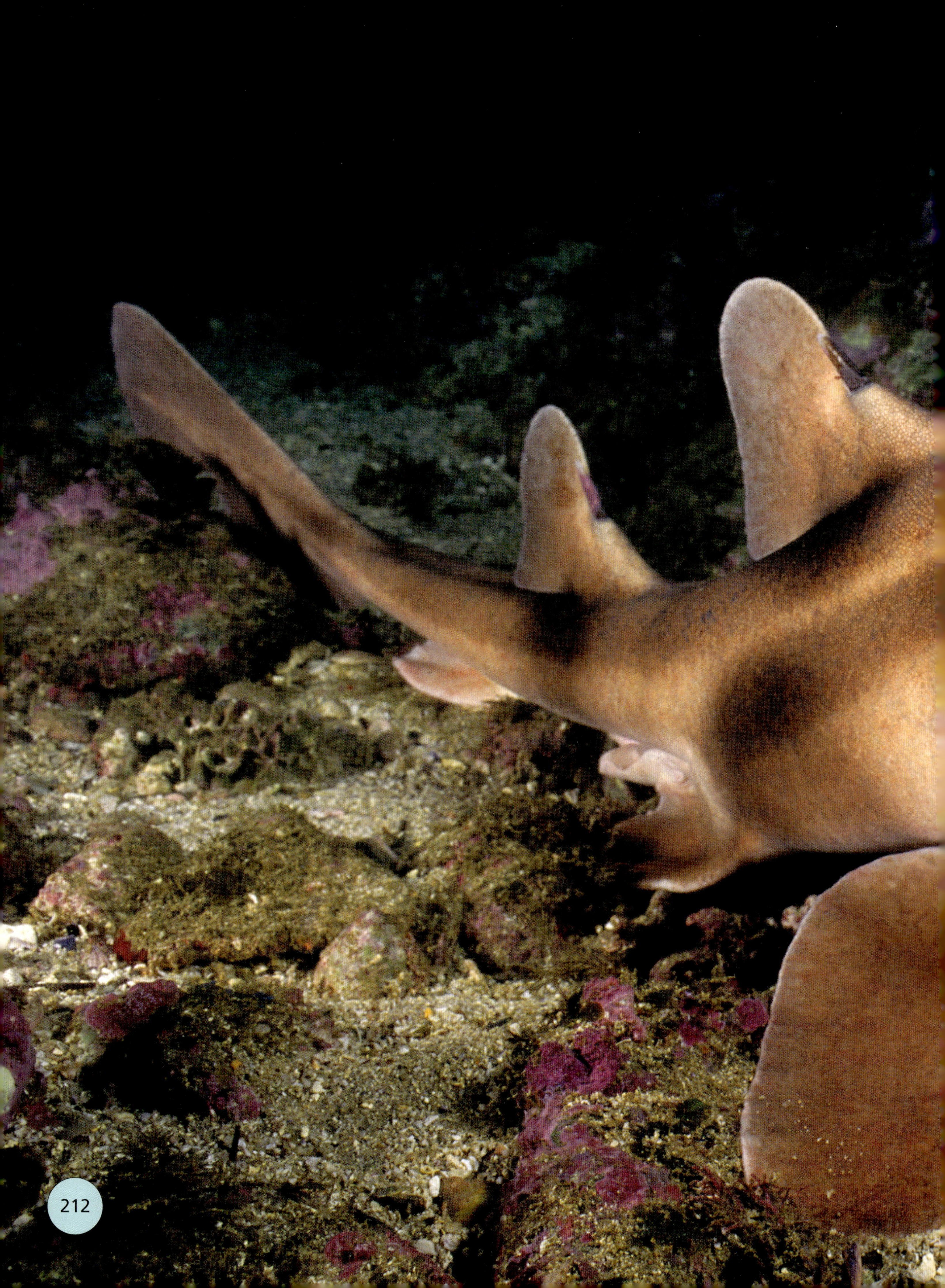

Bullhead sharks

213

Bullhead sharks

- **There are nine species** of bullhead sharks, including the horn shark, the Galapagos horn shark and the Port Jackson shark.

- **These stocky sharks** all have a pig-like snout and a small mouth in front of their eyes.

- **The prominent brow ridges** are polished smooth in species that rest by day in caves, or under ledges of rock or coral.

- **Bullhead sharks** are more active by night than by day.

- **They live in shallow coastal waters**, which are usually less than 100 m deep.

- **These sluggish sharks** wriggle slowly over the sea bed hunting for prey, or clamber over the bottom on their paddle-like front fins.

- **Bullheads are small sharks**, growing to lengths of 1.2–1.7 m.

- **The sharp spines** on their back fins deter predators from trying to eat them.

Bullhead sharks

➤ **Bullheads have two different** sorts of teeth. The pointed front teeth are used to hold prey, while the large, blunt back teeth are used for crushing shellfish and other small sea creatures.

➤ **Female bullhead sharks** lay eggs inside leathery egg cases, which are shaped like screws. They are such an awkward shape that it takes the mother several hours to lay each egg case.

▼ *A male crested bullhead shark eating the egg case of another species, a Port Jackson shark.*

Horn shark

- **The horn shark** is a small shark. Males grow up to 60 cm long, while females are larger, reaching lengths of at least 80 cm. They can reach a maximum length of 1–1.2 m.

- **These sharks live** only in the east Pacific Ocean, in rocky habitats.

- **They live** in warm, shallow coastal waters about 2–11 m deep.

- **Young horn sharks** prefer sandy places, but adults are more common on rocky reefs. This reduces competition for food.

- **Adult horn sharks** are more active at night, while young horn sharks tend to come out during the day.

- **Bat rays make hollows and pits** in the sand as they feed and this makes it easier for young horn sharks to find prey. They can also hide from predators in the hollows.

- **Crabs and sea urchins** are the preferred prey of horn sharks.

- **Horn sharks are named** after the poisonous spines, or horns, in front of both of their back fins.

- **Horn sharks have pig-like snouts** and large lumps above their eyes that look rather like eyebrows.

- **After laying her eggs**, the female horn shark picks them up with her mouth and places them into a rock crevice to keep them safe.

Bullhead sharks

Spine

DID YOU KNOW?
Some horn sharks have red-stained teeth because of all the sea urchins they eat.

▲ The flexible, muscular pectoral fins of the horn shark help it to crawl over the sea bed as it searches for prey.

218

Bullhead sharks

▲ A horn shark props itself up on its strong front fins as it rests on the sea bed off the coast of California. Its huge, pig-like nostrils are very good at picking up the scent of food.

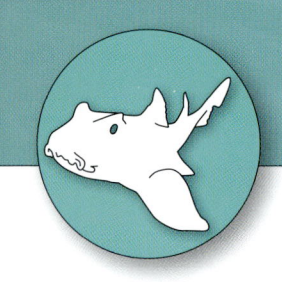

Port Jackson shark

- **The Port Jackson shark** is a type of bullhead shark.

- **It is named after Port Jackson** (the inlet containing Sydney harbour in Australia) where it was first discovered, and lives mainly in southern Australia.

- **It has a unique black striped saddle-like pattern** on its back and a dark stripe under each eye.

- **The eye stripes** may reduce glare as the shark swims over shiny sea beds. Soldiers apply grease paint under their eyes for a similar reason.

- **A Port Jackson shark** can eat and breathe at the same time. It takes water in through the first gill slit and pumps it out through the other four gill slits, leaving the mouth free for feeding.

- **Port Jackson sharks** mostly come out at night to feed on sea urchins and small fish. They spend the day resting, often in groups in or near caves.

- **Mating and egg-laying** happens in late winter and spring.

- **Female Port Jackson sharks** gather at traditional egg-laying sites, and lay spiral-shaped egg cases.

Bullhead sharks

- **The egg cases** are wedged firmly into crevices on rocky reefs, with the pointed edge down.

- **The young hatch out** of the eggs after about one year developing inside the egg cases. Males take up to ten years to mature, while females take up to 14 years.

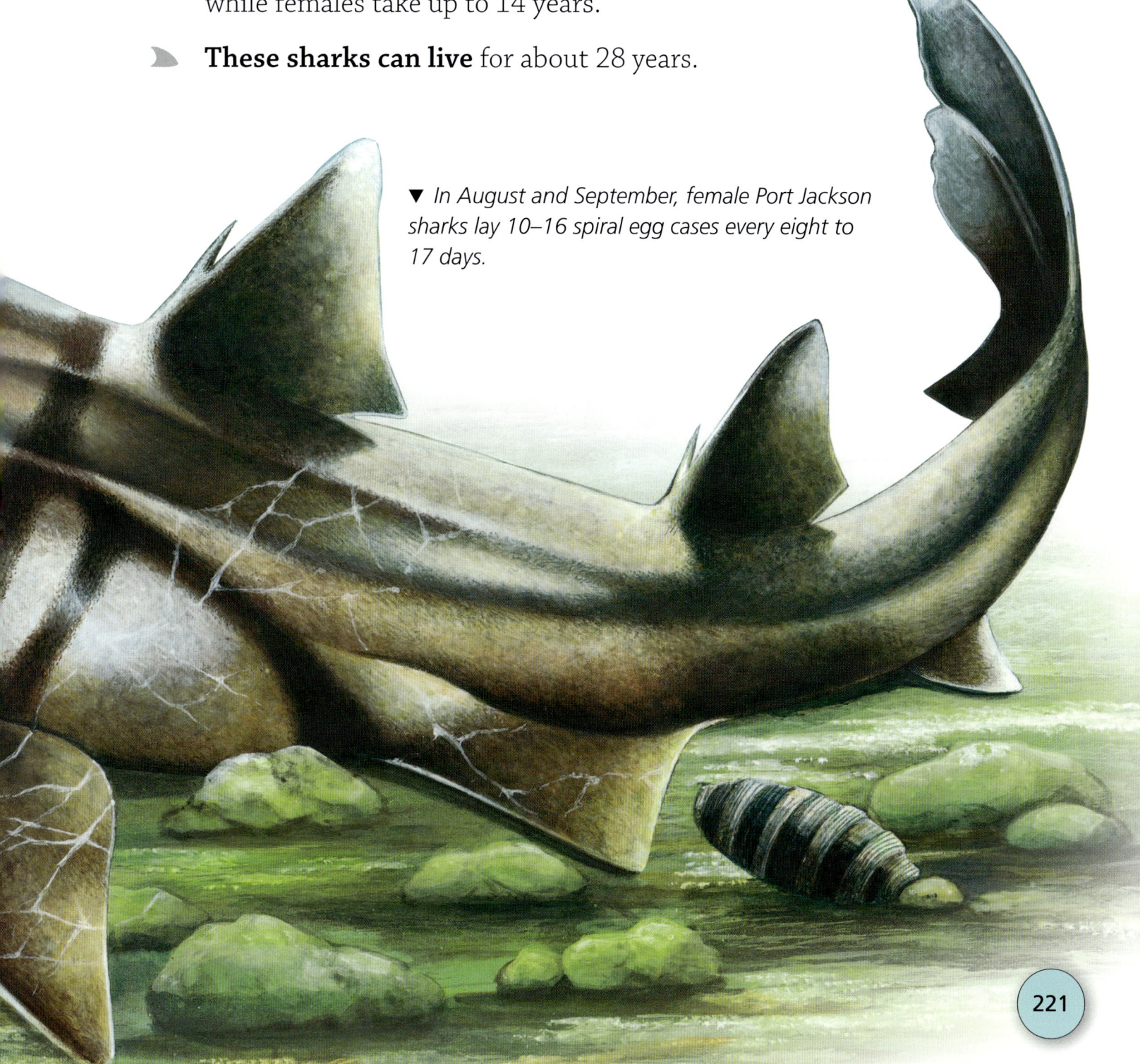

- **These sharks can live** for about 28 years.

▼ *In August and September, female Port Jackson sharks lay 10–16 spiral egg cases every eight to 17 days.*

222

Bullhead sharks

▼ The Port Jackson shark has a distinctive black pattern, and its snout is similar to that of the horn shark, its close relative. These common sharks are often kept and bred in captivity.

224

Carpet sharks

Carpet sharks

- **The carpet sharks** are a varied group of about 40 different species of shark.

- **Species include** blind sharks, wobbegongs, nurse sharks, bamboo sharks and the zebra shark, as well as collared and long-tailed carpet sharks.

- **Many types** are less than one metre long, but this group also includes the whale shark, which is the biggest shark of all.

- **They live in warm tropical seas**, such as those around Australia, Indonesia and Arabia, and often inhabit shallow waters around reefs and sandbars.

▼ *The wobbegong shark's clever camouflage helps it to catch unsuspecting prey, such as this fish, as it swims by.*

Carpet sharks

Large dark patch

▲ The spotted skin of an epaulette shark helps it to blend in with the patterns on the sea bed.

- **Carpet sharks** often lie still on the sea bed. Many species have a slightly flattened body shape that helps to camouflage them.

- **Most carpet sharks** feed on crabs, shellfish, octopus and sea worms.

- **Some carpet sharks lay eggs** in cases, while others give birth to pups.

- **Many carpet sharks** have beautiful speckled markings, which resemble the patterns of carpets or tapestries.

- **Long-tailed carpet sharks** have extra-long tails, with long, fine fins that resemble fronds of seaweed.

- **The barbelthroat carpet shark** has barbels on its throat.

> **DID YOU KNOW?**
> Collared carpet sharks can change colour to match their surroundings.

Epaulette sharks

- **Epaulette sharks** get their name from the dark patches on the sides of their body above the pectoral fins, which are like epaulettes (cloth flaps) on a jacket.

- **Their large, dark 'eye spots'** may help to startle a predator or divert its attention away from the shark's real eyes.

- **Epaulette sharks** belong to the group of long-tailed carpet sharks.

- **Growing to a maximum length** of 107 cm, the epaulette shark is more active at dusk or night.

- **It lives in shallow coral reef areas** of northern Australia and New Guinea, where it hunts for worms, shrimps and crabs among corals and rock pools.

- **The eggs of the epaulette shark** take from 115–130 days to hatch.

- **Epaulette sharks** use their strong, paddle-like front fins to crawl and clamber about, rather like salamanders.

- **When they are scared**, they will crawl away rather than swim.

Carpet sharks

- **Michael's epaulette shark** has a pattern of spots covering its body, with a large black 'eye spot' on the side behind its head. It lives in the waters around Papua New Guinea.

- **Henry's epaulette shark** has a double 'eye spot' on either side of its body, just behind the gills.

▼ Henry's epaulette shark 'walking' over a coral reef in Indonesia.

Blind sharks

- **Another type of carpet shark** is the blind shark. It is not actually blind. If caught and pulled out of the water, it closes its eyes very tightly, which makes it appear to have no eyes.

- **Blind sharks live** off the coast of Australia and are often found in shallow water near the shore. They hide in caves or crevices during the day and hunt at night.

- **There are only two species** of blind shark. One is simply known as the blind shark, while the other is called Colclough's shark or the blue-grey carpet shark.

- **Both types feed** by snuffling along the sea bed for cuttlefish, shellfish, squid, sea anemones and crabs.

- **The blind shark** is a yellowish colour underneath and brownish on top, with pale spots.

- **Young blind sharks** have dark stripes or bands across their bodies, which fade as they grow older.

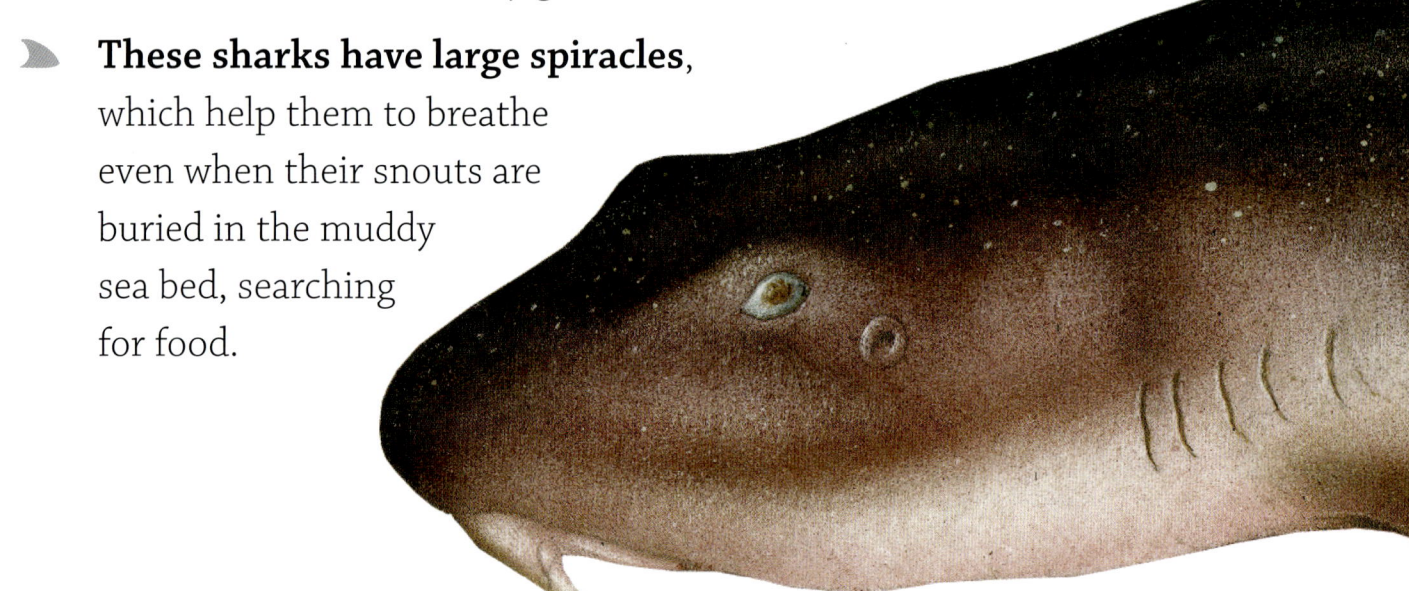

- **These sharks have large spiracles**, which help them to breathe even when their snouts are buried in the muddy sea bed, searching for food.

Carpet sharks

- **They have long sensory barbels** under their mouths, which help them to feel for food.

- **Female blind sharks** give birth to between six and eight pups at a time.

DID YOU KNOW?
Blind sharks can survive long periods out of water.

▼ Blind sharks can grow up to 120 cm in length but most are less than 80 cm long.

Wobbegongs

- **Wobbegong sharks**, also known as wobbies, belong to the carpet shark family.

- **The name 'wobbegong'** was given to these sharks by the Australian Aborigine people. It is thought that the word means 'shaggy beard'. Wobbegongs are often found in shallow, sandy water around the coast of Australia.

- **Wobbegongs can be quite large**, and some, such as the tasselled wobbegong, grow up to 4 m in length. They all have large, flattened bodies to help them hide on the sea bed.

- **Wobbegongs have lots** of whisker-like barbels around their mouths. The barbels of the spotted wobbegong are branched and frilly.

- **The tasselled wobbegong** has tassel-like barbels around its face, like a beard.

- **Wobbegongs are powerful sea bed predators**, feeding on smaller fish and other sea creatures, such as crabs, lobsters, octopus and squid. They suck in prey and spear it on their large teeth.

- **The strong jaws** of the wobbegong can easily bite off a person's hand or foot.

- **Wobbegongs sometimes bite people** who accidentally step on them. For this reason, they have a reputation as being dangerous. They may attack if they feel threatened.

Carpet sharks

- **Wobbegongs use their strong fins** to clamber around on the sea bed, sometimes even moving out of the water.

- **The female spotted wobbegong** has large litters of up to 37 pups.

▼ The beautiful gulf wobbegong lives on coral reefs around the coast of southern Australia. It sometimes attacks divers.

▶ A tasselled wobbegong using its broad front fins like wings to 'fly' over a coral reef. The tassels of skin around its jaws disguise the shape of its mouth, helping it to ambush its prey.

Carpet sharks

235

Bamboo sharks

- **Bamboo sharks** are part of the long-tailed carpet shark family, along with epaulette sharks, and the hooded and speckled carpet sharks.

- **They are harmless** to humans.

- **Bamboo sharks have** leg-like, muscular fins, which they use for clambering over coral reefs.

- **Young brown-banded bamboo sharks** have bold, dark-brown bands for camouflage, but the patterns fade to a plain brown colour in adults.

- **These sharks can survive** out of water for up to half a day, allowing them to feed in small pools on coral or rocky reefs.

- **The blue-spotted bamboo shark** has large white or blue spots on its dark brown skin.

- **It comes out at night** to feed on small fish and crabs, but hides away in rocky crevices by day. Its teeth are good for grabbing soft-bodied prey, but can also crush hard prey.

- **Female white-spotted bamboo sharks** release one or two round egg cases every six or seven days for about two months.

Carpet sharks

◗ **The young hatch** after about 100 days developing inside their protective egg case.

◗ **The white-spotted bamboo shark** is caught for food and for people to use in traditional Chinese medicine.

▼ The stripes on this young brown-banded bamboo shark help to break up its body shape as it rests among the eelgrass on the sandy sea bed.

238

Carpet sharks

▲ The brown-banded bamboo shark lives on coral reefs in the Pacific Ocean, from east India to northern Australia and Japan. It has a long, thick tail.

Nurse sharks

- **Unlike most carpet sharks**, nurse sharks don't have carpet-like markings. They are usually brownish-grey, and sometimes have a few spots.

- **Nurse sharks hunt at night**. During the day, they often lie on the sea bed in groups.

- **Nurse sharks** can reach 4 m in length.

- **These sharks have two barbels** beneath their noses. They use them to smell and feel for prey.

- **Nurse sharks** live in the east Pacific Ocean and the Atlantic Ocean.

- **They live in warm, shallow water** (usually up to about 12 m deep). Nurse sharks use their muscular pectoral fins to clamber about on rocky and coral reefs, and between mangroves.

- **Crabs, lobsters and sea urchins** are the preferred food of nurse sharks. They have broad, flat teeth to grind up hard shells.

- **If a nurse shark bites**, it hangs on with a clamp-like grip. It can be almost impossible to dislodge it.

- **The nurse shark** uses its snout to find prey and sucks food in rapidly. It can even remove conch snails from their shells.

- **Females give birth** to between 20 and 30 pups at a time, after a pregnancy lasting six months.

▶ *This nurse shark is using its strong pectoral fins to climb over rocks and coral on the sea bed.*

Carpet sharks

DID YOU KNOW?
Nurse sharks are named after the loud sucking noise they make when feeding, which sounds rather like a human baby drinking milk from its mother.

Tawny nurse shark

- **Part of the carpet shark group**, tawny nurse sharks are related to nurse, blind and whale sharks.

- **At 3 m in length**, the tawny nurse shark is quite large. It lives in warm tropical seas close to the shore.

- **The tawny nurse shark** is also known as the spitting shark because it spits water as a defence if captured.

- **After spitting**, the tawny nurse shark is said to grunt. It is one of the few sharks thought to make a noise.

- **The tawny nurse shark** has fairly long sensory barbels on its mouth to help it feel for food.

- **Its prey includes corals**, crabs, octopuses, sea urchins and reef fish. Sometimes it even eats sea snakes.

- **The colour of the tawny nurse shark** may slowly change to different shades of brown to match its surroundings and provide good camouflage.

▶ *Tawny nurse sharks live near the coast in shallow waters up to 30 m deep. They have a wide range, from Australia, Indonesia and Japan to eastern Africa, the Red Sea and India.*

Carpet sharks

- **Tawny nurse sharks** rest in groups during the day, sheltering in caves or rocky crevices.

- **Female tawny nurse sharks** give birth to between one and 26 pups at a time. The young are 40–60 cm long at birth.

- **Tawny nurse sharks** are usually docile with divers, but may bite if they are disturbed too much.

DID YOU KNOW?

The tawny nurse shark has a powerful, sucking mouth, which it uses to extract prey such as fish and octopuses from their hiding places.

Zebra shark

- **The zebra shark** grows up to 3 m in length. Like thresher sharks, zebra sharks have very long tails.

- **Distinctive dark and pale stripes** give zebra sharks their name. They only have these when they are young – as they become adults, the stripes separate into blotches.

- **The broad tail fin** of a zebra shark is as long as its body.

- **The zebra shark** is sometimes called the leopard shark because adults have brown spots on yellowish skin.

- **The striped skin** of newborn zebra sharks and the way they swim makes them look like banded sea snakes. As these sea snakes are very poisonous, this resemblance may help to protect them.

- **Zebra sharks** feed on shellfish, crabs, small fish and possibly sea snakes. These sharks usually live on their own.

- **A zebra shark's egg cases** are a purplish-brown colour. They have tufts of hair to help them lodge firmly among rocks and seaweed.

Carpet sharks

▲ Adult zebra sharks have distinctive spotted skins. They are more active at night and can swim strongly to search for food.

▶ **Female zebra sharks** can produce female pups without their eggs being fertilized by a male zebra shark.

▶ **Scientific research** has shown that the zebra shark and the whale shark are, surprisingly, closely related.

▼ A stripy zebra shark pup, which has just hatched out of its egg case.

246

Carpet sharks

▲ Zebra sharks spend most of the day resting on the sea floor. They can breathe easily as they face into the current and pump water over their gills.

Whale shark

- **Whale sharks** are the biggest kind of shark and the largest fish on Earth. They grow to an enormous length of 14 m and have the same mass as a double-decker bus.

- **Their closest relatives** are zebra sharks and short-tail nurse sharks – not other filter-feeders such as basking sharks or megamouths.

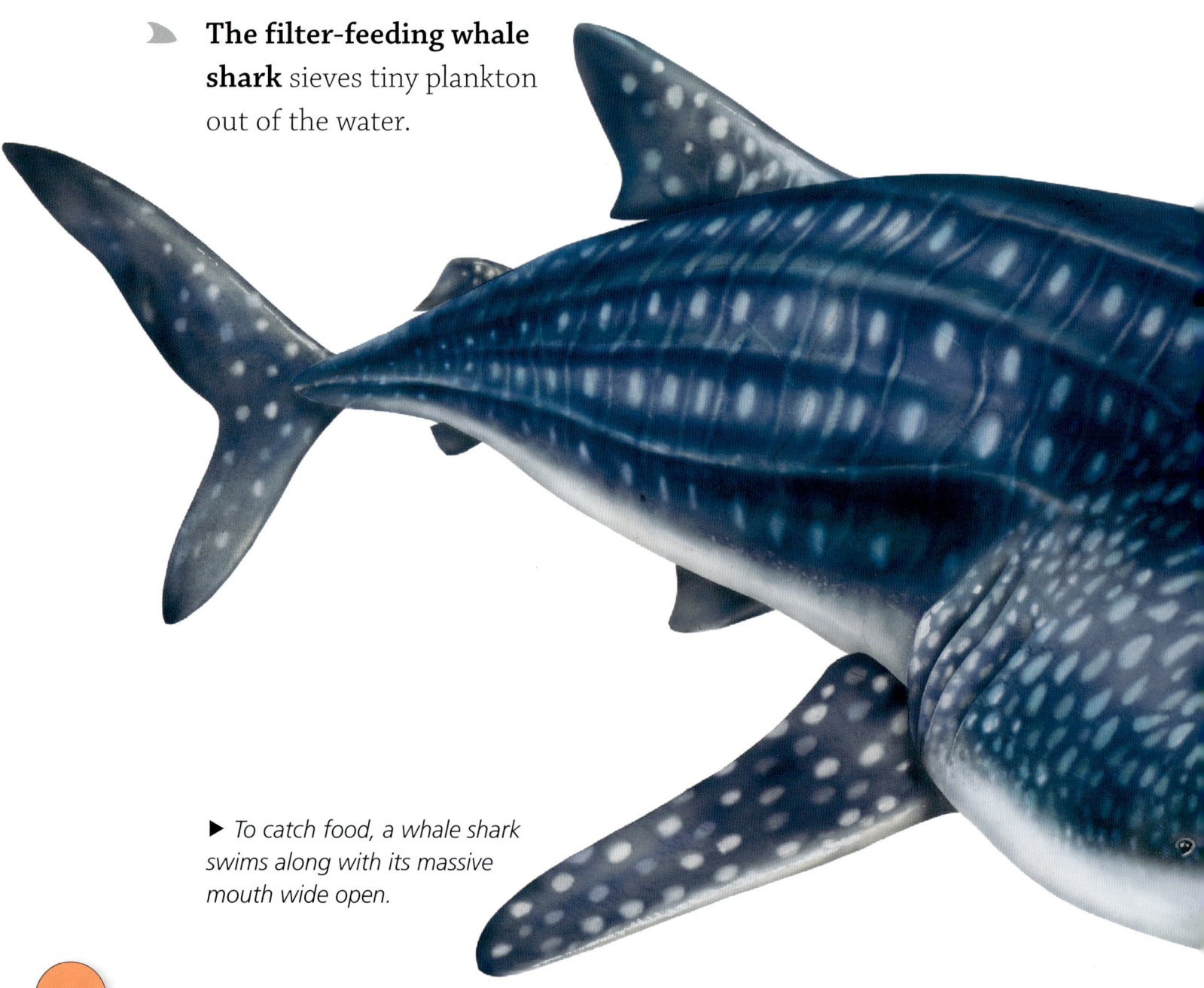

- **The filter-feeding whale shark** sieves tiny plankton out of the water.

▶ To catch food, a whale shark swims along with its massive mouth wide open.

Carpet sharks

- **These huge sharks** are harmless to humans.

- **Although a whale shark** has around 3000 tiny teeth, they are of little use. Instead it uses bristles in its gills to trap food.

- **Scientists think that some whale sharks** could live to be 100 years old or more.

- **Whale sharks scoop up food** at or near the surface of the water, sometimes hanging vertically and bobbing up and down.

- **The whale shark** has an extra-large liver full of oil to help it swim along slowly at the surface without sinking.

- **A whale shark's liver** makes up about 20 percent of its body weight and may weigh as much as a small car.

- **One female whale shark** was found with 300 pups inside her.

Huge mouth, up to 1.5 m across

DID YOU KNOW?
A whale shark's skin is around 10 cm thick, making it the thickest of any living creature.

250

Carpet sharks

◀ Whale sharks suck water in through their massive mouths, trapping food on their gills. They may gather in groups of up to 100 where there are large concentrations of food.

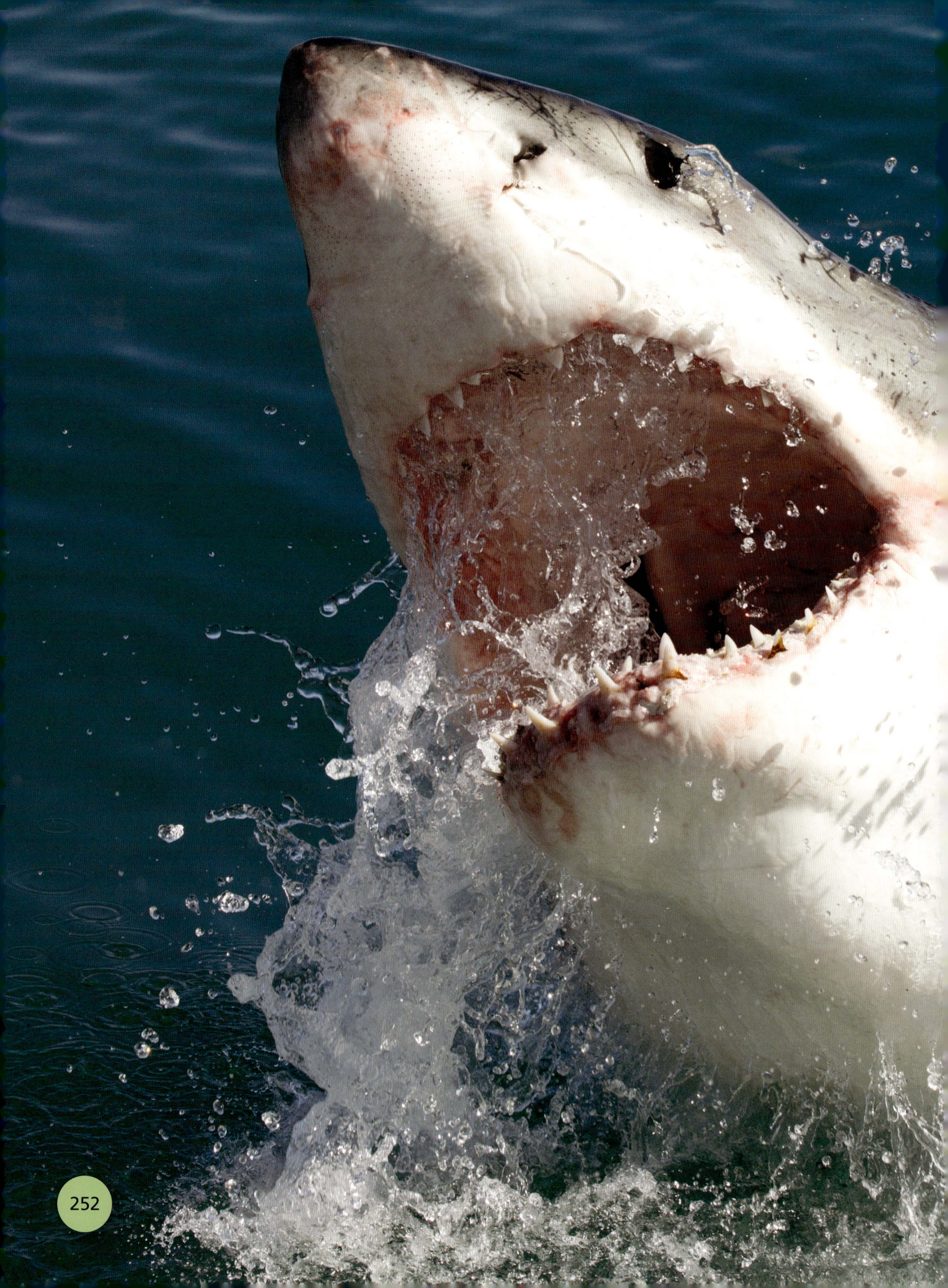

Mackerel sharks

Mackerel sharks

- **The mackerel shark family** consists of 15 species. They are mainly active, fast, open-ocean predators that live near the surface of the sea.

- **The most famous shark**, the great white, belongs to this family, as do mako, salmon and porbeagle sharks.

- **Two filter-feeding sharks** – the megamouth shark and the basking shark – are also in the mackerel shark family.

- **One very unusual mackerel shark** is the goblin shark, with its sensitive, blade-like snout.

- **The diet of mackerel sharks** varies from dolphins, seals, birds and turtles, to other sharks, rays, fish and small sea creatures.

- **Some of the larger mackerel sharks**, such as the great white, sometimes bite people.

- **Many mackerel sharks** live in groups and some, such as thresher sharks, hunt together.

Mackerel sharks

- **Some mackerel sharks**, such as the shortfin mako, migrate long distances.
- **Mackerel sharks** give birth to pups rather than laying eggs.
- **Most mackerel sharks** are threatened by over-fishing.

▼ *Measuring up to 3.5 m in length, the porbeagle shark is warm-blooded and a fast swimmer.*

Goblin shark

- **With its incredibly long**, flattened and pointed snout, the goblin shark looks very strange.

- **The long snout** looks like a weapon, but in fact, scientists think it helps the shark find prey using its sense of electrical detection.

- **Goblin sharks** have pale-pink skin that is much softer and flabbier than most other sharks'. It bruises easily.

- **Goblin sharks feed on fish**, squid and crustaceans such as crabs and lobsters.

- **Like many sharks**, the goblin shark pushes its jaws forwards as it attacks.

- **They have sharp teeth** at the front of their mouths for grabbing prey and smaller teeth at the back for chewing.

- **When they are born**, goblin sharks are 80–90 cm long, but they grow to lengths of at least 4 m.

- **Goblin sharks** live in the Atlantic Ocean, Pacific Ocean and western Indian Ocean.

- **The goblin shark's large liver** takes up 25 percent of its body weight, but scientists don't know why it is so big.

- **Scientists still do not know** much about these sharks as they are rarely caught.

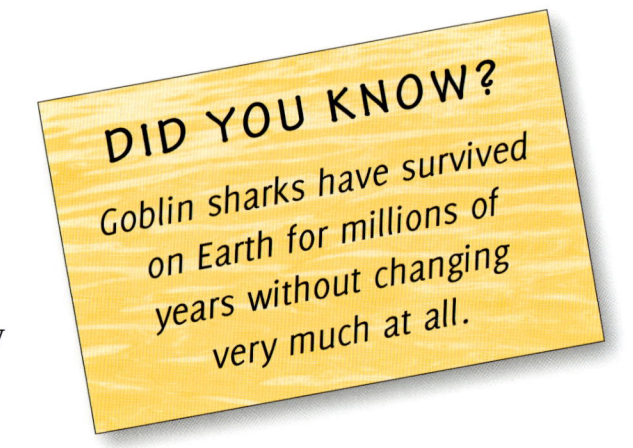

DID YOU KNOW?
Goblin sharks have survived on Earth for millions of years without changing very much at all.

Mackerel sharks

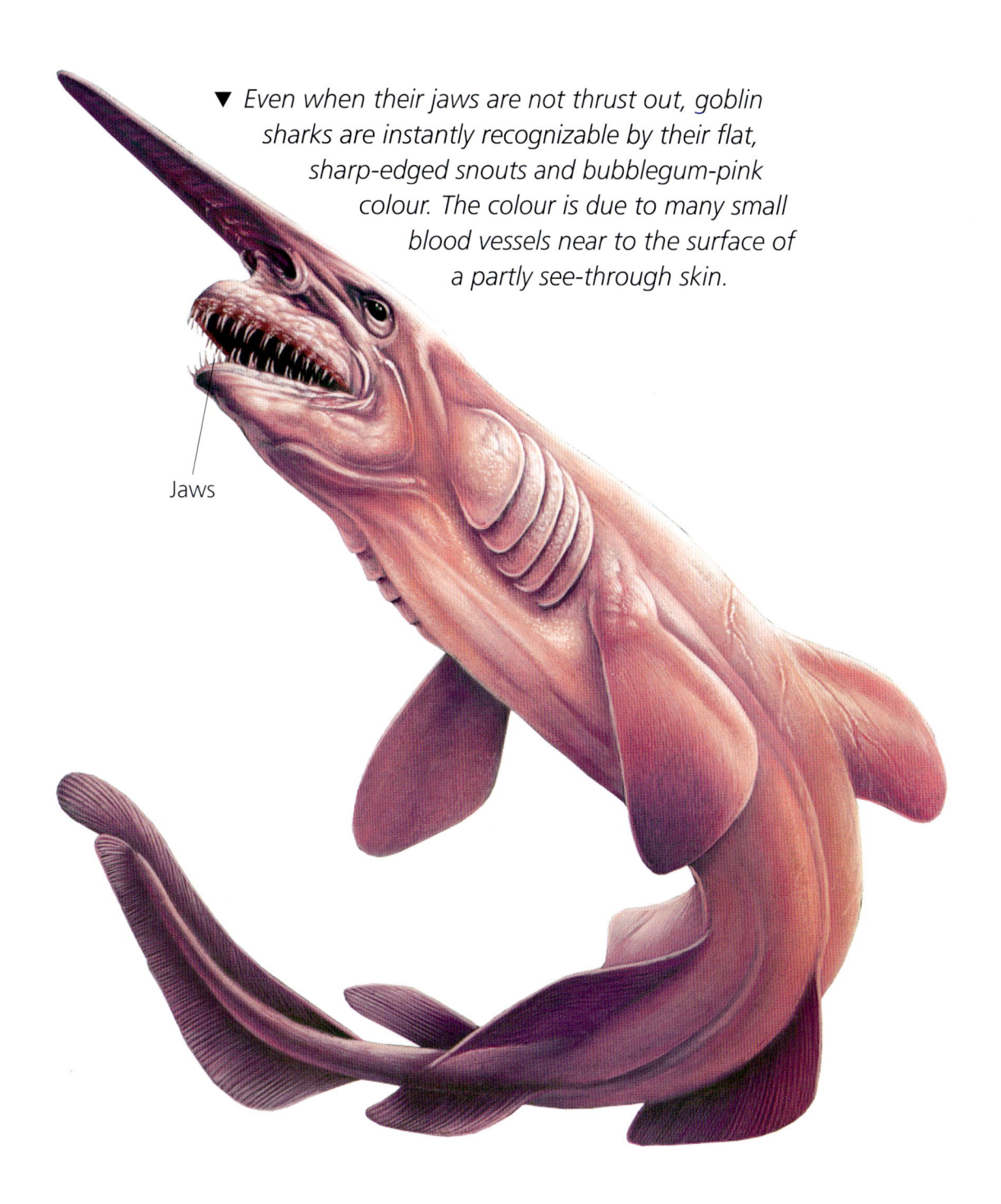

▼ Even when their jaws are not thrust out, goblin sharks are instantly recognizable by their flat, sharp-edged snouts and bubblegum-pink colour. The colour is due to many small blood vessels near to the surface of a partly see-through skin.

Jaws

Sand tiger shark

- **A typical sand tiger shark** is around 2–3 m long. It has brownish markings, but is not stripy like a tiger.

- **Sand tiger sharks** are not closely related to tiger sharks. They belong to a different order, and are more closely related to makos and great whites.

- **They are named** after their habit of swimming over the sandy sea bed, and because of their large, sharp teeth.

- **Their diet is mainly fish**, but occasionally sand tigers kill and eat bigger animals such as sea lions.

- **The species is popular** in aquariums. They are exciting to watch and survive well in captivity.

- **The sand tiger shark** has lots of gaps between its irregular, projecting teeth, giving it a 'snaggle-tooth' appearance.

DID YOU KNOW?
Sand tiger sharks have been known to approach divers who are spear-fishing and grab the fish off their spears.

Mackerel sharks

- **Sometimes, sand tiger sharks** feed together, surrounding prey to make it easier to catch.

- **Sand tiger sharks** can swallow air from the surface to help them hover at a particular depth in the water without using up a lot of their energy.

- **Male sand tiger sharks** guard females after mating, which gives their pups a better chance of surviving until they are born.

- **Female sand tiger sharks** give birth to two pups every other year after a pregnancy of between nine and 12 months. Pups hatch out of eggs inside the mother, and feed on the eggs and smaller pups that are produced after them.

▼ *A mouthful of sharp, pointed teeth helps the sand tiger shark to keep hold of slippery fish easily.*

Thresher sharks

▶ **There are three species** of thresher shark – the common, the pelagic and the bigeye.

▶ **Thresher sharks** are recognized by their extremely long tails. The upper lobe can be up to 50 percent of the shark's entire body length. Including the tail, these sharks can grow up to 6 m long.

▶ **They use their long tails** to round up shoals of small fish, such as sardines or herrings. Then they stun the fish by beating (or 'threshing') them with their tails before eating them.

▶ **Although threshers are big**, their mouths are small, so they only eat little prey.

Tail can be up to 3 m long

Mackerel sharks

- **Two or more thresher sharks** may work together to catch fish.

- **Thresher sharks** migrate away from the tropics to cooler waters in spring, and return to warmer waters in autumn.

- **Although thresher sharks** rarely attack humans, they have been known to injure fishermen by hitting them with their tails.

- **Common threshers** are the best-known sub-species, and are often seen near the seashore.

- **Pelagic threshers** get their name because they prefer to stay in the pelagic zone – the open sea – away from the seashore.

- **Bigeye threshers** often live in deep water. Their large eyes are up to 10 cm across.

> **DID YOU KNOW?**
> Thresher sharks have a reputation for being very cunning. Because of this, the ancient Greeks and Romans called them 'fox sharks'.

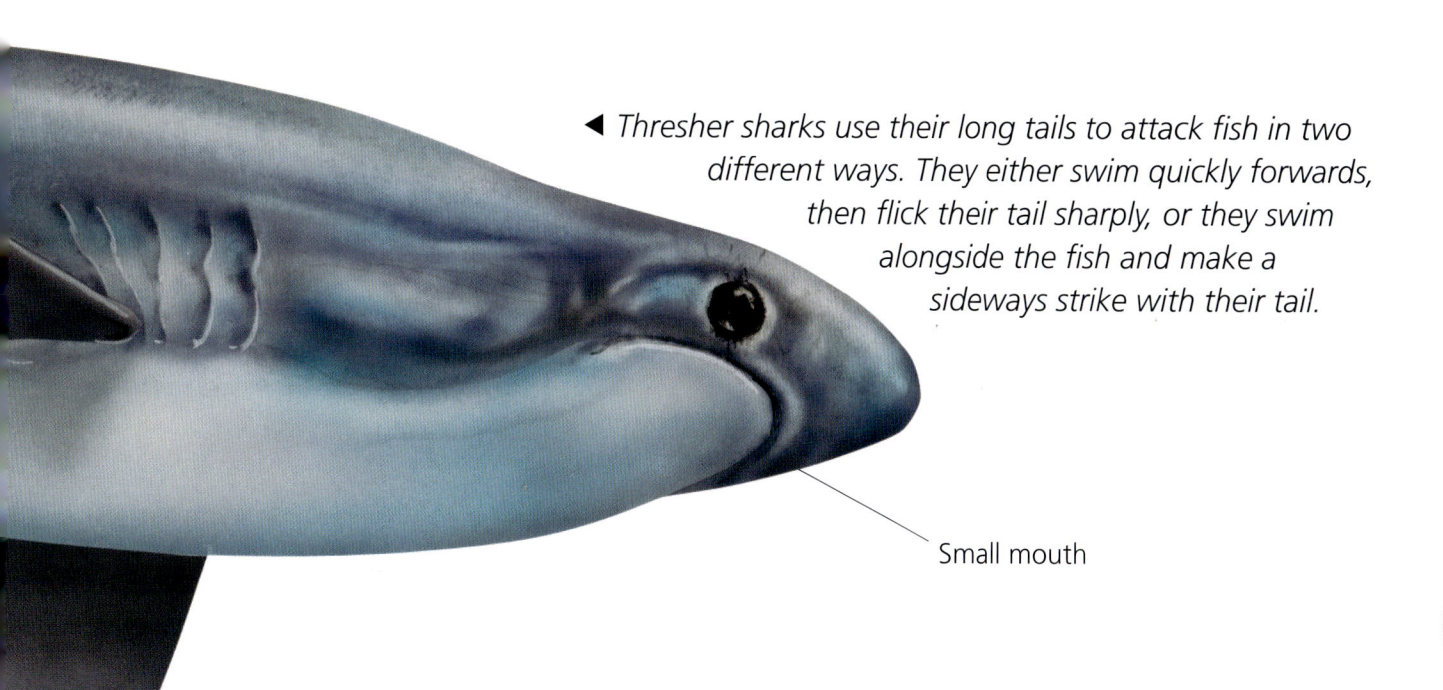

◀ Thresher sharks use their long tails to attack fish in two different ways. They either swim quickly forwards, then flick their tail sharply, or they swim alongside the fish and make a sideways strike with their tail.

Small mouth

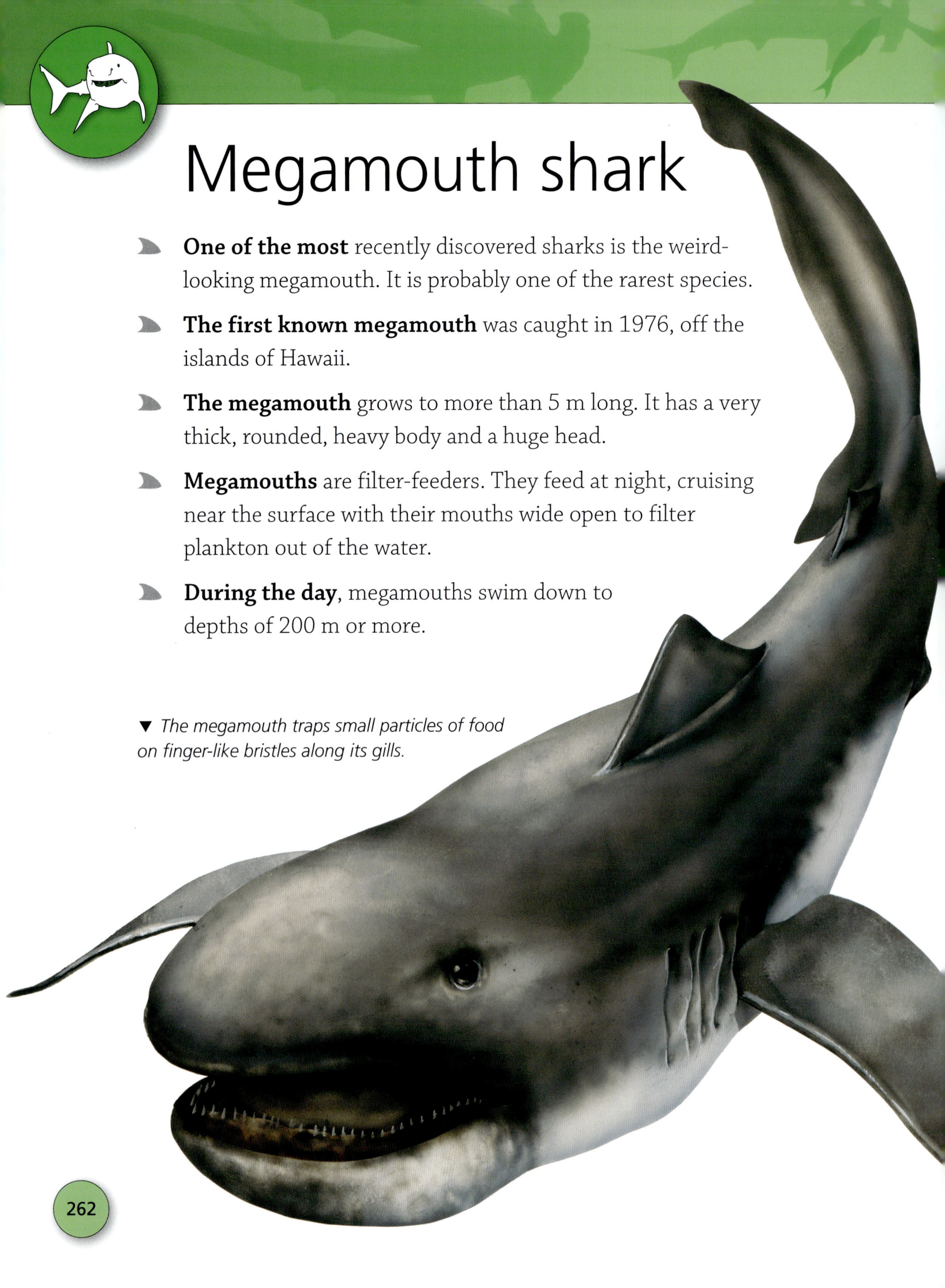

Megamouth shark

- **One of the most** recently discovered sharks is the weird-looking megamouth. It is probably one of the rarest species.

- **The first known megamouth** was caught in 1976, off the islands of Hawaii.

- **The megamouth** grows to more than 5 m long. It has a very thick, rounded, heavy body and a huge head.

- **Megamouths** are filter-feeders. They feed at night, cruising near the surface with their mouths wide open to filter plankton out of the water.

- **During the day**, megamouths swim down to depths of 200 m or more.

▼ *The megamouth traps small particles of food on finger-like bristles along its gills.*

Mackerel sharks

▲ The shark symbols on this map show where megamouth sharks have been found in the world's oceans. They have probably been lurking in the oceans for millions of years.

- **The megamouth** gets its name due to its huge mouth, which can be up to 1.3 m wide.

- **The scientific name** for the megamouth is *Megachasma pelagios*, which means 'huge yawner of the open sea'.

- **The mouth** is at the front of the snout, not underneath, as in most sharks.

- **Megamouths have been caught** around the world in the Pacific, Atlantic and Indian oceans.

DID YOU KNOW?
The inside of a megamouth's mouth may be silvery or reflective, or even glow-in-the-dark, in order to attract prey.

264

Mackerel sharks

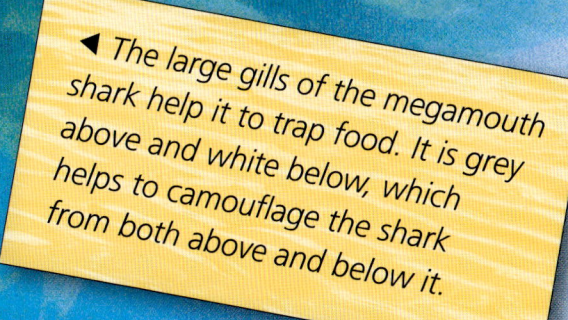

◀ The large gills of the megamouth shark help it to trap food. It is grey above and white below, which helps to camouflage the shark from both above and below it.

Crocodile shark

- **Scientists are trying** to find out more about the little-known crocodile shark.

- **When fully grown**, this species is still quite small – around one metre long.

- **The crocodile shark** has huge eyes compared to its body size. They take up almost half of its head.

- **Females usually give birth** to four babies at a time.

- **Small fish**, squid and shrimps are its main diet.

- **Before 1936**, crocodile sharks were unknown, until one was discovered in a Japanese fish market.

- **The crocodile shark's name** comes from the Japanese word, *mizuwani*, meaning 'water crocodile'. Like a crocodile, it has pointed teeth and snaps its jaws.

Mackerel sharks

- **Crocodile sharks** don't attack people, but if caught they may bite fishermen on the hand.

- **One of its closest relatives** is the megamouth shark – even though they are very different in size and feeding habits.

- **Crocodile sharks** may migrate to the surface to feed at night and swim back down to deeper water during the daytime.

DID YOU KNOW?
Crocodile sharks have been known to bite through undersea communications cables.

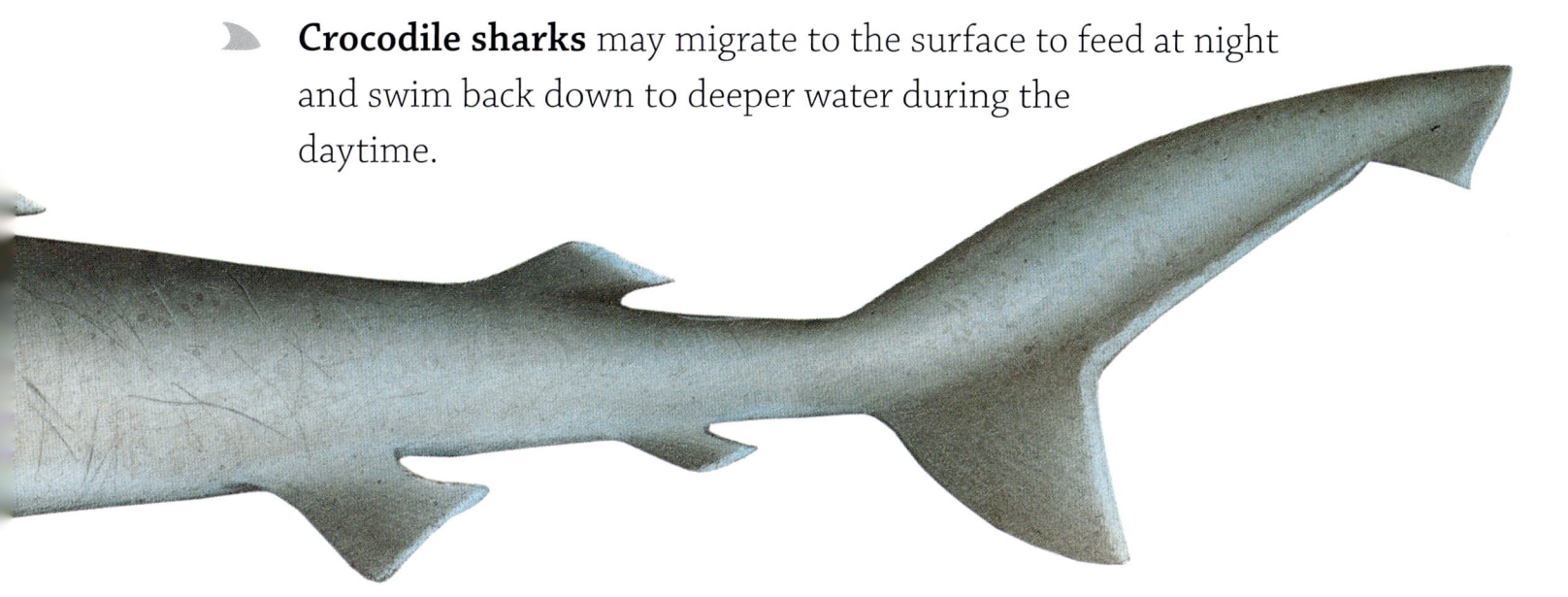

▲ *Its big teeth and large eyes make it look threatening, but the crocodile shark is no bigger than a medium-sized dog.*

Basking shark

- **Basking sharks get their name** because they appear to 'bask', or lie in the sun, close to the surface of the sea when they are feeding.

- **They are the second-biggest shark** after the whale shark, growing up to 12 m in length.

- **Basking sharks** are filter-feeders, and feed by sieving plankton out of the water.

- **These placid animals** do not attack humans. They lack big teeth for biting or chewing.

- **Basking sharks** will sometimes leap right out of the water, and then fall back down with a huge splash.

- **Other names for this species** are bone shark, elephant shark, bigmouth shark, or sunfish – because people used to think it enjoyed lying in the sun.

- **Occasionally basking sharks** have been seen swimming in large groups of 50 or more.

- **The basking shark** has huge gill slits that almost go right around its head. It traps food on slimy bristles, called gill rakers, in front of its gills. A basking shark has more than 5000 gill rakers.

Mackerel sharks

- **The basking shark** filters over 1.5 million litres of water in one hour. That's as much water as there is in an Olympic-sized swimming pool!

- **Unlike its cousin**, the great white, the basking shark is a gentle giant.

DID YOU KNOW?
Basking sharks have huge livers that weigh up to 2000 kg. The liver may contain 2682 l of oil!

▼ Basking sharks have enormous mouths up to one metre wide, which they open widely when feeding. Their gill rakers are shed and re-grown at regular intervals.

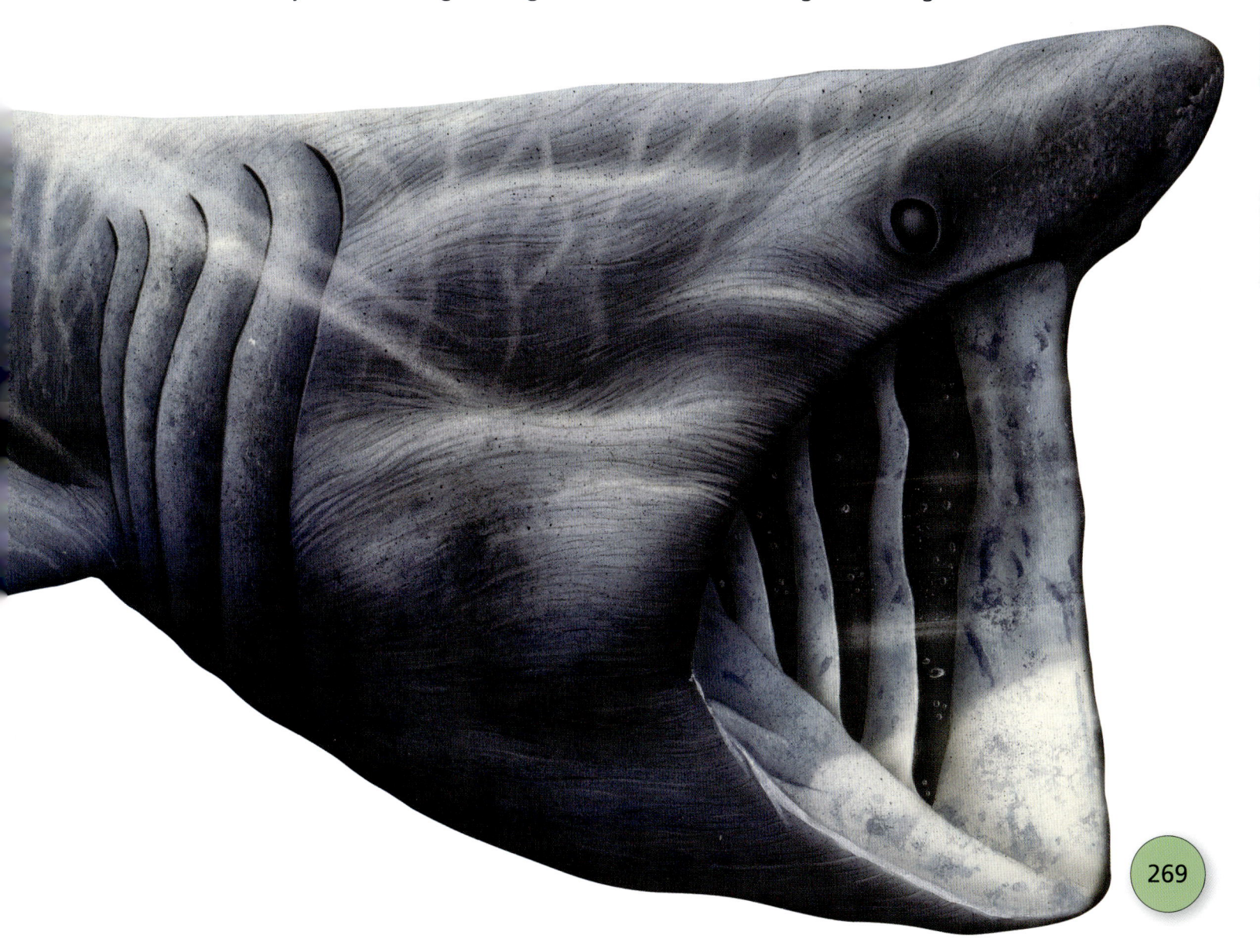

270

Mackerel sharks

▼ Basking sharks are sometimes seen feeding in surface waters off the coast of Cornwall, UK, during the summer months. This huge shark has a pointed nose and darker blotches of colour on its back and sides. It is a lighter colour on the underside.

Great white shark

- **The great white** is among the best-known of all sharks.

- **Belonging to** the mackerel shark group, great whites are fast, fierce hunters.

- **A typical great white** is around 4–5 m long – slightly longer than a car.

- **The biggest great whites** on record were over 7 m long.

- **Great whites** are often found in medium-warm waters, such as those around Australia and Japan.

- **When swimming**, great whites will sometimes poke their heads out of the water or leap high into the air.

- **Great white sharks** are warm-blooded and keep a high body temperature, even in cold water.

- **This helps to speed up** their digestion, especially of fatty foods (such as seals), which are hard to digest but full of energy.

- **Female great whites** give birth to between two and 13 pups at a time after a pregnancy of about 12 months.

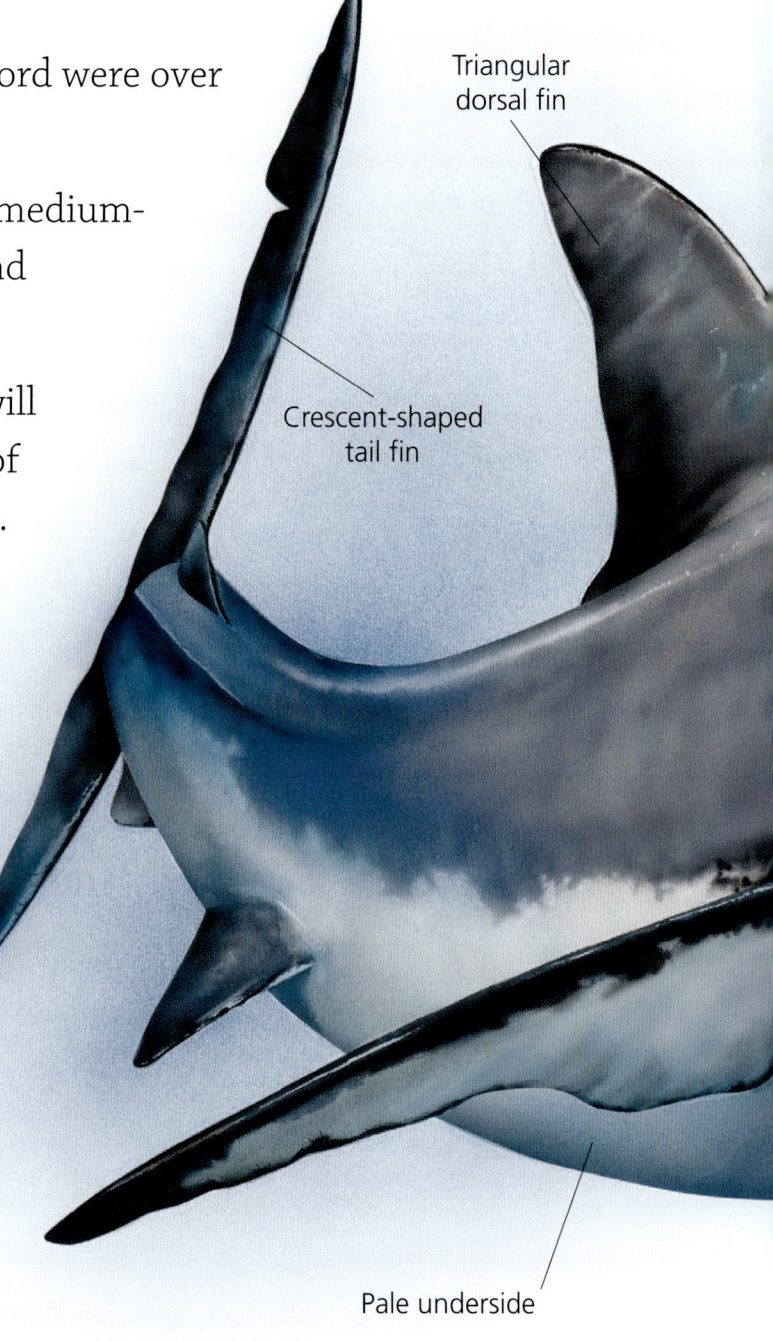

Triangular dorsal fin

Crescent-shaped tail fin

Pale underside

Mackerel sharks

➤ **It is difficult** to keep a great white in captivity. If they are put into an aquarium, they live for only a few days.

▼ *A great white shark's body is sturdy, powerful and built for hunting.*

Dark-grey upper body

Wide mouth with rows of large, serrated teeth

Wing-like pectoral fins

DID YOU KNOW?
One great white shark swam 17,703 km from southern Africa to Australia in less than nine months.

Champion hunter

- **The great white shark** is the biggest hunting fish in the sea.

- **It hunts in the daytime** and catches a wide variety of prey, from fish such as tuna, rays and smaller sharks, to marine mammals such as seals and dolphins, birds and turtles.

- **A great white** is not white all over. It has a white belly, but its back is a dark blue-grey colour. This is called countershading, which makes it hard for prey to see the shark from above or below.

- **In every bite**, a great white uses about 80 teeth. When its teeth wear out or break they are replaced, so it may use up to 30,000 teeth in a lifetime.

- **The biggest teeth** of a great white are up to 5 cm long.

- **In the top jaw**, a great white's teeth are shaped like triangles, with jagged edges like a saw for cutting into its prey.

- **The lower jaw** is full of smaller, more pointed teeth, which are good for holding slippery prey.

- **A great white can take big bites** because its loose jaws slide forwards to open very wide. This takes just a few seconds.

- **With large prey,** a great white may take a bite and then let go, leaving the animal to die from loss of blood before starting to feed.

- **In the final stages** of an attack, a great white rolls its eyes back into their sockets to avoid them being damaged if the victim tries to escape or fight back.

▶ A great white shark attacking a seal decoy in a science experiment. The shark is moving so fast that it can't stop when it grabs the seal, so it jumps right out of the water.

Mackerel sharks

▼ A great white shark, showing the distinct line between its grey back and white underside. The sharp, pointed teeth in its lower jaw are clearly visible, as is its very dark eye.

Mackerel sharks

Mako sharks

- **Swift and fierce makos** are strong, muscular hunting sharks that can swim at great speed.

- **One shortfin mako** travelled over 13,000 km in six months, swimming to and fro between New Zealand and Fiji.

- **Makos are closely related** to great whites, and they live and hunt in a similar way. They will sometimes attack humans, but their diet is predominantly fish.

- **They have long**, streamlined, graceful bodies and pointed snouts, and can grow up to 4 m in length.

- **Known for their vivid colours**, makos are dark purple-blue on top and silvery-white underneath.

- **A mako's smooth teeth** are very narrow and pointed to help them grab slippery fish in their jaws.

- **The name 'mako'** comes from the Maori word for 'shark'. Makos are common around New Zealand, the home of the Maori people.

Mackerel sharks

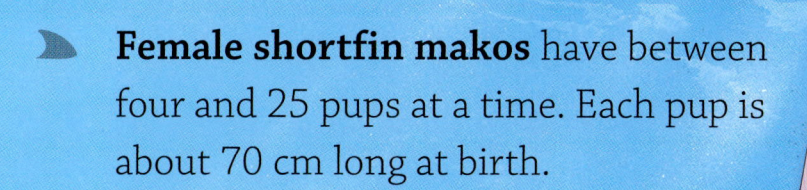

- **Female shortfin makos** have between four and 25 pups at a time. Each pup is about 70 cm long at birth.

- **People often fish** makos as a sport and they are also caught for food.

DID YOU KNOW?
There are two species of mako – the shortfin and the longfin. The longfin has longer pectoral fins and bigger eyes.

▼ A fast-swimming, active shark, the short-finned mako has large eyes, a long, pointed snout and large, dagger-like teeth. Its crescent-shaped tail fin enables it to swim at high speed.

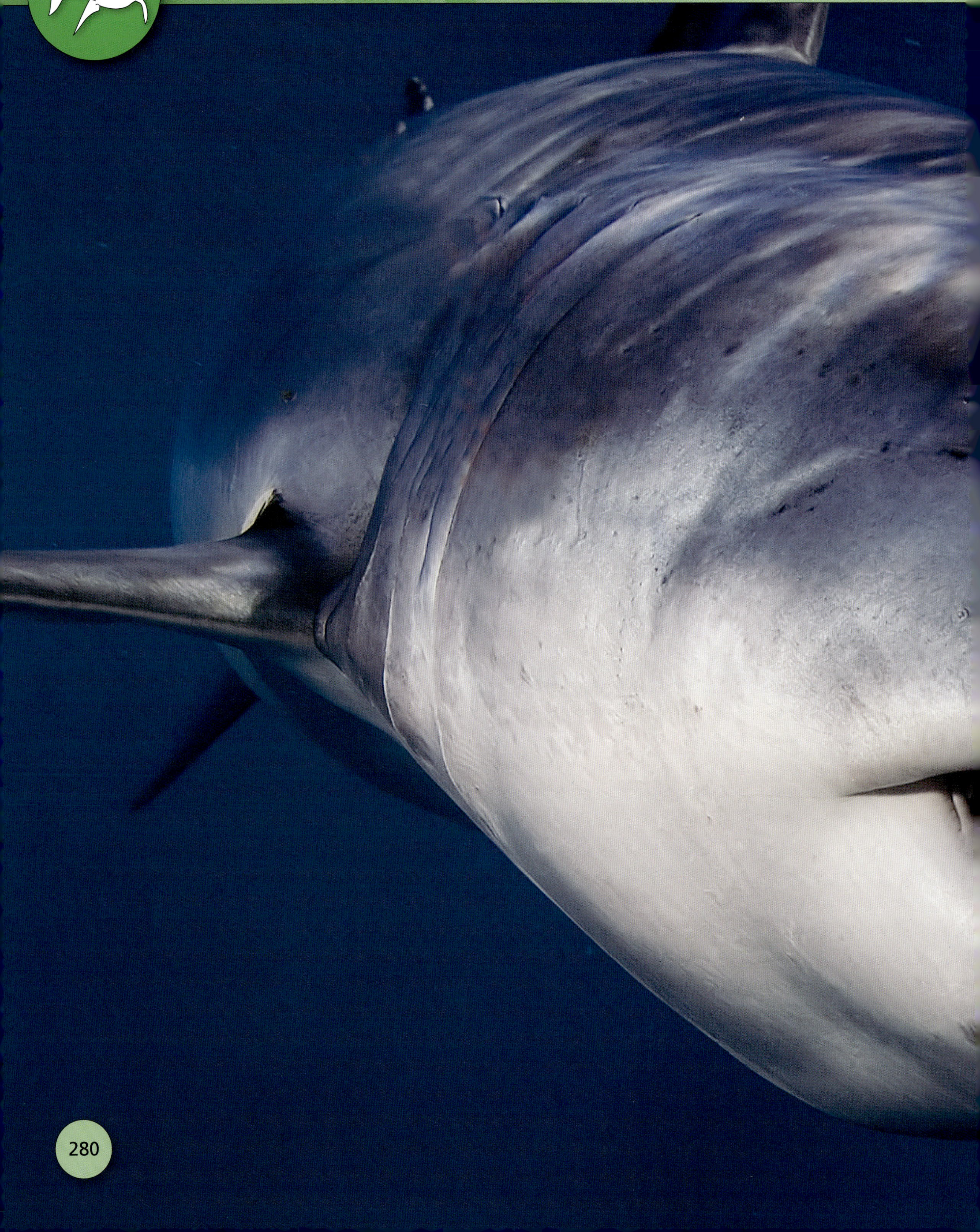

Mackerel sharks

▼ The tiny holes (called ampullae of Lorenzini) on the snout of this shortfin mako detect the electrical signals given off by its prey. Shortfin mako sharks are white under the snout and mouth, whereas the longfin mako is a dusky colour in these areas.

Salmon shark

- **The salmon shark** is closely related to the great white, makos and porbeagle sharks.

- **It has a heavy body**, a short, cone-shaped snout and long gill slits. Two keels (ridges) on the tail help it to swim at great speeds.

- **Salmon sharks** live in the North Pacific Ocean, in cool coastal waters and the open ocean, from the surface down to depths of at least 375 m.

- **Like its close relatives**, the salmon shark is warm blooded. This helps it to hunt prey in very cold water because its warm body temperature keeps its muscles working well.

- **Salmon sharks** feed mainly on schools of fish, such as salmon, herring and sardines.

- **They sometimes feed** in groups numbering 30 or 40 individuals.

- **This shark migrates** with the seasons, following its prey. Adults move further north than young sharks.

- **Female salmon sharks** give birth to between two and five pups every spring.

- **The pups** are 65–80 cm long when they are born.

- **Adult salmon sharks** grow to lengths of about 2.5 m, with some reaching lengths of 3 m.

▶ *The salmon shark has a distinctive white patch on the side of its body, at the base of its pectoral fins. Each year, large numbers of these sharks gather at river mouths along the northwest coast of North America to catch salmon returning to the rivers to breed.*

Mackerel sharks

283

Porbeagle shark

- **Like great whites**, porbeagles are grey on top and white underneath. They also have a white mark on their dorsal fins.

- **Porbeagle sharks** grow up to 3 m in length. They have a second keel on their tails, which helps them to swim fast.

- **These sharks prefer** cooler seas, such as the north and south Atlantic Ocean. Porbeagles can keep their body temperature warmer than their surroundings.

- **Porbeagles are inquisitive** and may attack humans. However, attacks are rare because people don't usually venture into their cold water habitats.

- **Their diet** is mostly fish and squid. They will chase shoals of mackerel over long distances.

- **Porbeagles have** long, sharp teeth to spear prey and stop it from escaping.

- **Their smooth-edged teeth** cannot cut the flesh, so prey is usually swallowed whole.

- **Porbeagles migrate** with the seasons, moving to coastal waters near the shore in summer and swimming to deeper water for the winter months.

- **Female porbeagles** give birth to between one and five pups after a pregnancy of 8–9 months.

Mackerel sharks

- **Porbeagles are among** the few fish that are thought to play. They roll over at the ocean surface, chase one another and wrap themselves in seaweed!

▼ *A porbeagle shark chases a shoal of fast-swimming mackerel.*

DID YOU KNOW?
The porbeagle shark may live for up to 65 years!

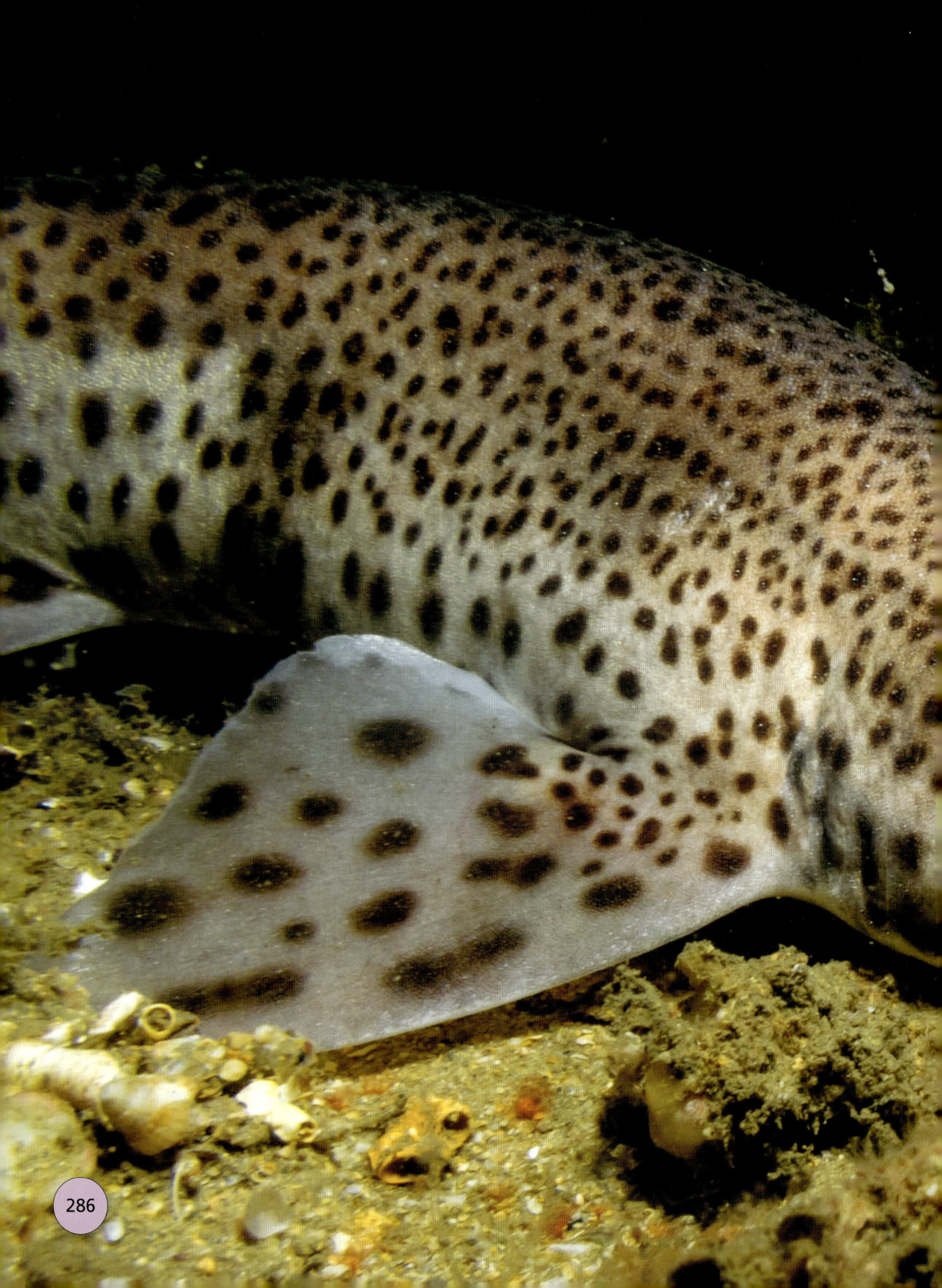

Ground sharks

Catsharks

- **Catsharks are the largest shark family**, with more than 160 species. Some have unusual names, including ghost catshark, demon catshark, bighead catshark, spongehead catshark and even Pinocchio catshark!

- **Catsharks are named** after their cat-like eyes.

- **They are usually** less than one metre in length, although some are only 30 cm long and a few reach 160 cm.

- **Catsharks eat** small fish and crabs.

- **Sometimes confused with dogfish**, catsharks can be identified by the fact that they lack spines on their dorsal fins and are usually slimmer than dogfish.

▼ The coral catshark lives among the coral reefs of the western Pacific Ocean, from Pakistan and India to New Guinea and southern China. It hunts at night for small fish, shellfish and shrimp.

Ground sharks

- **Dogfish are** also usually dull colours, but many catsharks have beautiful markings. The chain shark has patterns on its skin that look like silver chains.

- **Some catsharks** that live near the shore sleep in groups in rock crevices by day and come out at night.

- **Most catsharks** lay eggs in cases with long tendrils that curl round plants on the sea bed.

- **A few catsharks**, such as the lollipop catshark and the African sawtail catshark, give birth to pups.

- **Catsharks are not dangerous** to people and some are kept in aquariums.

▶ A baby smallspotted catshark develops inside its egg case for about nine months before it is ready to hatch out.

290

Ground sharks

◀ The dark spots on the long, thin body of this smallspotted catshark help camouflage it among weeds on the sea bed. It feeds on shellfish, crabs and worms as well as fish.

Swellsharks

- **Also known as balloonsharks**, swellsharks are slow-moving sharks, about 50–100 cm in length.

- **This species is named** after its ability to swell to twice its normal size by pumping water into its stomach.

- **This ability may startle** or frighten a predator, giving a swellshark time to escape.

- **If in danger**, a swellshark puffs itself up into a ball inside a rocky crevice so it can't be pulled out of the rocks.

- **At the surface**, the swellshark can also inflate its body with air instead of water. This works well – but must be noisily belched out when the threat has passed.

- **A closely related species**, the draughtsboard shark has dark and light checkerboard markings. It is said to bark like a dog as air escapes from its stomach.

- **Swellsharks have** long, wide mouths, which they use to gulp down mouthfuls of small fish before swallowing them whole.

Ground sharks

- **They have** up to 60 small, sharp teeth, with dagger-like points, in each jaw.

- **Swellsharks hide** in seaweed, caves and rocky crevices by day and come out at night to hunt for fish, crabs, shrimps and prawns.

- **Female swellsharks** usually lay two eggs in large, purse-shaped egg cases. The eggs take seven to ten months to hatch.

▼ The swellshark grows to a maximum length of about one metre. This sluggish shark is spotted and blotched all over, helping it to blend into a rocky sea bed covered with seaweed.

294

Ground sharks

▼ The swellshark lives on rocky sea floors in the eastern Pacific Ocean. Although this one is easy to see against a background of purple sea urchins, its markings usually give it good camouflage.

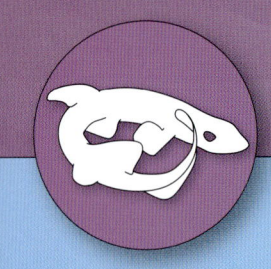

Houndsharks

- **There are more than 40 species** of houndshark, including the whiskery shark, the tope, the gummy shark and the leopard shark.

- **They are small** to medium-sized sharks, ranging from 40 cm to 150 cm in length.

- **Their oval eyes** have nictitating eyelids for protection.

- **Most types live** on shallow sea beds, but there are a few deep-water species that swim at great depths, possibly deeper than 2000 m.

- **Some species are very active** and swim most of the time. Others swim close to the sea bed and may rest on the bottom.

- **Instead of sharp**, biting teeth, most houndsharks have flat teeth for crushing prey, such as shellfish, crabs and lobsters.

Ground sharks

- **Gummy sharks** were named because they seemed to have no teeth. They actually have flat, grinding teeth instead of sharp, pointy ones.

- **Female houndsharks** give birth to between one and 52 pups.

- **Female gummy sharks** are pregnant for about one year. The pups are 30–35 cm long when they are born.

- **Houndsharks** are not dangerous to people.

DID YOU KNOW?
The sailback houndshark is named after the huge triangular fin on its back, which looks like the sail on a boat.

▼ A spotted houndshark swimming over a sandy sea floor near the Galapagos Islands. These stout houndsharks also live along the coasts of Peru and northern Chile.

Whiskery shark

- **The whiskery shark** is a species of houndshark that lives in Australia.

- **It has a variety** of common names including flake, snaky and sundowner.

- **The whiskery shark** is the only houndshark to have long barbels on its nose.

- **The barbels** help this shark to catch octopuses – its preferred food. It also eats squid, fish and lobsters.

- **The whiskery shark** has a stout body, which is almost a humpbacked shape. The two dorsal fins are quite large and a similar size and shape.

- **The short, arched mouth** of this shark is full of very sharp, blade-like teeth.

Ground sharks

- **Whiskery sharks** live on or near the sea bed in areas with rock, seagrass and seaweed, to depths of about 220 m.

- **Female whiskery sharks** give birth to between four and 29 pups at a time, after a pregnancy of seven to nine months.

- **The pups** are 20–27 cm long when they are born, but usually grow to lengths of about 135 cm.

- **The whiskery shark** grows up to a maximum length of 160 cm, and may live for as long as 15 years.

- **The oval eyes** of the whiskery shark are protected by a nictitating membrane.

▲ *Younger whiskery sharks have dark blotches all over their bodies for camouflage, but these blotches fade with age to a more general, brownish colour.*

DID YOU KNOW?
Whiskery shark pups double or triple in size in the first 15–17 months of their lives.

Tope shark

- **The tope shark** is a species of houndshark that lives all over the world in warm waters.

- **It usually swims** in small schools, so one of its alternative names is the school shark.

- **People catch a lot** of these sharks for their meat, liver oil and fins, which are used to make soup. As a result, the tope shark is also sometimes known as the oil or vitamin shark, and as the soupfin shark.

- **The tope shark** has a long, slim snout and its second dorsal fin is much smaller than its first.

▲ Tope, or school, sharks are strong swimmers and can swim up to 56 km in one day.

Ground sharks

- **It has a large, arched mouth**, with plenty of small, blade-like teeth for catching fish.

- **Tope sharks may make** long migration journeys to find food or safe places to have their young.

- **They also make** shorter daily migrations, from deep water in the day, to shallower water at night.

- **Females give birth** to between six and 52 pups once every three years, after being pregnant for about one year.

- **The pups are 30–40 cm** long when they are born, but grow up to be 120–180 cm.

- **Pups stay mainly** in shallow nursery areas near the shore for about two years, before joining schools of young tope sharks.

302

Ground sharks

▼ The large, oval eye of a tope shark dominates its very long snout. Tope sharks are blue-grey to light brown above and pale or white below. They can live for up to 60 years.

Smoothhound sharks

- **Smoothhound sharks** are a group of houndsharks that are important predators in coastal waters.

- **They feed on crabs**, lobsters, shrimps, squid and fish.

- **The starry smoothhound** will eat a crab whole, including the shell and any anemones living on it!

- **The common smoothhound** is usually found on or near the sea bed in water 5–50 m deep. It lives near the shore around river mouths and shallow bays that have sand, mud or gravel under the water.

- **After a pregnancy** of 10–11 months, female common smoothhounds give birth to between four and 15 young, each measuring about 40 cm in length.

- **The starry smoothhound** is named after the many small, white spots on its back and sides.

Ground sharks

▼ *Female Gulf of Mexico smoothhound sharks are usually less than 118 cm long, but males are much smaller, reaching maximum lengths of only about 80 cm.*

- **The dusky smoothhound** lives in the Atlantic Ocean. It is a very active shark, always on the move looking for food.

- **The striped smoothhound** has dark bars across its back when young but the spotless smoothhound has plain, grey-brown skin.

- **The Venezuelan dwarf smoothhound** is 22 cm long at birth and only about 50 cm when fully grown.

- **The sharptooth smoothhound** has sharp points sticking up from its flat, crushing teeth.

Leopard shark

- **The leopard shark** is named after its spotted skin.

- **It is one of the most common sharks** on the west coast of North America, from Oregon to central Mexico.

- **The leopard shark** swims in waters low in oxygen, such as river mouths and bays. It has extra red blood cells to help it absorb enough oxygen.

- **It is an active**, strong-swimming shark, and may follow the tide in and out to find prey on shallow mudflats.

- **Leopard sharks** may form schools with smoothhound sharks, spiny dogfish and bat rays.

- **Its teeth are flat** and it feeds on crabs, shrimps, clams, worms, octopuses and fish.

Ground sharks

- **On the coast of California**, leopard sharks suck innkeeper worms from their U-shaped burrows in the mud and swallow them whole.

- **Leopard sharks** sometimes rip the breathing siphons off clams and eat them, discarding the rest of the clam and its shell.

- **Female leopard sharks** give birth to between four and 37 pups at a time.

- **Pups are about 20 cm long** at birth, but may grow to be 130 cm or even 200 cm long.

▼ The leopard shark has relatively small eyes because it lives in shallow, bright, sunlit waters.

DID YOU KNOW?
Larger leopard sharks nip the front fins of smaller individuals as a sign of dominance.

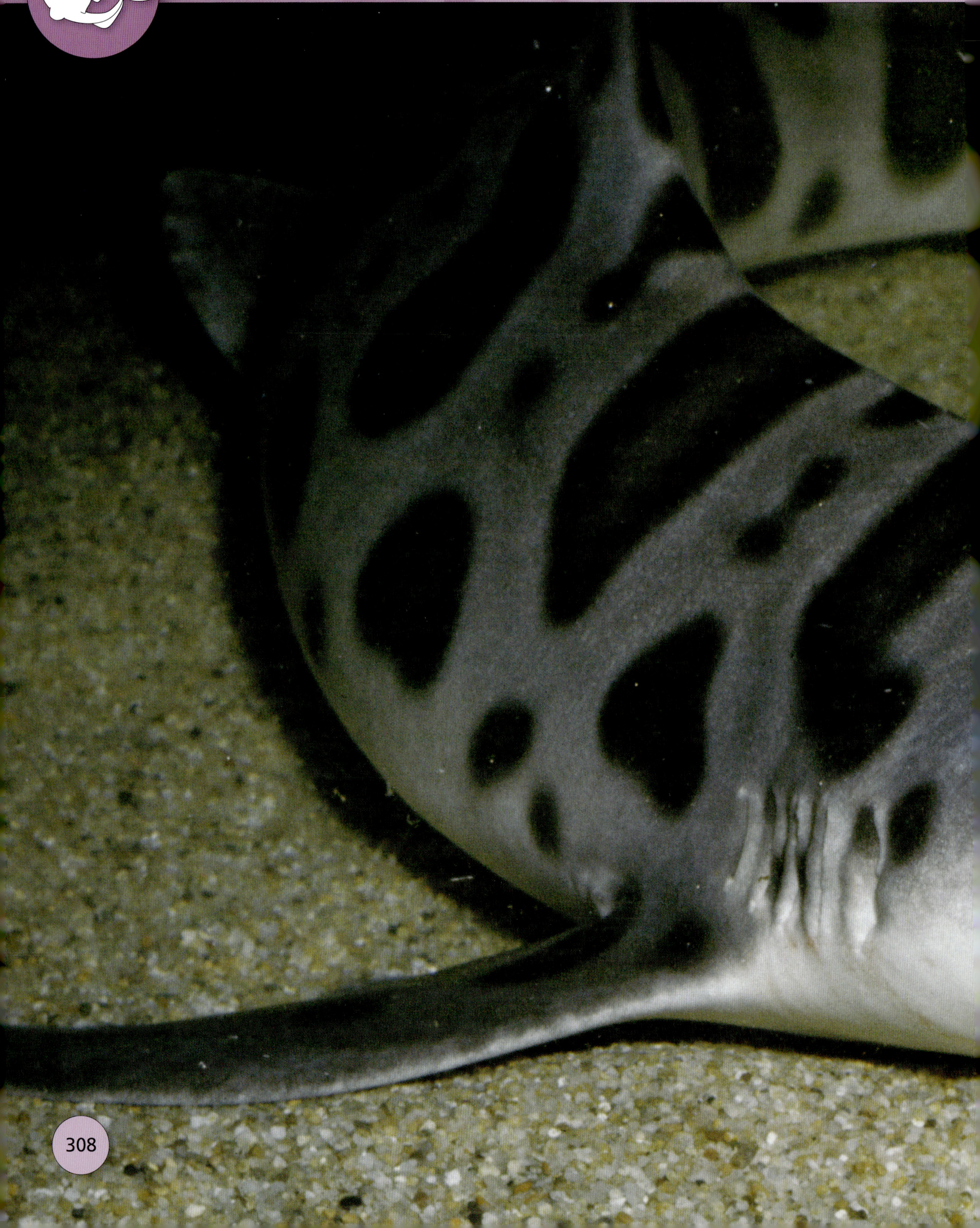

Ground sharks

▼ The leopard shark's markings are so varied that they can be used to identify individuals, like human fingerprints. Its oval eyes are protected by a layer called a nictitating membrane.

Weasel sharks

- **Most weasel shark species** are small, usually no more than one metre in length.

- **There are about eight different species**, including the hooktooth, the snaggletooth and the sicklefin weasel shark.

- **Weasel sharks** live in coastal waters of the east Atlantic Ocean and the west of the Pacific Ocean.

- **They have oval eyes** with nictitating eyelids, which they can draw across their eyes for protection.

- **The hooktooth shark** has very long, hooked lower teeth, which stick out from its long mouth.

- **The straight-tooth weasel shark** has pointed lower teeth, but they do not stick out of its short, arched mouth.

- **The Atlantic weasel shark** has a specialized diet of squid and octopuses.

- **It has a striking pattern** of yellow stripes along its back, which is light grey or bronze.

- **The female snaggletooth shark** gives birth to between two and 11 pups at a time, after a pregnancy of seven to eight months.

- **Most weasel sharks** are harmless to humans, apart from the snaggletooth shark, which is large enough to be a threat. It reaches a maximum length of 2.4 m.

Ground sharks

▼ Weasel sharks are related to bull and lemon sharks. They are recognized by the natural dent where the tail meets the body. This is called the precaudal pit.

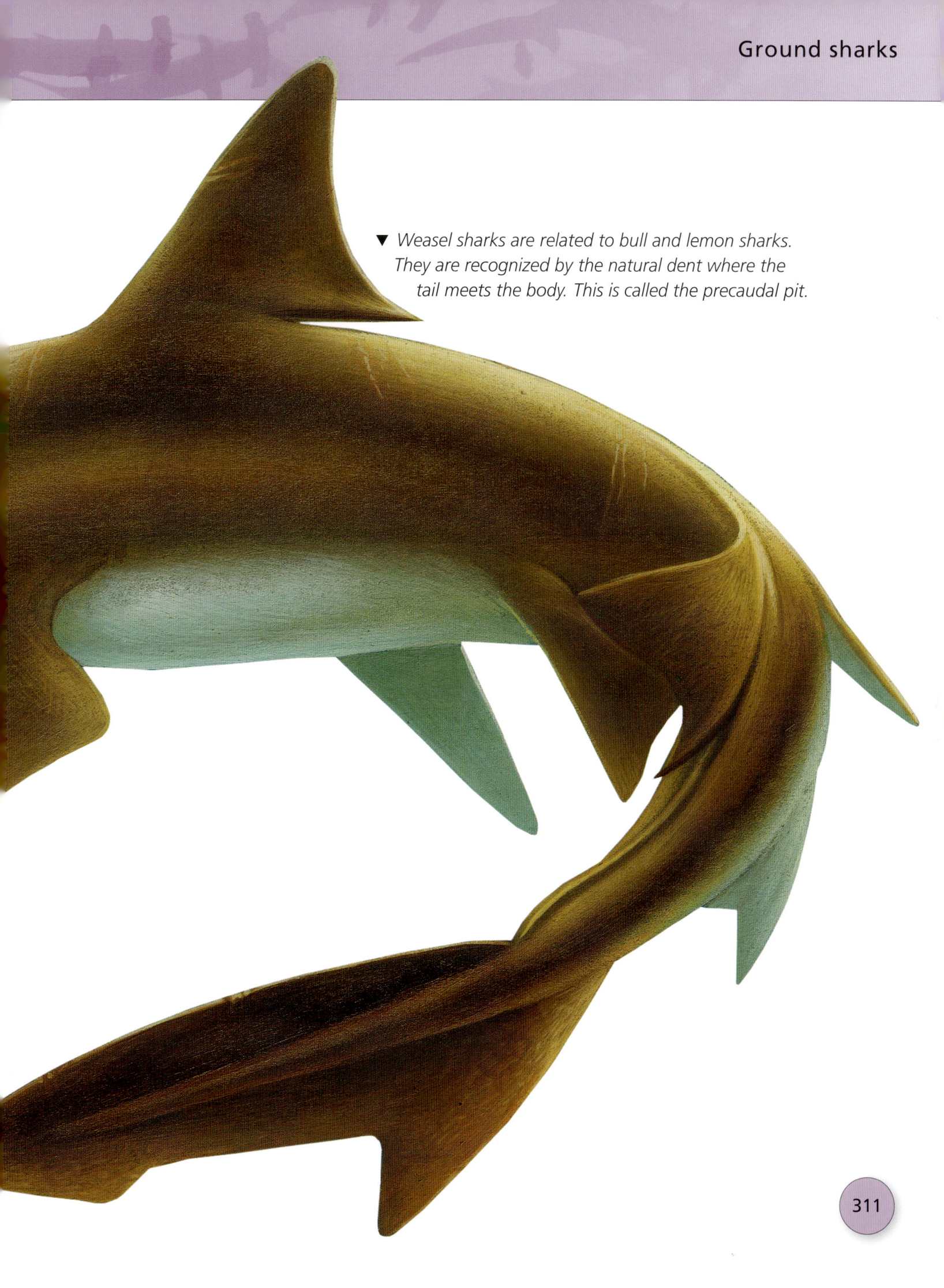

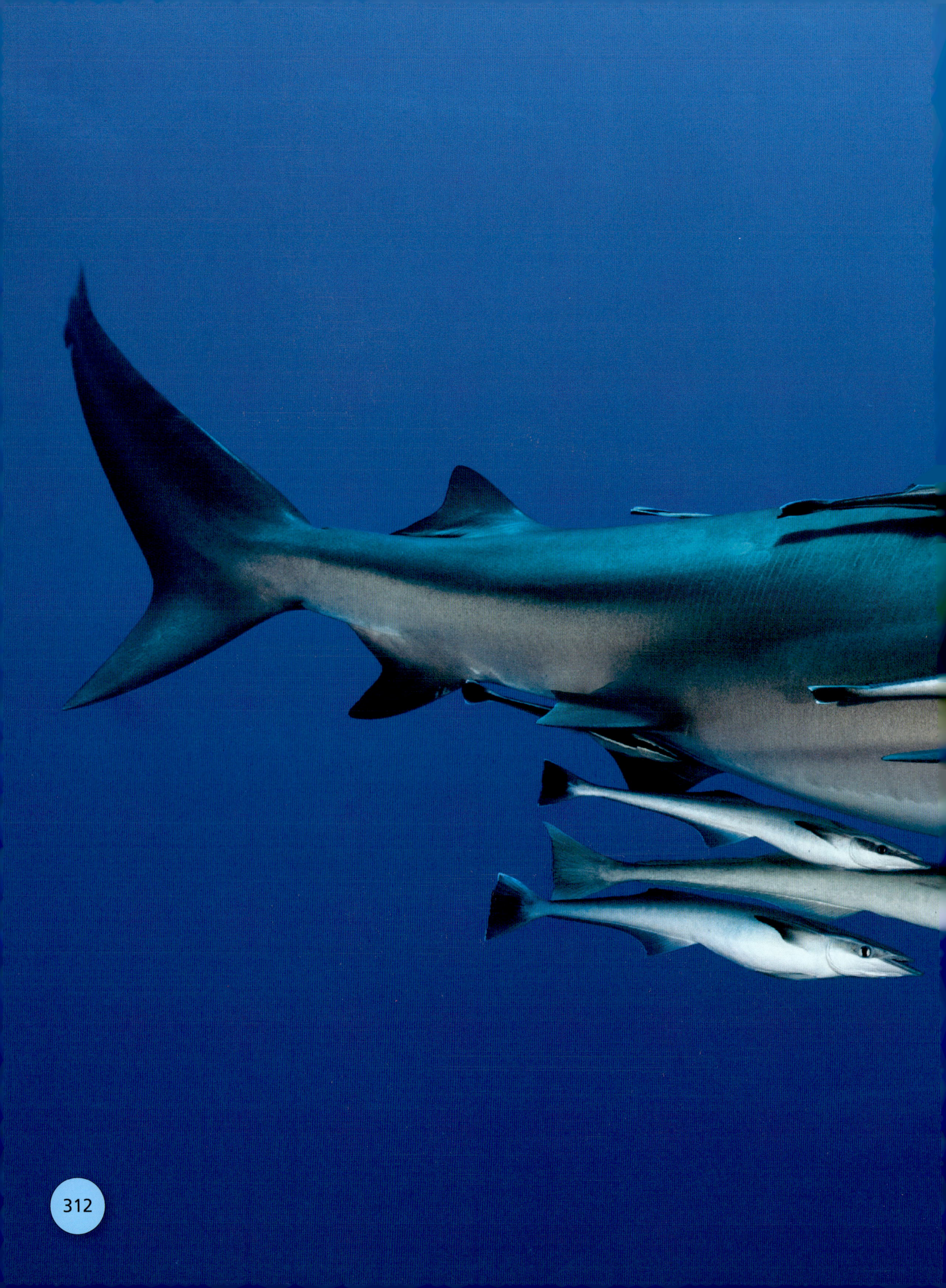

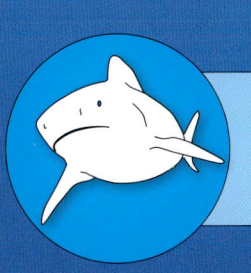

Requiem sharks

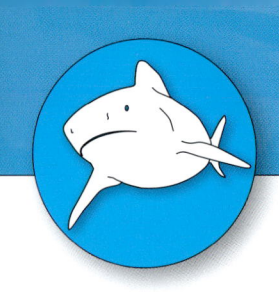

Requiem sharks

- **There are at least 56 species** in the requiem shark family (Carcharhinidae). It was probably named after the French word for shark, *requin*.

- **The family includes** some of the most typical and well-known sharks, such as blue sharks, lemon sharks, tiger sharks, bull sharks and reef sharks.

- **Requiem sharks** are sometimes called whaler sharks.

- **Sharks in this family** are usually large and chunky-looking, with bodies 1–3 m long.

- **Their skin is usually plain**, without any patterns, although they are dark on top and light beneath. This countershading camouflages them from above and below.

- **Sharks in this family** have long, arched mouths with sharp, blade-like teeth.

Requiem sharks

- **Their eyes** are usually round with nictitating eyelids.

- **They have two fins** on their back. The second dorsal fin is usually smaller, and the top lobe of their tail fin is much larger than the bottom lobe.

- **Most requiem sharks** live in tropical waters, both near the shore and out in the open ocean, with most living in sunlit surface waters rather than the deep ocean.

- **A few requiem sharks** – the bull shark and the river sharks – are the only species that can live in freshwater for long periods of time.

DID YOU KNOW?
Bull sharks living in rivers produce 20 times more urine than those living in the sea!

◄ The bull shark is a fierce predator, which attacks animals as large as cattle and hippos. Smaller prey includes baby sharks, such as lemon shark and sandbar shark pups.

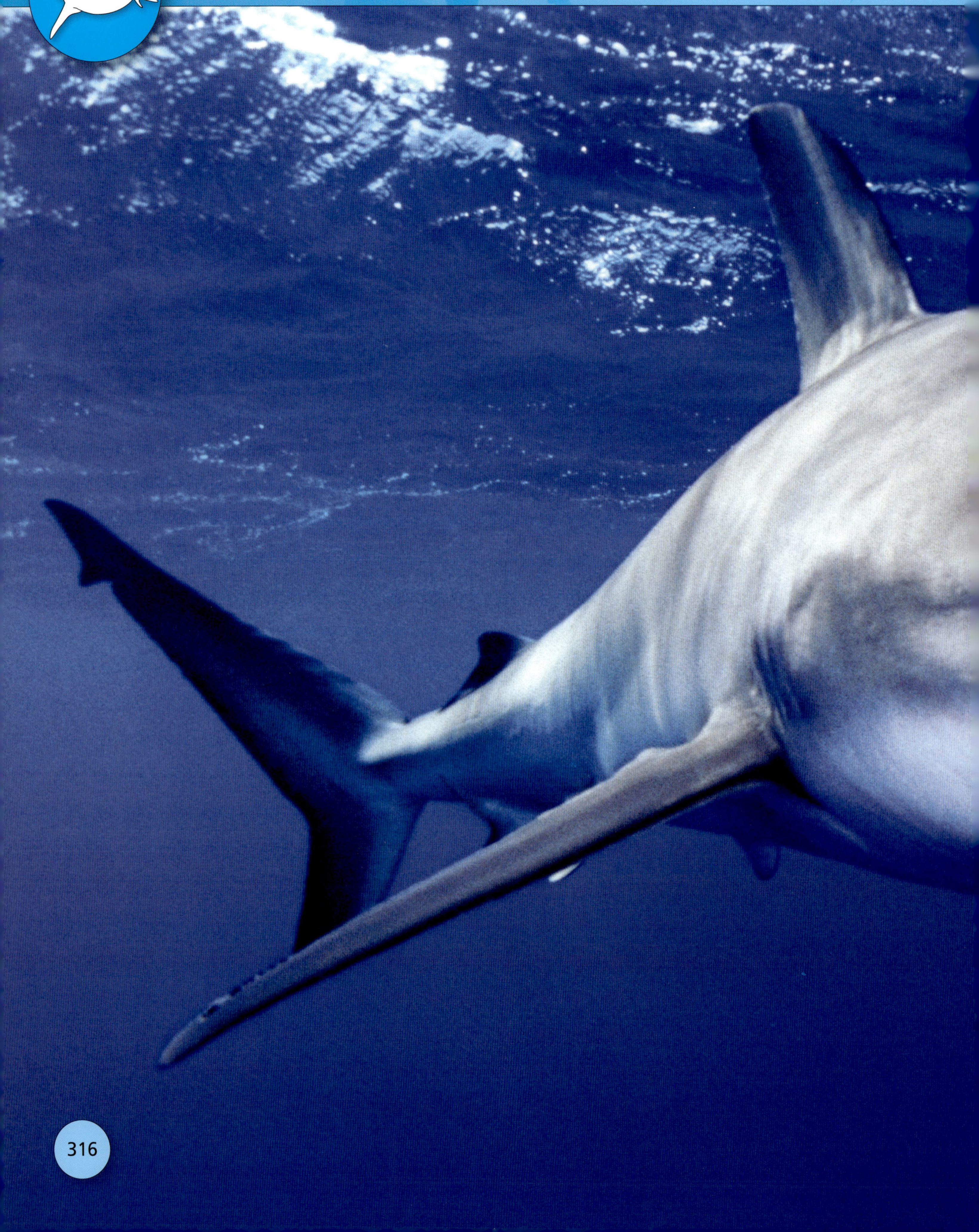

Requiem sharks

▼ The Galapagos shark has all the typical features of requiem sharks – a large, chunky body, plain skin, round eyes, a long, arched mouth and a large dorsal fin.

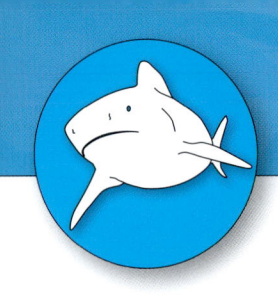

Blacknose shark

- **The blacknose shark** is named after the black spot under the tip of its snout. It also has black tips to its second dorsal fin and the top lobe of its tail.

- **This shark lives** near the coasts of the western Atlantic Ocean, from the southern USA down to southern Brazil.

- **It swims in shallow water** from 18–65 m deep, mainly over sand or coral, and feeds on small fish.

- **The blacknose shark** is a small shark. It grows to about 1–1.2 m in length.

- **It is harmless** and other larger sharks often attack and eat it.

- **The blacknose shark** arches its body and raises its snout in a threat display, warning other males or human divers to 'back-off'.

- **Female blacknose sharks** give birth to between three and six pups after a pregnancy of 10–12 months.

- **Blacknose sharks** live for about 10–20 years.

- **People catch a lot** of these sharks for food and they are also kept in aquariums.

Requiem sharks

▼ The blacknose shark feeds on small fish, including anchovies and porcupine fish. It is a fast swimmer, and sometimes swims with other blacknose sharks in large schools.

Silvertip shark

- **This wide-ranging** shark lives in the tropical Pacific Ocean.

- **It lives near the shore**, around islands and on the edge of coral reefs, rather than in the open ocean.

- **Silvertip sharks** swim mainly in shallow waters, from the surface down to depths of 600–800 m.

- **This shark is named** after the striking white tips and trailing edges on all its fins, except its small dorsal fin near the tail, which is black.

▶ A large, bulky shark, the silvertip is bold and aggressive and may sometimes attack human divers.

Requiem sharks

- **Silvertip sharks feed on fish**, including smaller sharks, as well as eagle rays and octopuses.
- **Its top teeth** are shaped like triangles, while its bottom teeth are thin, pointed spikes, which are good for holding slippery prey.
- **Silvertip sharks** are more aggressive than Galapagos sharks or blacktip sharks, and adults often have a lot of scars from fights with other sharks.
- **This large shark** starts life as a pup about 60–80 cm long.
- **Female silvertips** usually give birth to five or six pups at a time.
- **The pups** grow up to be about 2 m long as adults, but some reach lengths of 3 m.

DID YOU KNOW?
Silvertip sharks are threatened by people catching too many of them for their large fins and meat.

322

Requiem sharks

▼ A silvertip shark being followed by a shoal of trevally fish. The trevallies eat the shark's leftover food and even scratch against its rough skin to get rid of parasites living on their own skin.

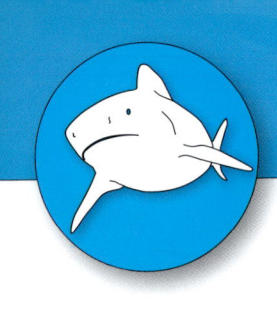

Grey reef shark

- **The grey reef shark** is grey above and white below, with a black edge to its strong tail fin and blackish tips to its other fins.

- **It lives in the Pacific Ocean**, close to the shore or around coral reefs, to depths of up to 140 m.

- **The grey reef shark** lives in deeper water than the blacktip reef shark.

- **It feeds mainly** on the sea bed, catching reef fish, squid, octopuses and crabs.

- **The jagged top teeth** are wider than the thin, pointed bottom teeth.

- **Grey reef sharks** spend the day in groups in or near reefs, and are more active at night.

- **Pregnant females** also spend their time in large groups in shallow, warm water.

- **Grey reef sharks** are inquisitive and often swim close to divers. If they feel threatened, they will arch their back, lower their front fins and wag their head and tail in broad sweeps.

Requiem sharks

- **These sharks** can be aggressive and may bite people.

- **Grey reef shark pups** are 45–60 cm long when they are born, but grow to lengths of 1.4 m or perhaps up to 2.5 m.

▼ A group of grey reef sharks swimming above a coral reef in the Indian Ocean. These active sharks like to live in groups and are strong swimmers.

DID YOU KNOW?
Grey reef sharks are worth much more kept alive as a tourist attraction than if they are killed for the fishing industry.

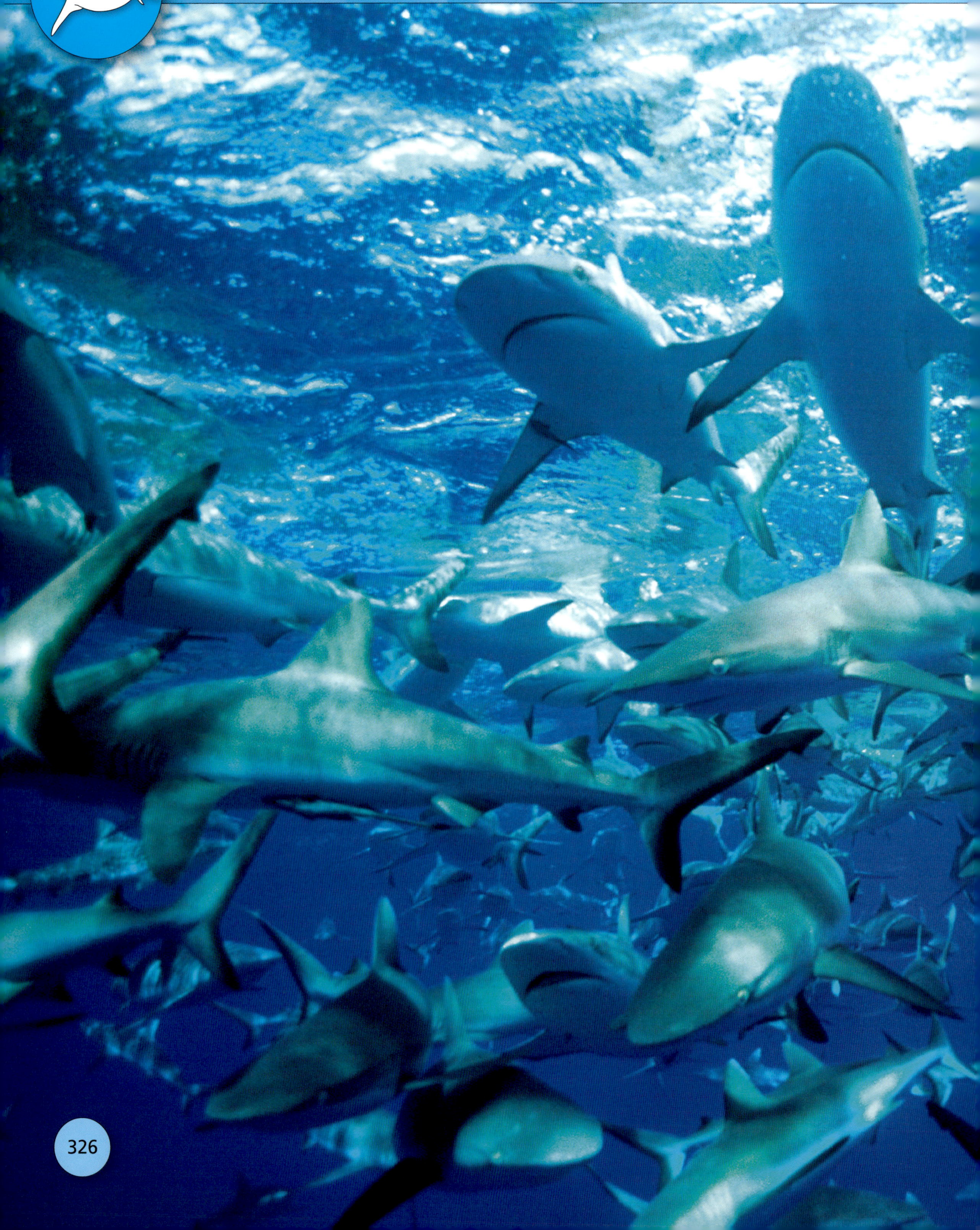

Requiem sharks

◀ Grey reef sharks are very social sharks, often seen swimming in schools like this one during the day. These large reef sharks may work together to trap fish near coral reefs.

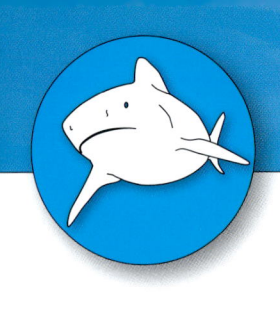

Spinner shark

- **This very active shark** is named after the way it spins through schools of fish with its mouth open when feeding.

- **It spins right out** of the water at the end of a feeding run, turning round and round up to three times before falling back into the water.

- **Spinner sharks** follow schools of mackerel and other fish on their migration journeys, so they always have plenty to eat.

- **As well as fish**, spinner sharks also eat stingrays, squid and octopuses.

- **They have narrow, pointed teeth** in both jaws to help them keep a tight grip on slippery fish.

▶ *The spinner shark is sometimes confused with the blacktip shark because of its black fin tips. It has long gill slits in front of its pectoral fins.*

Requiem sharks

- **The narrow, pointed snout** of the spinner shark helps it to swim quickly and catch speedy fish.

- **Spinner sharks** live in warm to hot waters in the Atlantic Ocean, Mediterranean Sea and the western Pacific Ocean.

- **Young spinner sharks** prefer lower water temperatures to the adults.

- **Female spinner sharks** give birth to between three and 15 pups at a time, after a pregnancy of 11–15 months.

- **Adult and young spinner sharks** have obvious black tips to most of their fins.

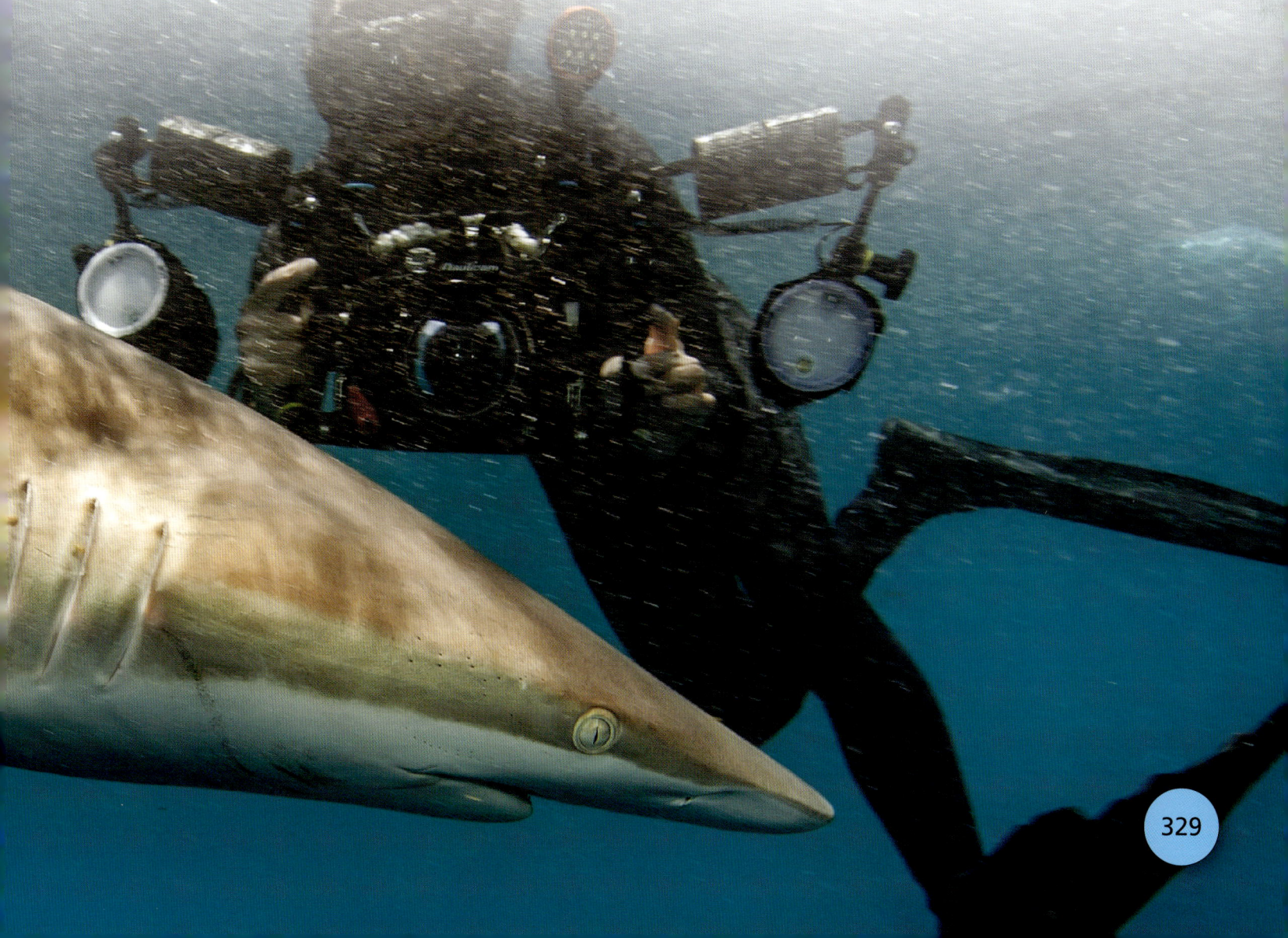

Bronze whaler shark

- **The bronze whaler shark** has several alternative names, including narrowtooth shark, cocktail shark and copper shark.

- **Its stocky body** is bronze-grey to olive-grey on top and white below, with a white band along its sides.

- **The teeth of bronze whaler sharks** are different from other requiem sharks because they are hook-shaped and narrow.

- **Bronze whaler sharks** feed mainly on squid, octopuses and fish such as sardines, mullet and flatfish.

- **Adult bronze whaler sharks** also feed on stingrays and sawfish.

- **During the winter**, large numbers of bronze whaler sharks follow shoals of sardines as they move along the coast of southern Africa.

- **This shark** can be dangerous to humans and becomes aggressive if food is around.

- **Female bronze whaler sharks** give birth to litters of 13–24 pups every other year.

- **Young bronze whaler sharks** usually swim in water less than 30 m deep.

- **Adults are not usually found** in such shallow waters and prefer to swim in waters that are at least 100 m deep.

▶ Long pectoral fins help bronze whaler sharks to glide easily through the water and migrate long distances with the seasons.

Requiem sharks

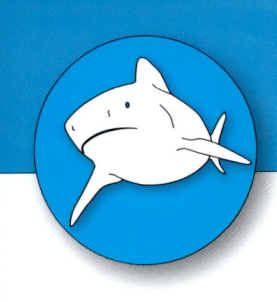

Silky shark

- **Named after its smooth skin**, the silky shark's denticles are small, tightly packed and overlapping.

- **Silky sharks** live all over the world in tropical oceans.

- **The silky shark** is most common in shallow waters less than 200 m deep. It is not as fully adapted to the open ocean as its cousin, the blue shark.

- **In the Red Sea**, the silky shark is often photographed by divers on coral reefs off the shore.

- **Silky sharks are active**, bold and inquisitive sharks.

- **Due to its large size** (up to 3 m) and aggressive behaviour, the silky shark could be dangerous to humans.

- **When they are in groups**, silky sharks sometimes open their jaws wide and puff out their gills. They also suddenly shoot up to the surface and then glide back down again. Scientists are not sure what these displays mean.

- **Silky sharks** are sometimes found swimming with schools of scalloped hammerhead sharks or tuna.

- **They mainly eat fish**, but also feed on squid, octopus and crabs.

- **Millions of the fins** of silky sharks are used to make shark's fin soup. This threatens the future survival of the species.

▶ *The rounded snouts and white undersides of silky sharks are clearly visible in this group, swimming just below the surface of the Caribbean Sea.*

Requiem sharks

Galapagos shark

- **The Galapagos shark** lives mainly around tropical islands (including the Galapagos Islands) in all the world's oceans.

- **It often lives** in places with strong ocean currents, from near the shore to depths of up to 180 m.

- **Galapagos sharks** are found in loose groups, but do not behave as a co-ordinated group.

- **Sometimes these inquisitive sharks** can be aggressive. They threaten divers by hunching their bodies, twisting and rolling, and possibly even biting.

- **Female Galapagos sharks** give birth to between four and 16 pups at a time.

- **The pups** are 60–80 cm long when they are born.

- **Young Galapagos sharks** swim in shallow nursery areas, which are less than 25 m deep.

- **Adults reach lengths** of 2.3 m, or even up to 3.7 m.

- **Galapagos sharks** feed mainly on bottom-dwelling fish.

- **They have long, rounded snouts** and large teeth that stand upright.

▶ Galapagos sharks often swim a few metres above the sea bed, but they will come to the surface to feed or investigate anything interesting going on.

Requiem sharks

DID YOU KNOW?
Galapagos sharks may be the same species as dusky sharks!

335

▶ Galapagos sharks have a streamlined body and live mainly in shallow waters over coral reefs and rocky sea floors. They mainly eat fish, but sometimes feed on sea lions and marine iguanas around the Galapagos Islands.

Requiem sharks

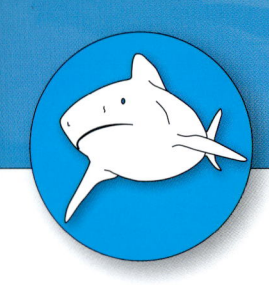

Bull shark

- **The bull shark** is a powerful, aggressive hunter. It gets its name because its body is thick, stocky and muscular, like a bull.

- **This species** is not especially long – bull sharks usually grow to between 2–3 m in length.

- **They are among the few species** that can survive in fresh water. Bull sharks swim hundreds of kilometres up rivers such as the Mississippi in North America, the Amazon in South America and the Zambezi in Africa.

- **Some bull sharks** have been found living in Lake Nicaragua, a large lake in Central America.

▼ *A very short, wide head, blunt snout and small eyes are characteristic features of the bull shark.*

Requiem sharks

▲ *A bull shark has a large, broad, triangular first dorsal fin on its back, but the second dorsal fin is much smaller.*

- **Bull sharks** are often known by other names, depending on where they live – such as the Zambezi River shark or the Nicaragua shark.

- **Some experts think** that bull sharks may be the most dangerous species. This is because they often lurk in shallow waters where humans swim.

- **Bull sharks usually swim** slowly near the sea bed in water less than 20 m deep, but they are agile and quick when chasing prey.

- **They eat a wide range** of food, from fish and sea turtles to birds, dolphins and dead whales.

- **Bull sharks have small eyes** because they often live in shallow, muddy waters, where eyesight is not that useful for hunting prey.

- **Fierce and strong**, bull sharks probably attack more people than any other shark. They have huge jaws and large, sharp teeth.

Blacktip reef shark

- **Blacktip reef sharks** have black tips on all their fins and are sometimes known as black sharks.

- **Like its cousin** the whitetip reef shark, the blacktip reef shark prefers warm, shallow water.

- **This shark** has long, slender teeth ideally suited to snapping up its main prey – fish that live around coral reefs.

- **Scuba divers** often encounter blacktip reef sharks, but they are rarely aggressive – although they have been known to bite.

- **Adults usually grow** to lengths of about one metre but some reach maximum lengths of up to 2 m.

- **Blacktip reef sharks** have small, oval eyes with a pupil like a vertical slit. Their eyes don't need to let in much light as they live in shallow, sunlit waters.

- **They are active**, strong swimmers, and their back fin often breaks through the surface in shallow water.

DID YOU KNOW?
Since the Suez Canal was built, blacktip reef sharks have been able to swim through it from the Red Sea to the Mediterranean Sea.

▲ *The black fin markings of the blacktip reef shark contrast strongly with its light coloured skin.*

Requiem sharks

▲ A blacktip reef shark hunting for fish over a coral reef.

Black tip to dorsal fin

- **Blacktip reef sharks** live in the western Pacific Ocean, the Indian Ocean and the eastern Mediterranean.
- **They live alone** or in very small groups.
- **Female blacktip reef sharks** give birth to between two and four pups at a time, after a pregnancy lasting 16 months.

342

Requiem sharks

▲ A small group of blacktip reef sharks in a shallow lagoon with pink whiprays. Blacktip reef sharks are powerful swimmers, sometimes jumping right out of the water when hunting.

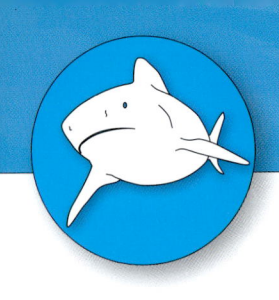

Blacktip shark

- **A larger species** than the blacktip reef shark, blacktip sharks usually reach lengths of 1.9 m, with maximum lengths of 2.55 m.

- **The blacktip shark** has less black on its fin tips than its cousin, the blacktip reef shark, and no black on the top lobe of its tail.

- **This species is widespread** in all hot and warm oceans, usually near the shore in water no deeper than 30 m.

- **Blacktip sharks** are fast swimmers, often living in large schools near the surface.

- **These sharks feed** mainly on fish, but also eat squid, octopuses and crabs.

Requiem sharks

- **Like spinner sharks**, blacktip sharks may sometimes leap out of the water and spin round after making a feeding run through a school of fish.

- **Female blacktip sharks** give birth to between four and seven pups after a 10–12 month pregnancy.

- **This shark** is not usually harmful to people, but may chase spear-fishers to steal their fish.

- **Blacktip sharks** are often caught by people for their meat, skins (which are made into leather), and liver oil, which is full of vitamins.

▼ Blacktip sharks have long, narrow, pointed snouts and small eyes. There is an obvious white band along the side of their bodies.

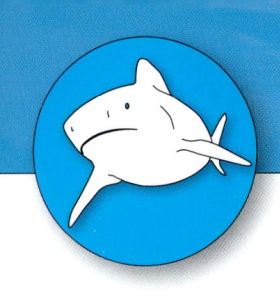

Oceanic whitetip shark

- **There are two different species** that both have the name 'whitetip' – the whitetip reef shark and the oceanic whitetip shark.

- **The oceanic whitetip** is a large hunter that lives in open oceans all over the world.

- **It usually grows** to about 2 m long, but can reach lengths of 3.5 m or even 4 m.

- **The oceanic whitetip** has obvious white rings at the tips of almost every fin on its body.

- **It also has distinctive** large pectoral fins, which are like paddles.

- **These large fins** are very valuable for making shark fin soup and the numbers of this shark have reduced dramatically as a result.

- **Oceanic whitetips** are inquisitive sharks and often follow schools of tuna and squid, two of their preferred foods.

▲ *A widespread and aggressive shark, the oceanic whitetip mainly feeds on fish, but also eats seabirds, turtles, sea mammals, dead animals and rubbish thrown into the sea by people.*

Requiem sharks

- **They also follow ships**, often in groups, like packs of dogs. This may be why sharks were once called 'sea dogs'.

- **Slow-moving sharks**, oceanic whitetips cruise near the surface with their huge pectoral fins spread out. They are active by day and at night.

- **Females give birth** to up to 15 pups at a time, which are able to have their own young when they are about 4–7 years old.

DID YOU KNOW?
The oceanic whitetip shark sometimes bites swimmers and boats.

▶ Striped pilot fish help to keep oceanic whitetip sharks clean and healthy by eating parasites, leftover food and other waste. In return, the shark protects the pilot fish from predators. This is a form of symbiosis – a partnership where both animals benefit.

Requiem sharks

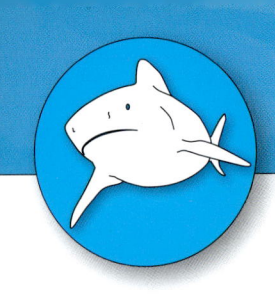

Dusky shark

- **Dusky sharks** probably live in all the world's oceans, but stay near the shore, up to depths of about 400 m.

- **They migrate** with the seasons, moving north in summer and back to warmer, tropical waters in winter.

- **Female dusky sharks** give birth in summer in shallow coastal waters. The young often form large feeding groups.

- **These sharks mature** between the ages of 17 and 24 years and live to a maximum age of about 34 years.

- **The top teeth of dusky sharks** are triangular with jagged edges; the bottom teeth are narrow and pointed for holding slippery prey.

▼ *The dusky shark is named after its dusky fin tips. The rest of its body is a uniform grey or bronze colour, with a white underside, making the shark well camouflaged.*

Requiem sharks

- **These sharks eat mainly fish** and other sharks. Bigger sharks often eat young dusky sharks.

- **Dusky sharks** are large sharks, growing to about 3 m in length, and sometimes reaching lengths of 4 m.

- **They can be very aggressive** and have attacked swimmers, surfers and divers.

- **Young dusky sharks** are sometimes kept in aquariums.

- **Dusky sharks** are very closely related to Galapagos sharks and recent scientific research suggests that they may be two forms of the same species.

Sandbar shark

- **A large, slow-growing coastal shark**, the sandbar shark often lives in bays, harbours and the mouths of rivers.

- **Sandbar sharks** grow to lengths of about 1.8 m, but can reach maximum lengths of up to 3 m.

- **It usually swims** near the bottom, at depths of up to 55 m, although it may reach depths of up to 280 m.

- **The sandbar shark** feeds mainly on small fish living on the sea bed, and also some shellfish and crabs. It feeds more at night than during the day.

- **This grey-brown** or bronzy-coloured shark has a stout body with no obvious markings.

- **The first dorsal fin** is very large and stands upright.

- **During the mating season**, a male will bite a female on her back until she swims upside down for mating.

- **Females give birth** every second or third year. They have between five and 12 pups after a pregnancy lasting 8–12 months.

Requiem sharks

- **At first**, young sandbar sharks live in shallow water near the coast, but they move to deeper, warmer water in winter.

- **Numbers of sandbar sharks** have been greatly reduced by people catching them for meat or their valuable fins.

▼ Sandbar sharks survive well in captivity and are often kept in aquariums, where the public can learn more about these spectacular sharks.

Night shark

- **The night shark** is a deepwater shark, found at depths of between 275 m and 365 m during the day and 185 m at night.

- **There are no recorded attacks** on humans by this species.

- **The night shark** has a very long, pointed snout that is longer than the width of its mouth.

- **Night sharks live** off the east coast of the Americas, from the USA south to Argentina, as well as off the west coast of Africa.

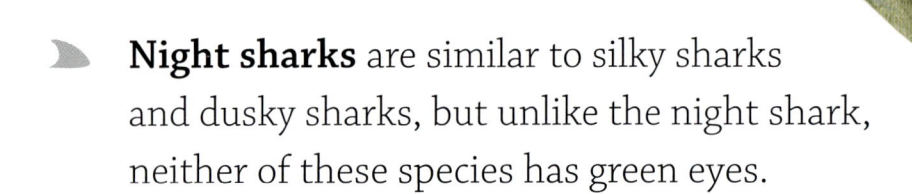

- **Night sharks** are similar to silky sharks and dusky sharks, but unlike the night shark, neither of these species has green eyes.

- **Night sharks** are slim, grey-brown sharks, with small dorsal and pectoral fins.

Requiem sharks

- **The night shark** has fifteen rows of teeth on each side of its top and bottom jaws. The triangular top teeth have jagged edges, while the bottom teeth are narrow and upright.

- **The night shark feeds on squid** and small fish, including flying fish and sea bass.

- **Female night sharks** give birth to between 12 and 18 pups at a time. The pups are 60–72 cm long at birth.

- **Adult night sharks** grow to about 2 m long, reaching maximum lengths of 2.8 m.

▲ Night sharks have large, green eyes, which probably help them to see in deep, dark waters.

DID YOU KNOW?
The name of the night shark comes from the fact that it is usually caught at night.

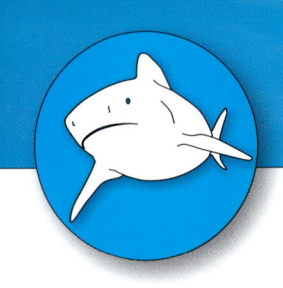

Tiger shark

- **The tiger shark** will attack almost anything, including humans, making it one of the most dangerous sharks.

- **These sharks** are usually about 3 m long, but they can grow up to 6 m.

- **They have massive heads** with a blunt snout, large eyes and a wide mouth.

- **The diet of tiger sharks** includes fish, seals, sea lions, turtles, shellfish, crabs, seabirds, dolphins, crocodiles, squid and jellyfish. They also take bites out of bigger animals such as whales. They have even been seen eating other tiger sharks.

- **Many unusual objects**, such as oil drums, tin cans, glass bottles, clothes, rubber tyres, coal, cushions, tools, and even pieces of armour, have been found in the stomachs of tiger sharks.

- **This species is found** in most of the world's warmer seas and oceans. It sometimes swims into river mouths.

- **Tiger sharks are named** after the striped markings of the young, which fade with age.

- **Females have large numbers** of pups – 35–55 pups at a time are common, but up to 82 pups may be born at one time.

- **Tiger sharks are strong swimmers**, able to reach speeds of more than 32 km/h in just a few seconds. However, they cannot swim this fast for very long.

- **Some tiger sharks** may travel many thousands of kilometres in one year, while others keep to a small stretch of coastline just 100 km long.

Requiem sharks

DID YOU KNOW?
Tiger sharks might mistake metal objects for living things because they give off a slight electrical signal, which these sharks detect with their electrical sense.

▲ Tiger sharks usually hunt alone, drifting slowly through the oceans until they spot a potential meal. This tiger shark is swimming in front of a group of lemon sharks, fighting for their share of food.

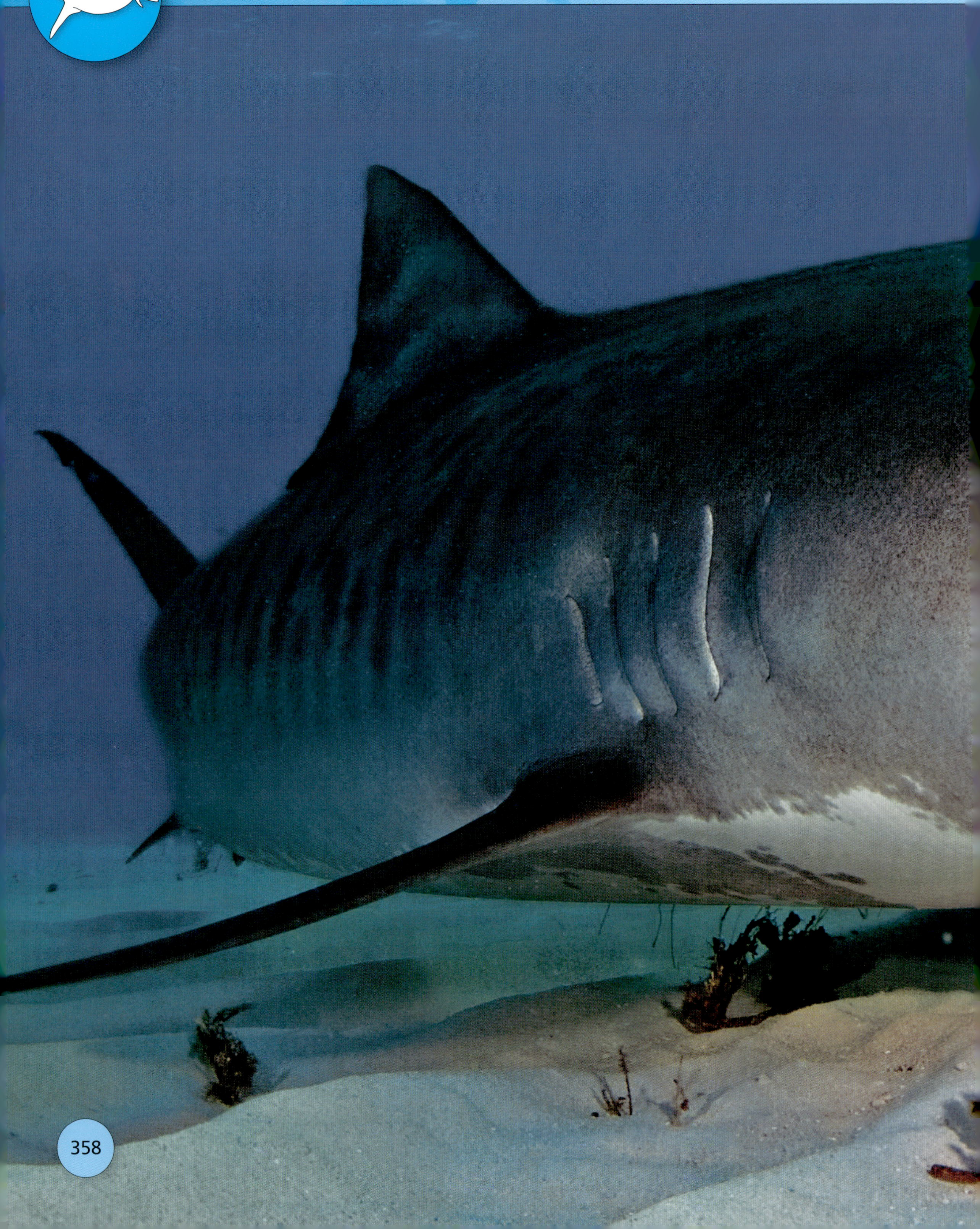

Requiem sharks

◀ A fearsome predator, the tiger shark has large jaws full of sharp teeth. Tiger sharks usually feed at night near the shore, moving to deeper water by day.

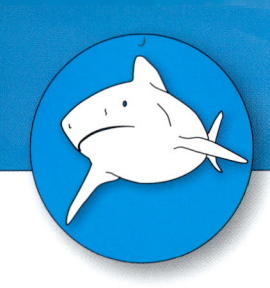

River sharks

- **Only a handful of sharks** (about six species) can survive in the freshwater of rivers.

- **River sharks** live in parts of south and southeast Asia, and Australia. They grow up to 3 m in length.

- **River sharks include** the Borneo river shark, the Ganges shark, the New Guinea river shark, the speartooth shark and the Irrawaddy river shark.

- **All these sharks** are very rare and in danger of dying out. This is probably due to people damaging their habitat and catching too many fish in the rivers where they live.

- **River sharks have tiny eyes** because eyesight is not an important sense in muddy river water. These sharks probably rely more on their electrical senses than their eyes.

Requiem sharks

- **The speartooth shark** is named after the tips of its lower teeth, which are shaped like tiny spears. The spear-like tips of the teeth have sharp cutting edges.

- **The eyes of the Ganges shark** point upwards. As it swims along the river bed looking for prey, its upward-facing eyes may help it to search for prey in the water above.

- **River sharks are secretive**, mysterious creatures and scientists know very little about them.

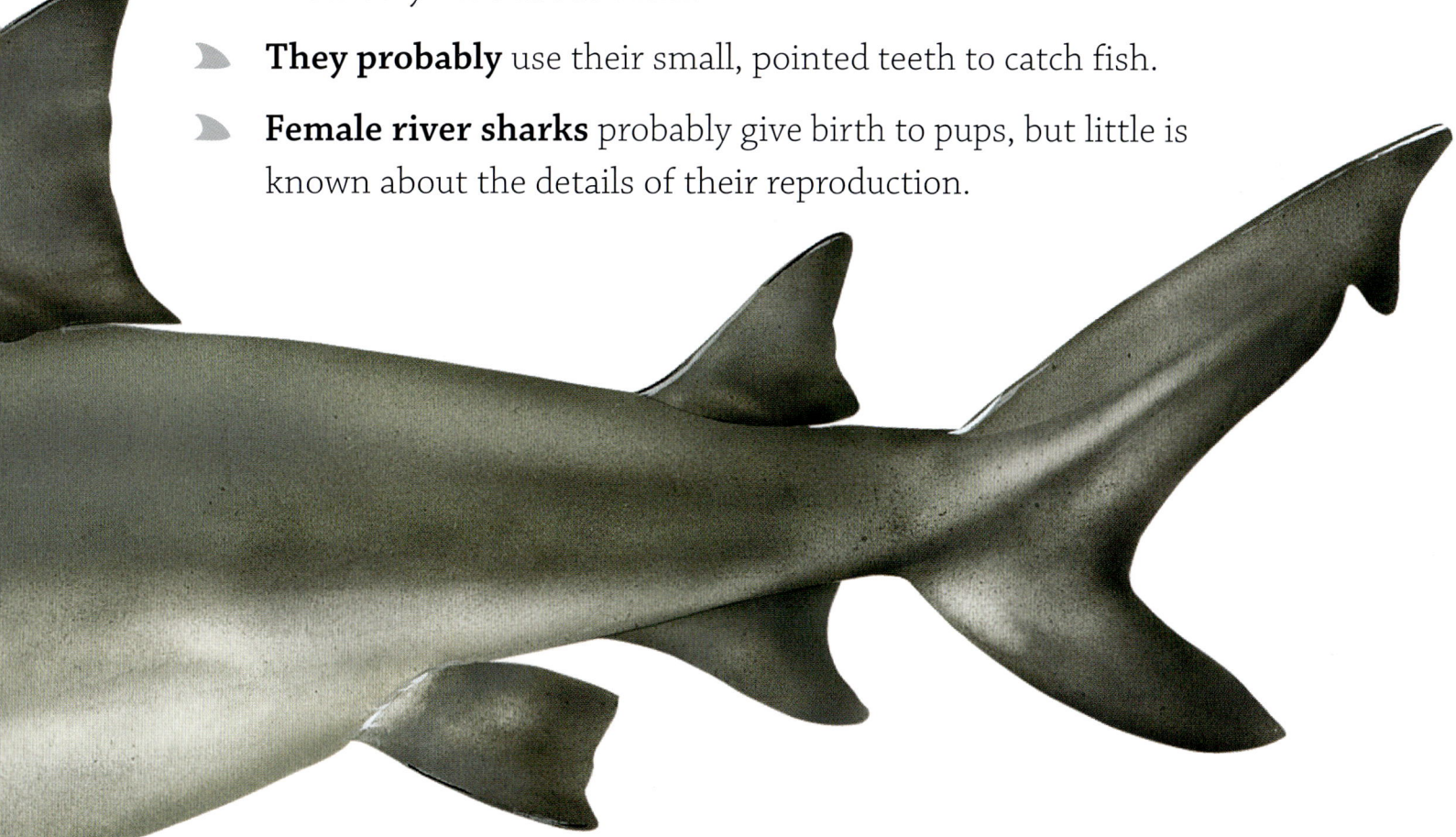

- **They probably** use their small, pointed teeth to catch fish.

- **Female river sharks** probably give birth to pups, but little is known about the details of their reproduction.

▲ The extremely rare speartooth shark lives only in a few rivers in New Guinea and the Northern Territory of Australia. It probably grows to lengths of 2 or 3 m.

361

Lemon shark

- **The lemon shark** gets its name from its yellowish colour, especially on its underside. It is related to tiger and bull sharks, and can grow up to 3 m in length.

- **Apart from the colour**, you can recognize a lemon shark by its two similarly sized dorsal fins. In most shark species, the first dorsal fin is much bigger.

- **Lemon sharks survive** well in captivity and may be kept in aquariums or sea life centres.

- **Since they can be kept in captivity**, scientists often study them.

- **When lemon sharks are young**, they eat small fish, sea worms and shrimps. As they get older, they feed on seabirds, rays and lobsters.

- **Lemon sharks** have been found with stings from stingrays embedded in their mouths.

▼ A lemon shark swims in shallow water near the shore.

Requiem sharks

- **Lemon sharks** are able to survive in shallow water with very low oxygen levels. This allows them to live around mangroves, coral reefs, bays and river mouths of Central and South America.

- **They live on their own** or in loose groups of up to 20 sharks.

- **Adult lemon sharks** may travel hundreds of kilometres in order to find a mate.

- **Female lemon sharks** give birth to between four and 17 pups at a time. The pups stay in sheltered nursery areas in shallow water for several years while they grow into adults.

▲ The lemon shark has a short nose and a mouthful of narrow, pointed teeth.

DID YOU KNOW?
When a male and female lemon shark meet to mate, they swim side-by-side so closely that they can look like a two-headed shark.

364

Requiem sharks

▼ A lemon shark with remora fish attached to its back. The remora fish help to keep the shark healthy by eating parasites and other debris, while the shark protects the remoras. This is an example of symbiosis.

Blue shark

- **One of the fastest sharks**, blue sharks can reach a top speed of almost 30 km/h.

- **Named after its deep**, silvery-indigo colour on top, this shark has a pale underside.

- **The migration route** of the blue shark is notoriously long. It travels across oceans, making trips of 3000 km or more. It can travel more than 60 km in one day.

- **Blue sharks eat mostly squid,** although they will feed on any kind of fish or other sea creature.

- **The blue shark has large**, sensitive eyes to find prey and finger-like bristles on its gills to stop small prey escaping from its gill slits.

- **It may circle round swimmers**, boats and divers for some time before closing in and biting.

- **The skin of a female** blue shark is twice as thick as that of the male. This helps to protect the females from bites during courtship and mating.

- **This species was once** extremely common, and is found in almost every part of every ocean. The population is now falling because it is so heavily overfished.

- **Blue sharks** are often caught by accident on hooks or in nets intended for tuna and swordfish.

- **Experts have estimated** that ten million blue sharks are caught and killed every year.

▶ *Blue sharks are sleek, slim and graceful, and grow up to 4 m in length.*

Requiem sharks

DID YOU KNOW?
Blue sharks have large litters of pups, sometimes giving birth to more than 100 at a time.

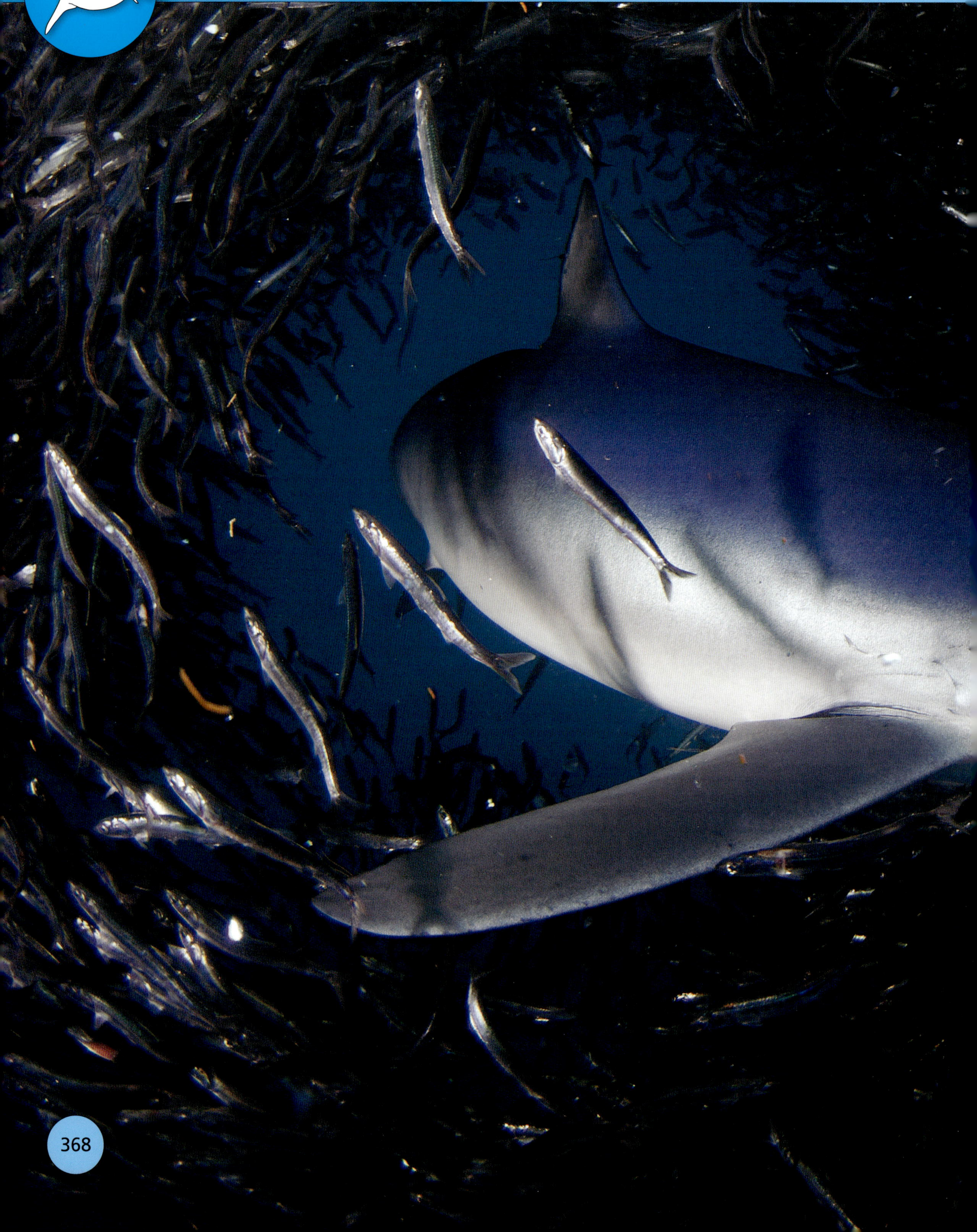

Requiem sharks

▼ A blue shark diving through a group of anchovies to grab a meal. The anchovies try to protect themselves by swimming in a tightly packed 'bait ball'. However, the ball is not completely shark-proof.

Whitetip reef shark

- **The whitetip reef shark** is a common shark, about 1.5 m long.

- **The distinctive white tips** on their tails and dorsal fins make them easy to recognize. Swimmers and divers often spot them because they inhabit coral reefs, sea caves and shallow water during the day.

- **At night, whitetip reef sharks** hunt for fish, crabs, prawns, squid and octopus. They rarely bother people, except to steal fish from fishing spears.

- **The second dorsal fin** on the whitetip reef shark's back is nearly as large as the first. This helps to distinguish this shark from silvertip and oceanic whitetip sharks.

- **The whitetip reef shark** has tough skin and flexible fins, which help it to move through small spaces among sharp pieces of coral on reefs.

Dorsal fin with white tip

▶ A whitetip reef shark lets a cleaner wrasse fish clean its teeth. As the wrasse is helping the shark, it doesn't get eaten.

Requiem sharks

- **When they rest during the day**, whitetip reef sharks pump water over their gills so they can keep breathing even though they are not moving.

- **Whitetip reef sharks** sometimes hunt in groups, both with their own kind or with other reef sharks.

- **These sharks are not usually aggressive** and tend to swim away from people. They will only bite if they feel very threatened.

- **Female whitetip reef sharks** give birth to two or three pups after a pregnancy of about five months.

- **Due to their docile nature**, whitetip reef sharks are a common species in aquariums and sea life centres.

Sharpnose sharks

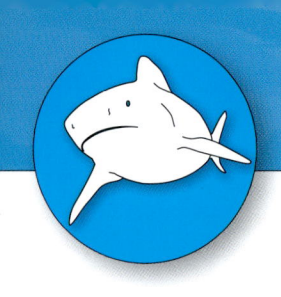

- **Sharpnose sharks are small**, slender sharks with long snouts, which are usually longer than the width of their mouths.

- **There are seven species**, including the milk shark, Atlantic sharpnose shark, Pacific sharpnose shark, Caribbean sharpnose shark and Australian sharpnose shark.

- **Most species** are less than one metre long, although the Pacific sharpnose shark may reach lengths of 1.5 m and the milk shark may grow as long as 1.75 m.

- **Sharpnose sharks are shy** and are not usually a threat to humans. In fact, they try to avoid contact with people.

- **They eat small fish**, shrimp, crabs, shellfish and worms.

- **Sharpnose sharks** have about 25 rows of small, triangular teeth in both jaws.

- **Predators of sharpnose sharks** include larger sharks and other large fish.

DID YOU KNOW?
Tiger sharks sometimes eat smaller sharpnose sharks.

Requiem sharks

- **Sharpnose sharks** live in shallow water up to 200 m deep, although the Caribbean sharpnose shark may venture into deeper waters up to 500 m deep.

- **Female sharpnose sharks** give birth to between one and seven pups (no more than ten) after a pregnancy lasting about one year.

- **The pups** are about 30 cm long when they are born.

▼ *The streamlined body and characteristically long, pointed snout of sharpnose sharks is very obvious in this Atlantic Ocean sharpnose shark.*

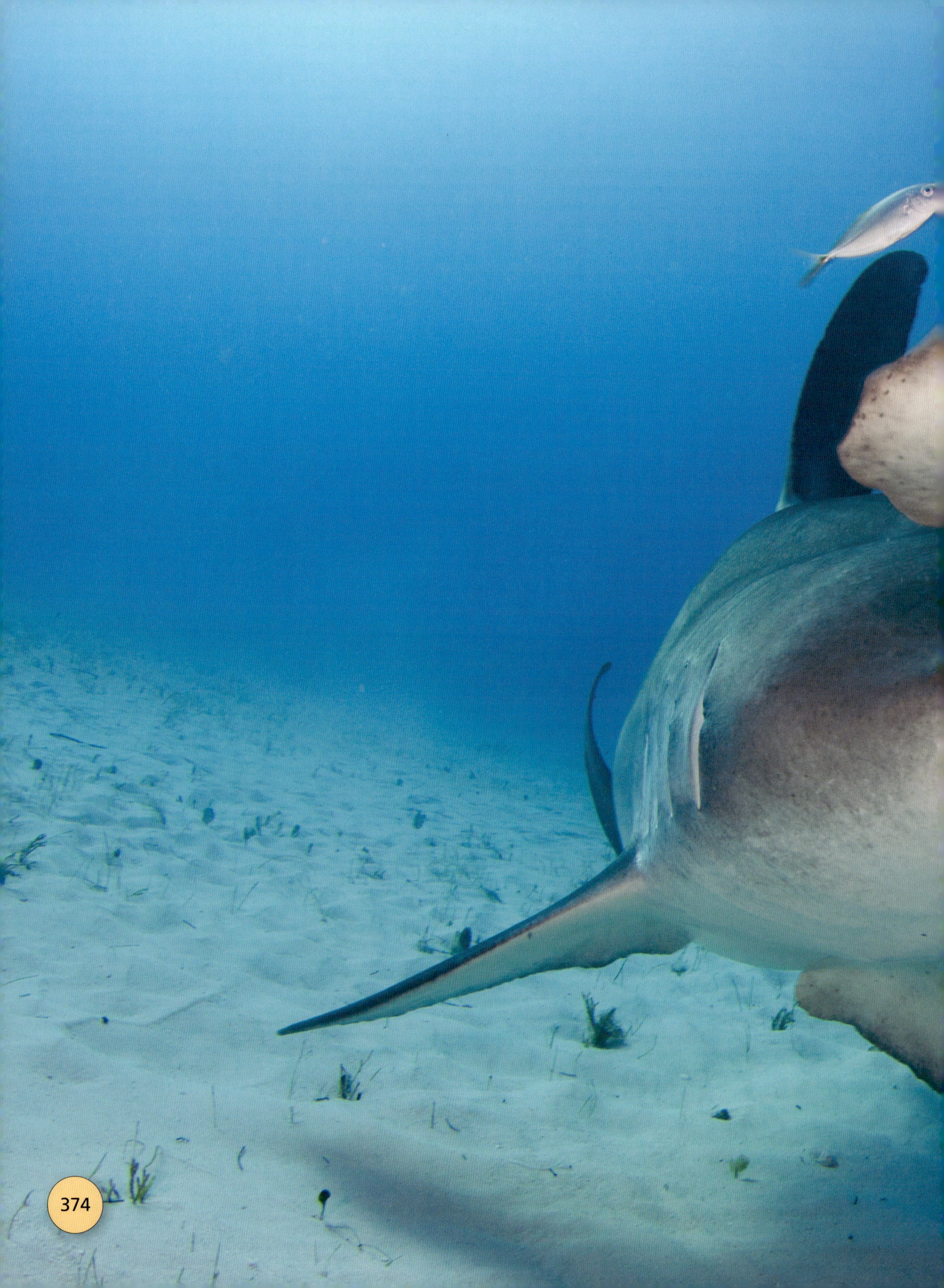

Hammerhead sharks

Hammerhead sharks

- **Hammerheads are probably** the strangest-looking sharks. The head is extremely wide and the eyes are at either end of the 'hammer'.

- **A hammerhead shark** has to turn its head from side to side in order to see forwards.

- **Experts think this head shape** may help the shark to find food, by spreading out their ampullae of Lorenzini over a wide area.

- **The shark's nostrils** are also spread wide apart on its head, giving it 'stereo' sniffing power and helping it to detect the scent of prey.

- **The hammer-shaped head** also works like underwater 'wings' to lift the shark upwards as it moves through the water.

- **Seen from the side**, they look similar to other sharks as the 'hammer' is so flat and streamlined.

- **There are nine species** of hammerhead, including great, scalloped, smooth, winghead and bonnethead sharks. Each species has a head of a slightly different size and shape.

Hammerhead sharks

- **During the day**, hammerhead sharks can often be seen swimming in large groups.

- **In hammerhead shark groups**, larger sharks tend to swim in the safest places in the middle of the group and smaller sharks around the outside. The sharks control their position in the group with displays, such as head shakes and swimming in large loops.

- **Hammerheads have taller dorsal fins** and smaller pectoral fins than most other sharks. This helps them to feed on the sea bed.

▲ The smooth hammerhead does not have a notch in the middle of its hammer-shaped head.

DID YOU KNOW?
A hammerhead can detect the electrical signals from the heart muscles of a stingray buried on the sea bed from 25 cm away.

Winghead shark

- **The winghead shark** is a small, stout hammerhead, which grows to a maximum length of about 1.8 m.

- **It has a longer**, slimmer 'hammer' than other hammerheads.

- **The winghead** is also called the slender hammerhead, the arrowhead or the arrow-headed hammerhead.

- **It has huge nostrils**, which are longer than its curved mouth.

Hammerhead sharks

- **Winghead sharks** live around coasts and islands in the Indian Ocean and the western Pacific Ocean.

- **They probably feed** on small fish, squid, octopuses, shrimps and crabs, but not much is known about the lives of these hammerheads.

- **Females give birth** to between six and nine pups after a pregnancy of 8–11 months.

- **The pups** are up to 40 cm long when they are born.

- **Pregnant females** sometimes fight each other.

- **This hammerhead shark** is not known to bite people, unlike its larger relative, the great hammerhead.

▲ The wide 'wings' on the head of this shark make it easy to recognize.

DID YOU KNOW?
The width of the winghead's hammer may equal nearly half the length of its body.

Bonnethead shark

- **Bonnetheads** are a type of hammerhead shark. They are also called bonnet sharks, bonnetnose sharks or shovelheads.

- **This shark's head** is a rounded bonnet shape and looks less like a hammer.

- **They are the smallest hammerheads**, averaging around one metre in length, reaching maximum lengths of 1.5 m.

- **Often found in shallow bays** and river estuaries, the bonnethead eats mainly crabs, shrimps and other crustaceans, as well as octopus and squid.

- **The bonnethead** lives around the tropical coasts of the Americas, in the eastern Pacific Ocean and western Atlantic Ocean, from southern California to Ecuador and from Rhode Island, USA, down to Brazil.

- **It has small, sharp teeth** in the front of its jaws to grab soft-bodied animals and large, broad teeth at the back of the lower jaw to crush hard-bodied prey.

- **Bonnetheads form huge groups** called schools, which may include thousands.

- **Scientists think this species** may have complex social systems, with different members of a group having different levels of dominance.

- **Fishermen have to be very careful** if they grab a bonnethead shark by the tail, as it can reach round and bite.

- **The scalloped bonnethead** is another type of hammerhead. Its head has curved or scallop-shaped lines on it.

Hammerhead sharks

▼ A bonnethead shark swallows a ray it has just found partially buried in the sandy sea bed. It isn't affected by the ray's painful sting.

Blue-spotted stingray

Scalloped hammerhead

- **Scalloped hammerheads**, or kidney-headed sharks, live all over the world in warm and hot oceans. They often swim near the shore but also reach depths of over 1000 m.

- **They tend to stay in deeper**, cooler water during the summer and move closer to the warmer surface waters in winter.

- **Scalloped hammerheads** are named after the groove at the front of the head, which gives them a scalloped, or 'scooped out', shape.

- **These hammerheads** sometimes use the magnetism given off by lava pushing through the sea bed as a 'magnetic highway'. This helps them to navigate between their daytime resting places and their night-time feeding areas.

- **They feed on fish**, other sharks, rays, and small sea creatures.

- **Scalloped hammerheads** swim in large schools when resting, which may be for safety or to help them find a mate. They separate at night to feed.

- **Female scalloped hammerheads** give birth to between 13 and 31 pups after a pregnancy lasting eight to 12 months.

Hammerhead sharks

- **The pups are born** in shallow waters near the shore. They are 42–55 cm long at birth.

- **They reach lengths** of about 1.5–2 m as adults, with a maximum length of up to 4 m.

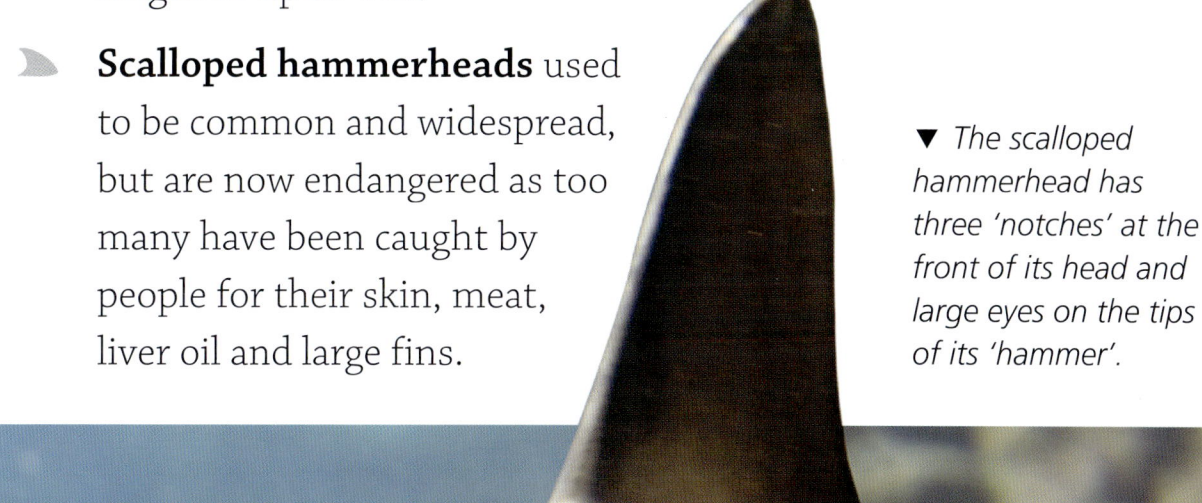

- **Scalloped hammerheads** used to be common and widespread, but are now endangered as too many have been caught by people for their skin, meat, liver oil and large fins.

▼ *The scalloped hammerhead has three 'notches' at the front of its head and large eyes on the tips of its 'hammer'.*

384

Hammerhead sharks

▲ The scalloped hammerhead's sharp teeth are ideal for spearing prey. Adult scalloped hammerheads are so large they have no natural enemies, but they are threatened by people catching them for their fins.

385

Great hammerhead

- **The great hammerhead** is the biggest hammerhead shark and can grow up to 6 m in length.

- **It is one of only a few shark species** that will attack humans, but is rarely aggressive.

- **The great hammerhead** has a relatively straight 'hammer' compared to other hammerheads. It has a notch at the front of its head in the middle.

- **It is light grey or grey-brown** on its back and white below, with few distinguishing markings.

- **Great hammerheads** live all over the world in tropical oceans.

- **They live close to the shore** but also in deeper water up to 90 m, or sometimes even 300 m, beneath the surface.

- **The diet of this active predator** is varied and includes stingrays and guitarfish from the sea bed, but also fish from all depths, such as groupers, jacks and grunts, and squid, as well as octopuses and lobsters.

- **Great hammerheads** migrate away from the tropics in summer to cooler waters, but return to warm, tropical waters for the winter.

- **Female great hammerheads** give birth to between six and 42 pups at a time, after a pregnancy lasting seven to 11 months.

- **The pups are 50–70 cm long** at birth and may sometimes be eaten by adult great hammerheads, which will behave as cannibals.

▶ The great hammerhead has about 25 triangular teeth with jagged edges in each jaw.

Hammerhead sharks

DID YOU KNOW?
The endangered great hammerhead is also called the squat-headed hammerhead. It can weigh up to 450 kg.

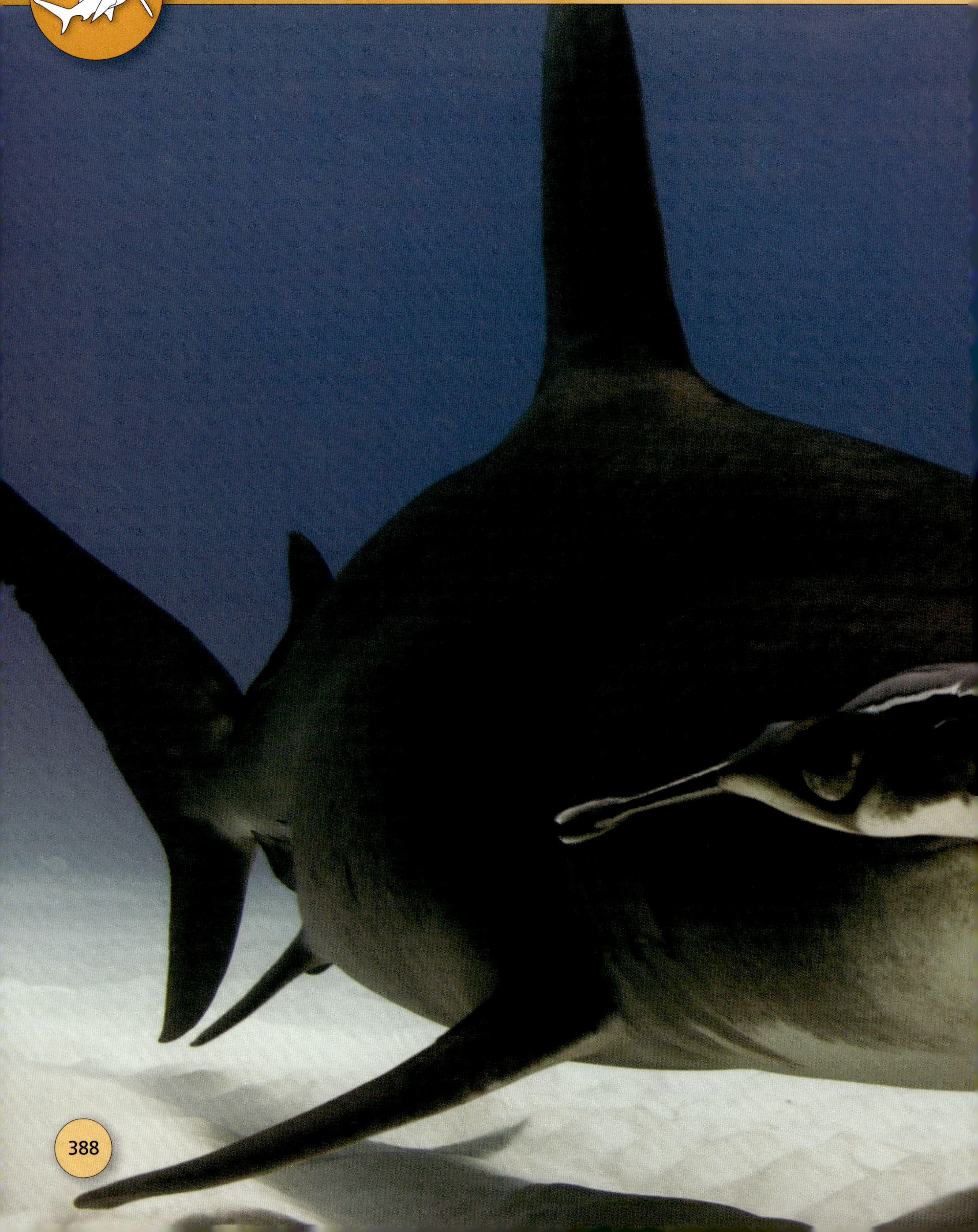

Hammerhead sharks

▼ The great hammerhead uses its 'hammer' to pin down its prey of stingrays. The shark then bites pieces from the stingray's wings so it cannot move.

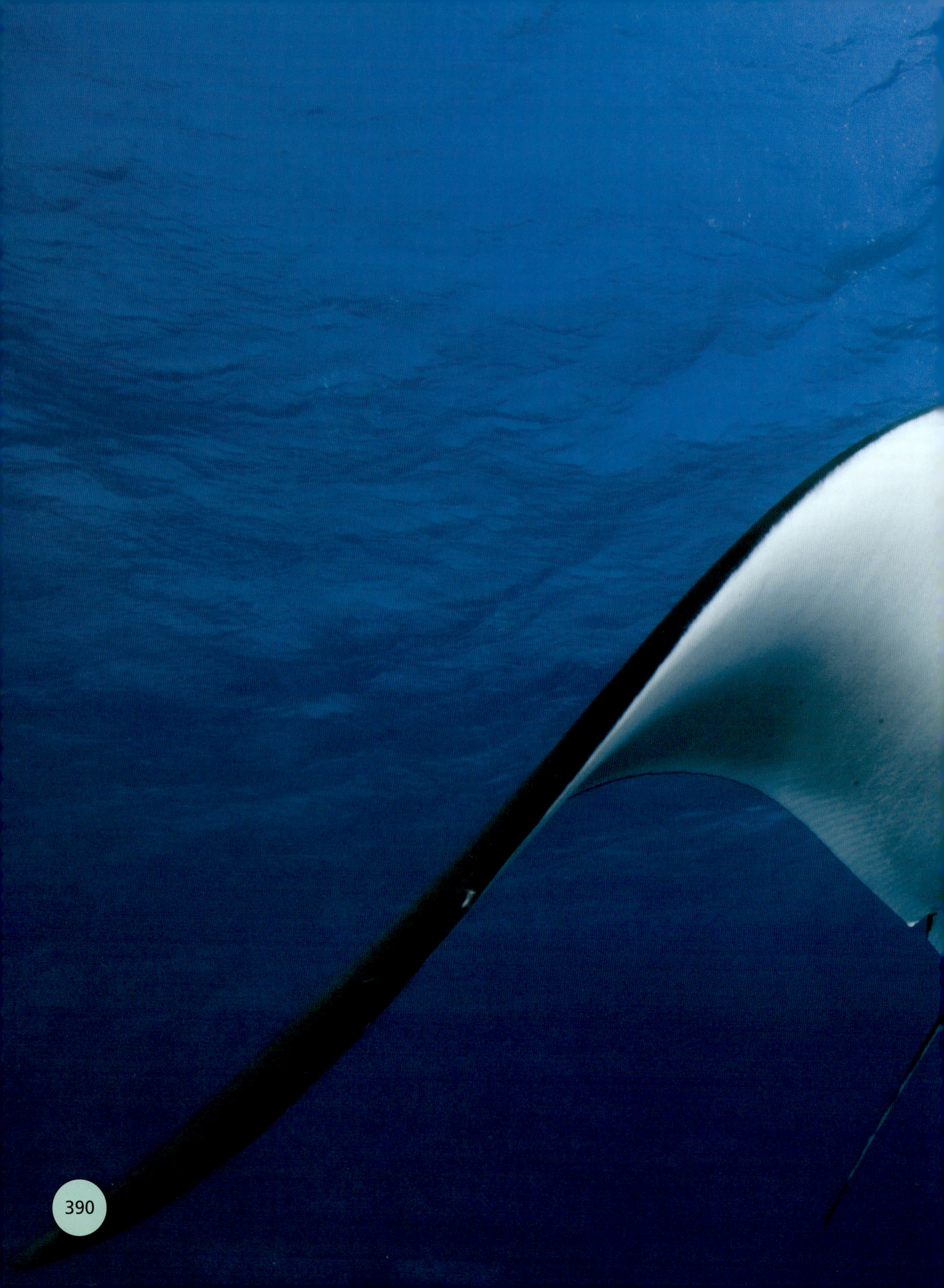

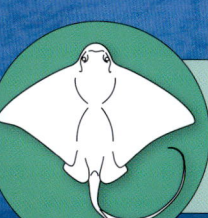

Shark relatives

Shark relatives

- **Sharks are closely related** to two other groups of fish – the batoids and the chimaeras.

- **The batoids include** rays, skates, sawfish and guitarfish. They range in size from plate-sized skates to giant manta rays.

- **There are more than 550 species** of batoids – more than the number of shark species.

- **Most batoids** have wide, flat heads and bodies, and long, tapering tails. They look similar to some types of shark, such as angelsharks.

- **Batoids feed** on bottom-dwelling sea creatures such as clams, shrimps and flatfish.

▶ Manta rays are the largest batoids and measure 4–9 m across their wings.

Shark relatives

▼ *The smalltooth sawfish reaches an average length of 5.5 m.*

- **Most batoids swim** by flapping their large, front fins. Some, such as sawfish, guitarfish and torpedo rays, use their tail for swimming, as sharks do.

- **Sharks are often difficult** to catch and keep in captivity, so scientists often study batoids instead. They are very similar to sharks, so they can provide clues to how sharks live.

- **Chimaeras are strange-looking**, long-tailed fish. Their name means 'a mixture', as they look a little like a cross between a shark and a bony fish.

- **The various species of chimaera** are also known as ratfish, ghost sharks, spook fish and even ghouls.

- **Like sharks, batoids and chimaeras** have light, flexible skeletons made of cartilage, instead of bone like other fish.

▶ A human diver looks tiny beside a giant oceanic manta ray. The paddle-like fins on the ray's head form a funnel, which directs the flow of plankton-rich water into its mouth. The slits under the ray's body are its gills.

Shark relatives

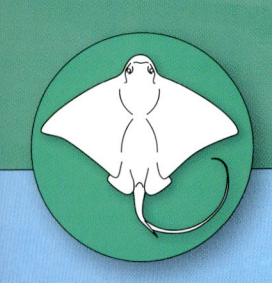

Rays

- **Rays are a type of batoid.** They are closely related to sharks.

- **With their huge, wing-like fins**, some ray species are wider than they are long.

- **A ray swims** using the rippling motions of its fins. It looks as if it is flying through the water.

- **Many rays** have a long, whip-like tail. Unlike sharks, they don't use their tails to push themselves through the water.

- **Rays have eyes** on the top of their heads and large spiracles to breathe through. This enables them to see and breathe without difficulty, even while lying flat on the sea bed.

DID YOU KNOW?
A group of stingrays is called a 'fever' of stingrays.

Shark relatives

- **Most rays are ovoviviparous** – they give birth to live young that have hatched from eggs inside the mothers' bodies, like some sharks do.

- **Rays live in seas** and oceans all around the world, from shallows near the shore to sea beds 3000 m deep.

- **Most species are solitary** and prefer to live alone. However some, such as golden cow-nosed rays, form huge groups of thousands of individuals.

- **Some rays**, such as the mangrove stingray and the manta ray, can leap right out of the water.

- **Many rays have colourful patterns** on their skin and live in shallow water. The Australian leopard whipray has leopard-like spots on its skin.

▼ *Rays have wide, flat bodies, which helps them to skim closely along the sea bed, searching for food.*

Manta rays

- **There are two species** of manta ray – the giant oceanic manta and the reef manta.

- **Manta rays are filter-feeders** – like the basking shark and the whale shark. They suck in water to filter out the tiny plankton.

- **Manta rays are nicknamed** 'devil rays' because of the horn-like fins on their heads.

- **The name 'manta'** comes from the Spanish word for cloak or blanket.

- **The biggest ray** is the oceanic manta ray. It is usually about 7 m wide and 7 m long (including its tail). The biggest are nearly 9 m wide.

- **The reef manta** is smaller than the oceanic manta, but still has an average wingspan of 3 m and a maximum wingspan of 4.5 m.

- **In both species of manta ray**, the wingspan is about twice the length of the body.

- **Manta rays often** visit cleaning stations where small fish feed on the dead skin and parasites on their skin and gills. Both the mantas and the small fish benefit from this behaviour.

Shark relatives

▲ Gill arches in the manta ray's mouth filter food from the water.

- **Manta rays have a docile nature** and are preyed on by killer whales and large sharks, such as the great white shark.

- **Female manta rays** give birth to one or two pups at a time. At birth, the pups measure up to 1.5 m from wingtip to wingtip.

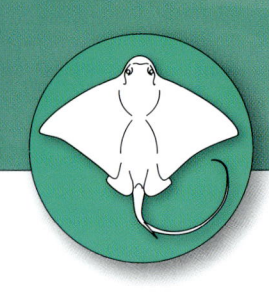

Electric rays

- **Electric rays** can generate electricity to give other animals a powerful electric shock. This ability can be used to deter predators or stun prey.

- **Short-nose electric rays** include some of the smallest rays, at less than 20 cm across.

- **There are over 60 species** of electric ray, including Atlantic torpedo rays, the lesser electric ray and the marbled electric ray.

- **Electric rays** live in shallow waters, but can also be found in waters at least 1000 m deep.

- **Most electric rays** bury themselves under sand on the sea bed during the day and come out at night to feed.

- **An electric ray** uses electricity to detect and stun its prey. Then it uses its front fins to guide the meal into its mouth, which is under the body.

- **Electric rays** also use their electricity to defend themselves from predators and to communicate with each other.

- **The electricity** is generated and stored in kidney-shaped electric organs at the base of their front fins.

Shark relatives

- **Some electric rays** produce as little as 37 volts or less, while Atlantic torpedo rays can generate as much as 220 volts of electricity.

- **The ancient Greeks** used the electricity from electric rays to numb the pain of operations and childbirth.

> **DID YOU KNOW?**
> The mouth of the Australian coffin ray is gigantic, which allows it to swallow prey half the size of its own body!

▼ A lesser electric ray lives in shallow coastal waters. It can generate a voltage of 14–37 volts in order to stun prey or defend itself from predators.

Stingrays

- **Stingrays have** a poisonous spine (or sometimes two or three) in the middle of their tails. It is used mainly for defence against attack.

- **River stingrays**, unlike other rays, live in freshwater. They are found in rivers in Africa and South America, especially the Amazon River.

- **Round stingrays** have almost completely round, flat bodies, like dinner plates.

- **Spotted eagle rays** are covered with beautiful pale spots on dark skin, but are white underneath.

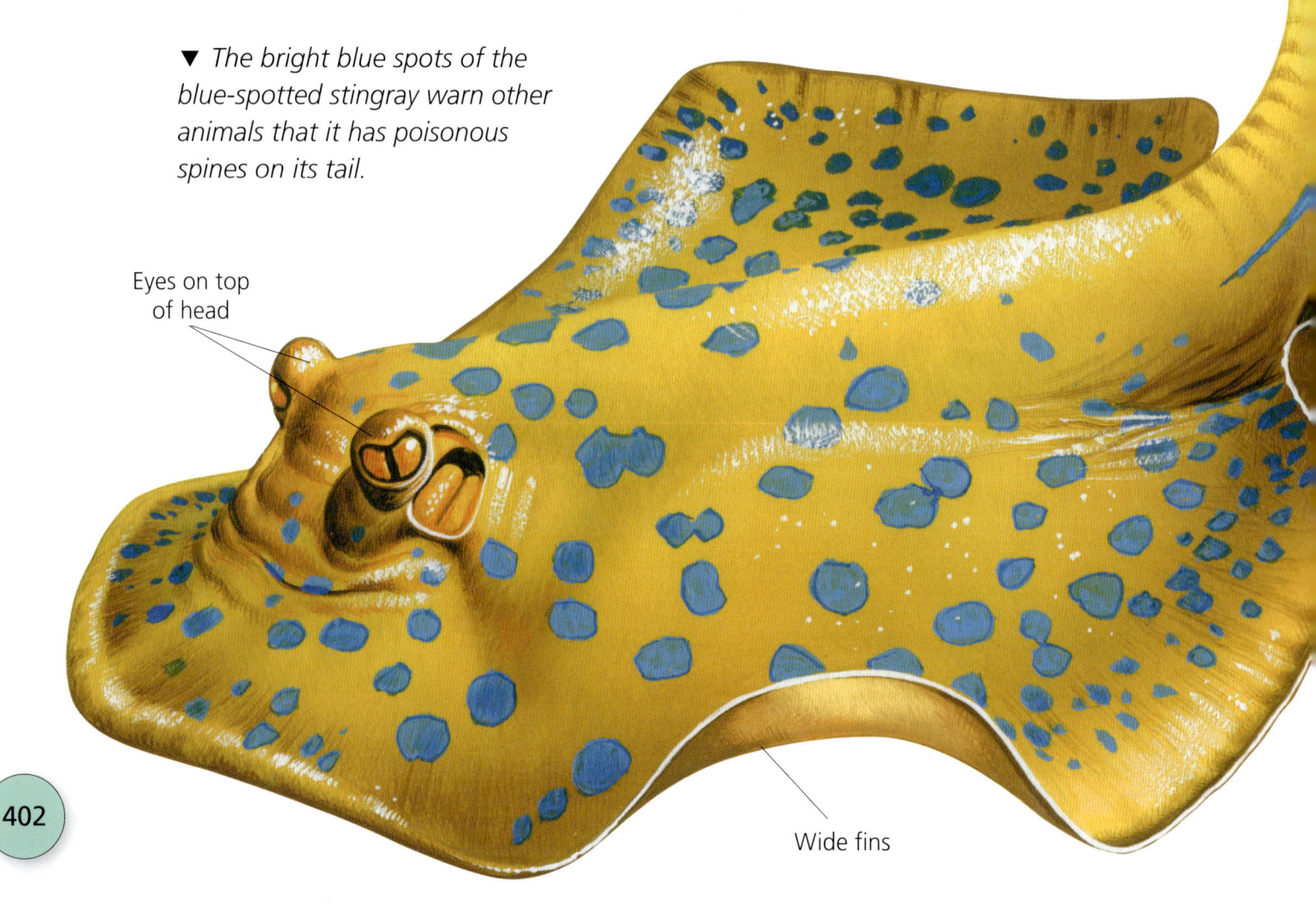

▼ *The bright blue spots of the blue-spotted stingray warn other animals that it has poisonous spines on its tail.*

Spines

Long tail

Eyes on top of head

Wide fins

Shark relatives

- **Most stingrays live** on the sea bed. They feed on shellfish and crabs, which they crush with their teeth.

- **The eagle, duckbilled and cownose rays** are nicknamed 'nutcracker rays'. This is because their teeth are joined together to form plates, which they use to crush their hard-shelled prey.

- **The pelagic stingray** is different. It lives in the open ocean and feeds mainly on squid.

▲ *The wingspan of spotted eagle rays is up to 3 m. These rays may jump right out of the water if a predator is chasing them.*

- **Most stingrays** only attack people in self-defence. If a person accidentally steps on a stingray buried in the sand, the stingray may flip up its dangerous tail to stab the person's legs or ankles with poison.

- **Female stingrays** give birth to between five and 15 young after a pregnancy of about nine months.

- **The mothers feed** the young a sort of 'milk' while they are developing inside their uterus (womb).

404

Shark relatives

▼ A blue-spotted stingray hunting in a shallow sandy area of a coral reef. Two hard plates inside its mouth crush the shells of its prey, including shellfish, shrimps and crabs.

Skates

- **Skates are similar to rays**, but they tend to have straighter edges to the front of their pectoral fins, and shorter tails.

- **Most types of skate** live in deep water, as far down as 3000 m.

- **Skates usually** lie on the sea bed waiting for prey such as crabs and shrimps to come close.

- **As its mouth is on its underside**, a skate does not lunge at its prey. Instead it swims over the victim and grasps it from above.

- **Like some sharks**, skates lay eggs with protective cases.

- **The egg cases** of the flapper skate are up to 25 cm long, and each contains as many as seven eggs.

▶ The common skate can be recognized by its unusually long and pointed snout. This species is now usually called the flapper skate.

Shark relatives

> **Skate egg cases** have stiff spikes to help them stick into the sea bed. They also have a sticky coating so that they soon become covered with sand or pebbles as a form of camouflage.

DID YOU KNOW?
The flapper skate is critically endangered due to over-fishing and habitat destruction.

> **Skate is a popular food** in some parts of the world – especially the fins, which are called 'skate wings'.

> **The largest skate** is the flapper skate, which reaches lengths of up to 2.8 m.

> **The Texas skate** has two big spots, one on each 'wing'. These spots look like the eyes of a larger animal, and may deter predators.

▼ Skate egg cases are sometimes called 'mermaid's purses'.

Guitarfish

- **Guitarfish are a family of rays** with over 40 different species.

- **The head of a guitarfish** is long, flat and guitar-shaped unlike the disc-shaped head of other rays.

- **The front fins of a guitarfish** are smaller than those of other rays and they use their tails for swimming (like sharks).

- **The giant guitarfish** reaches lengths of up to 3 m. It is found in the Red Sea and Indian Ocean.

- **During the day**, the shovelnose guitarfish lays buried in the sand, with only its eyes sticking out, waiting to ambush crabs or flatfish. At night, it swims over the sea floor, hunting for crabs, worms and clams.

- **Shovelnose guitarfish** crush crabs and shellfish with their many rows of pebble-like teeth.

- **The bowmouth guitarfish** (also known as the sharkfin guitarfish) has a mouth shaped like a longbow, and heavy ridges of sharp, spiky thorns on its head for defence.

- **It uses its large head** and front fins to trap prey against the sea bed, then quickly gulps down its meal.

Shark relatives

▸ **Female sharkfin guitarfish** have four to nine pups at a time. Each pup is about 45 cm long.

▸ **Young sharkfin guitarfish** have spots and bars on their skin, which gives them better camouflage than the adults, which are mainly grey.

▼ *The mottled, yellow-brown colours of the shovelnose guitarfish help it to blend into its sandy sea floor habitat.*

DID YOU KNOW?
The shovelnose guitarfish has been living on our planet for over 100 million years!

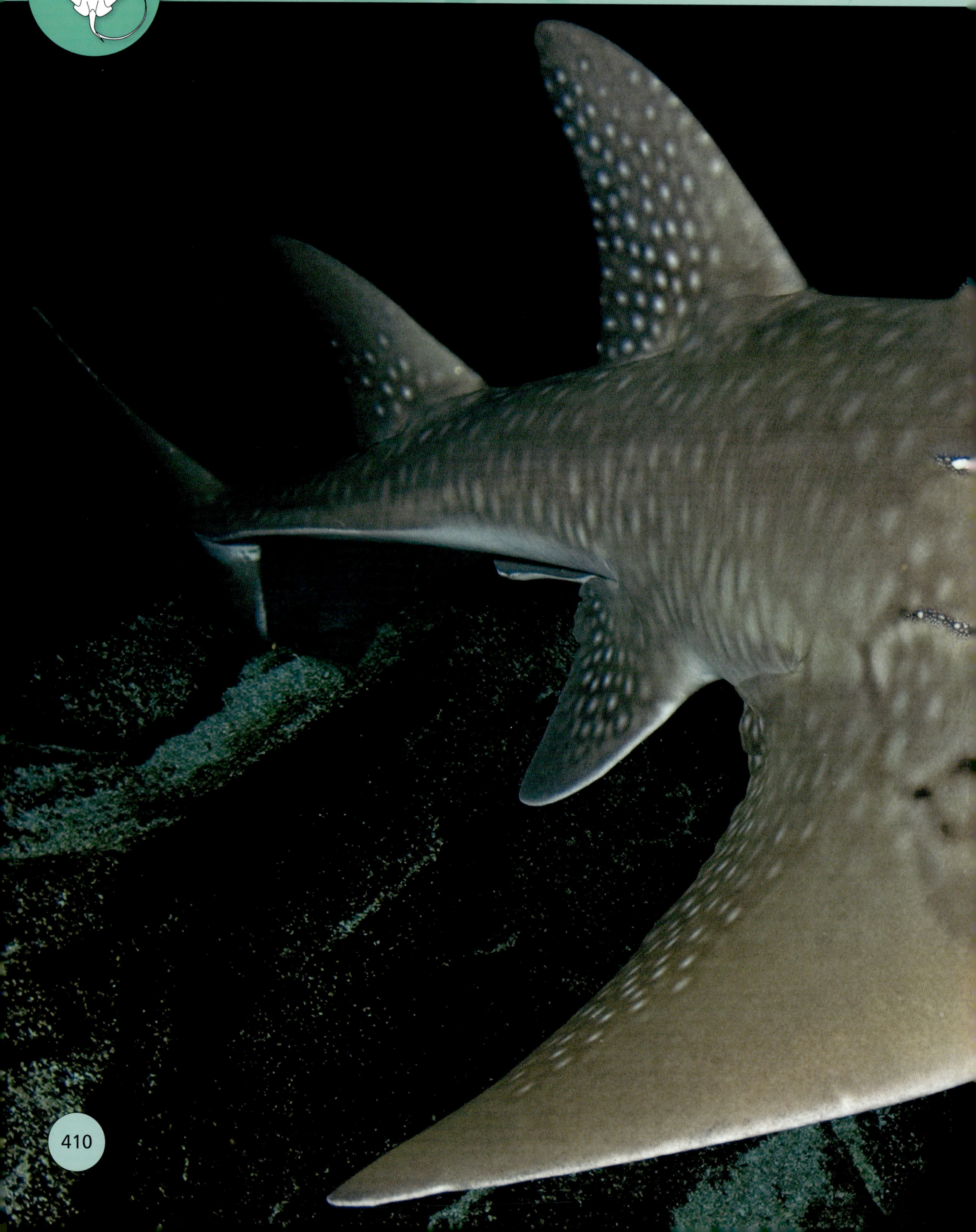

Shark relatives

▼ The bowmouth guitarfish has rows of ridged teeth for crushing crabs, shellfish and clams. This rare type of ray is a strong swimmer and grows up to 3 m long.

Sawfish

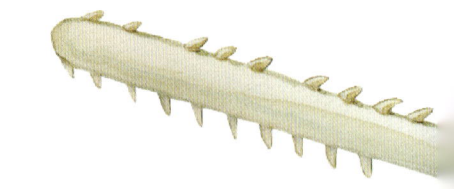

- **The seven species** of sawfish are a type of ray.

- **Sawfish get their name** from their long, saw-like snouts called rostrums, which are edged with sharp teeth, like those on a saw.

- **The green sawfish** grows to more than 7 m in length – longer than a great white shark.

- **Its saw can account** for up to one third, or more, of a sawfish's length.

- **Like rays**, sawfish have flattened bodies, but they look more like sharks than most rays do.

- **Although sawfish** resemble sawsharks, they are not the same. Sawfish are much bigger and lack barbels on their saws.

▼ The green sawfish has the largest snout, or rostrum, of any sawfish. Its rostrum reaches lengths of at least 1.6 m.

Shark relatives

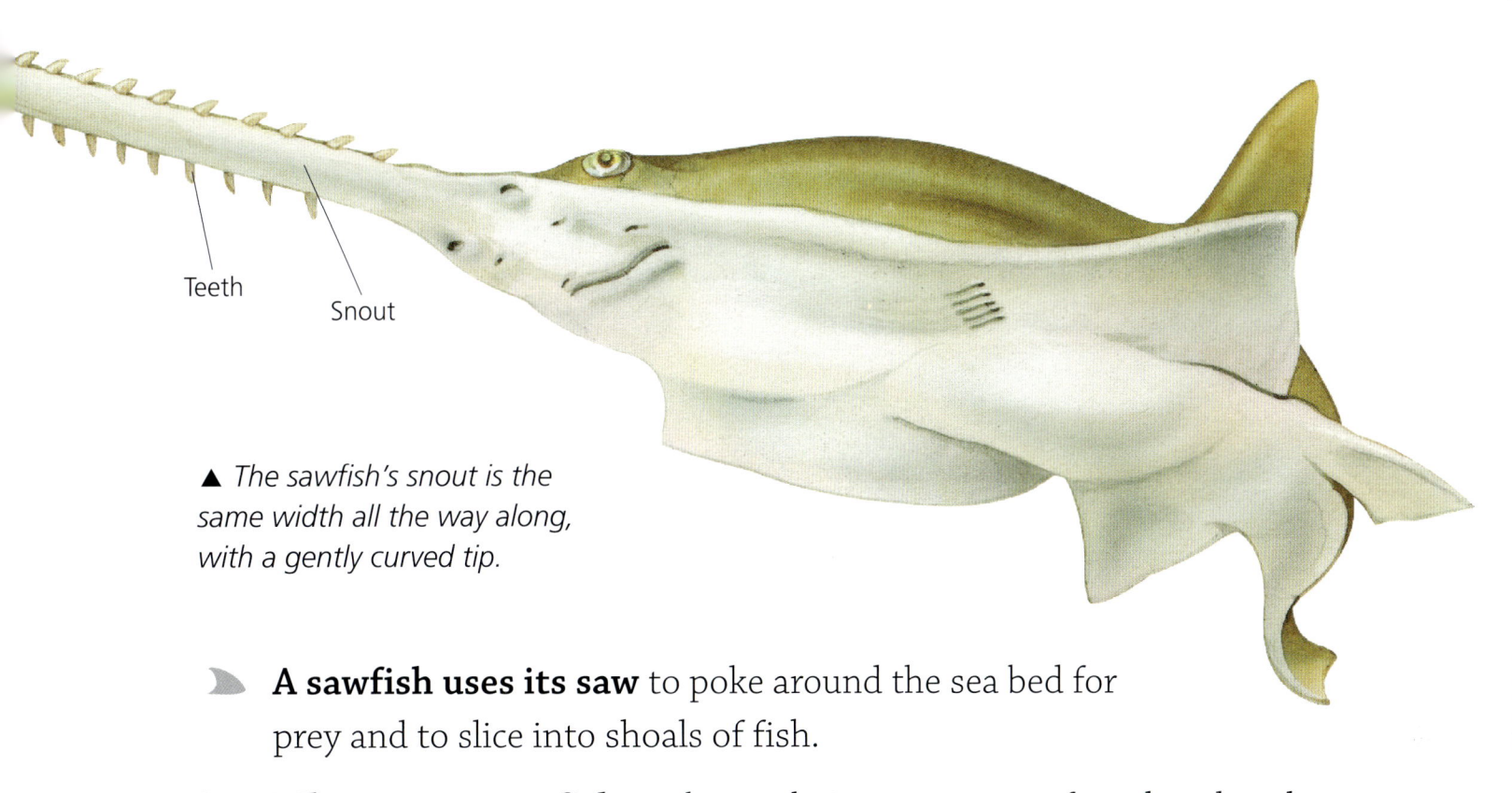

Teeth
Snout

▲ The sawfish's snout is the same width all the way along, with a gently curved tip.

▸ **A sawfish uses its saw** to poke around the sea bed for prey and to slice into shoals of fish.

▸ **When young sawfish** are born, their snouts are soft and enclosed in a covering of skin. This protects the inside of the mother's body from being injured by their sharp teeth. After birth, the protective skin soon falls off and the saw hardens.

▸ **The large-tooth sawfish** sometimes swims up rivers in Australia.

▸ **All species of sawfish** are endangered, due to over-fishing by people and habitat destruction of coastal regions, such as mangrove swamps, where they live.

413

Chimaeras

- **Although they are related** to sharks and rays, chimaeras have evolved separately for nearly 400 million years.

- **There are over 40 species** of chimaeras. They live in water ranging from 500 m deep to over 2500 m beneath the surface.

- **Chimaeras have** a very large head, smooth skin and a long body with a rat-like tail. They are sometimes nicknamed ratfish.

- **To swim along**, they flap their wing-like front fins, like rays.

- **Chimaeras have a plate-like gill cover** over their four gills (like bony fish).

- **Unlike sharks**, chimaeras cannot replace any teeth that are worn out or broken.

Shark relatives

- **Due to its plate-like, grinding teeth** and large nostrils, a chimaera's mouth looks like that of a rabbit. Another of their nicknames is rabbitfish.

- **The eyes of chimaeras** are usually green and very large, which helps them to pick up as much light as possible in the deep sea.

- **Most chimaeras** have a poisonous spine in front of their back fin.

- **Female chimaeras** lay eggs with leathery egg cases.

▼ The spotted ratfish is one of several types of chimaera. It has large eyes and long fins. Unlike many sharks and rays, chimaeras swim very slowly. They stay close to the sea bed, feeding on small fish and octopuses.

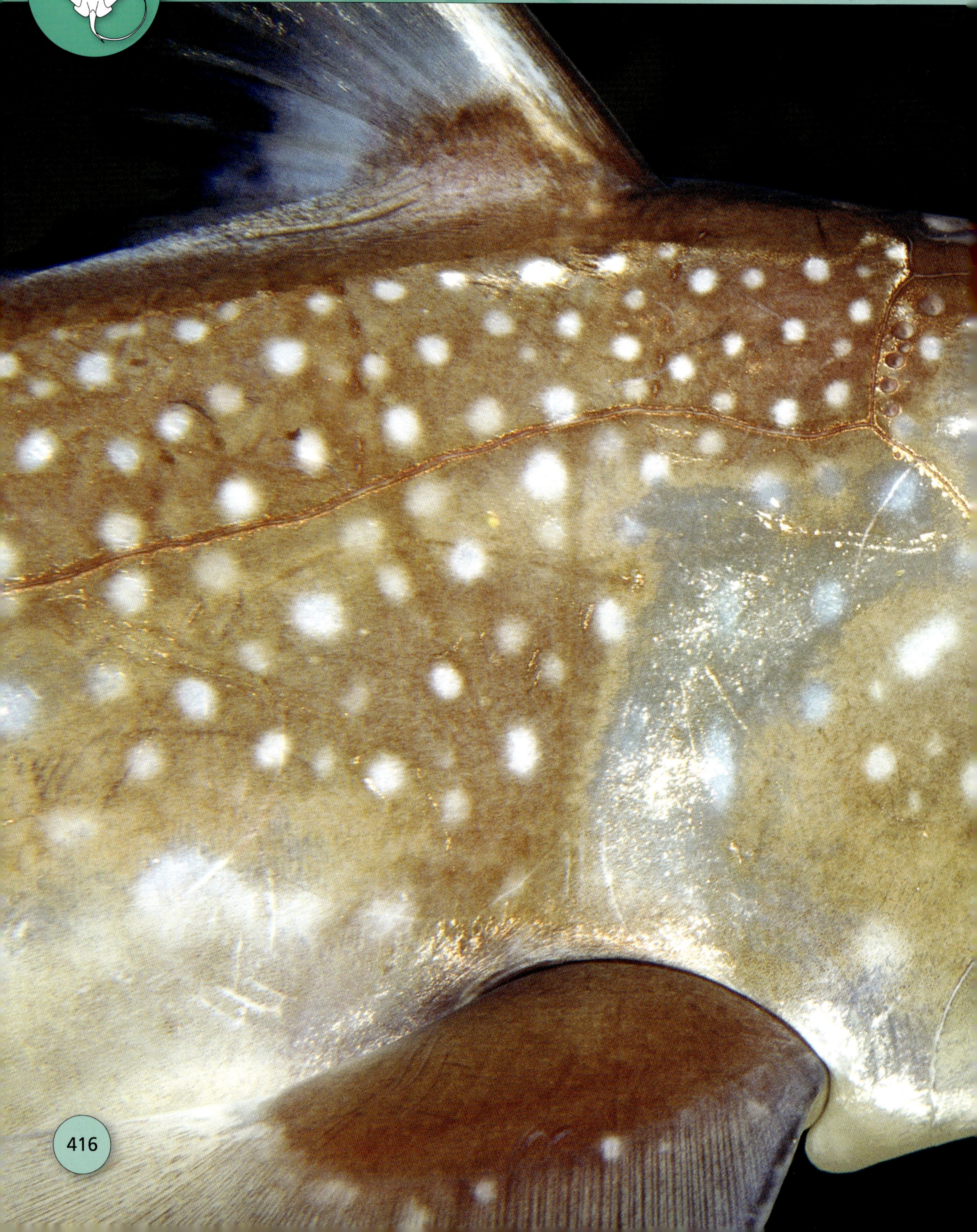

Shark relatives

▼ The spotted ratfish has a smooth, shiny skin, with no scales. Its large eyes reflect the light, like those of a cat. This helps it to find its way as it cruises slowly above the sea floor in the depths of the ocean.

Elephant fish

- **The elephant fish** belongs to a family of chimaeras called the plough-nosed chimaeras, which contains just three species.

- **It is named** after its long, fleshy snout, which is shaped rather like an elephant's trunk.

- **The elephant fish** uses its 'trunk' like a living metal detector. It snuffles through the mud on the ocean floor to detect the electrical signals given off by buried shellfish.

- **When it finds something to eat**, the elephant fish crunches up its prey using plate-like teeth.

- **Elephant fish** live in the southern hemisphere, in the oceans off southern South America, New Zealand, southern Australia and southern Africa.

- **They swim near the shore** and also in water as deep as 200 m.

- **Adults mate** in shallow water. Males have a retractable spiny clasper on their head to help them to hang on to females during mating.

- **Female elephant fish** lay their eggs in large, yellow-brown cases, about 10 by 25 cm in size.

Shark relatives

- **The eggs** take six to eight months to hatch and the young are about 12 cm long when they emerge from their egg cases.

- **Elephant fish** are often used to make 'fish and chips' in restaurants in New Zealand.

▼ *The elephant fish has large green eyes high up on its head, and large front fins, which it uses for swimming.*

DID YOU KNOW?
The elephant fish has hardly changed at all for about 400 million years.

420

Sharks and people

421

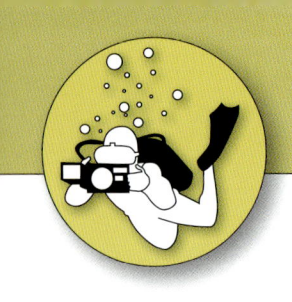

Living with sharks

- **Sharks have existed** on Earth for over 420 million years – much longer than modern humans, who evolved around 200,000 years ago.

- **It's a natural instinct** for people to be scared of sharks, as some are fierce hunters. Although sharks can be dangerous, attacks on humans are rare.

- **In the past**, sailors told tales of deadly attacks, but their stories were probably exaggerated.

- **People from the Pacific Islands** used shark teeth to make tools and weapons up to 5000 years ago.

- **In the 5th century BC**, the ancient Greek historian Herodotus wrote about how sharks attacked sailors when ships sank during battles at sea.

- **The ancient Greek scientist** Aristotle studied sharks and was one of the first to notice that they were different from other fish.

- **Due to modern fishing techniques**, humans are more dangerous to sharks than sharks are to humans. Many people are trying to ensure shark safety by raising awareness of their endangered status.

- **Today, people still use shark skin** to make leather goods and sell shark teeth as tourist souvenirs. The oil in a shark's liver is used in medicine.

- **However, people are learning** to respect sharks rather than fear them. Diving with sharks or watching them in aquariums helps people to find out why sharks are such an important part of the ocean ecosystem.

Sharks and people

▸ **Sports anglers** are being encouraged to tag any sharks they catch and return them to the ocean.

▼ *This shaman from Kontu in Papua New Guinea is hunting sharks and calling them using a conch shell. He will then slip a collar over the shark's head to capture it.*

DID YOU KNOW?
In ancient Japan, the god of storms was a shark, which was a symbol of fear.

Dangerous or not?

- **The great white shark** is often thought to be the most dangerous species because it is most often identified in attacks. This is because it is easy to recognize. Great whites are blamed for up to half of all serious shark attacks.

- **As well as attacking humans**, great whites have been known to attack small boats.

- **Great whites are deadly** to humans partly because we look similar in size and shape to their prey – seals and sea lions. The sharks simply get confused and attack the wrong prey.

▼ *The great white is dangerous compared to most other sharks – but still not as dangerous as many other types of animal.*

Sharks and people

▶ More people have been killed by the box jellyfish than sharks and crocodiles combined. This lethal jellyfish can kill a person in just a few minutes.

- **Many experts think** bull sharks are actually more dangerous than great whites – but they are not well-known as killers because they are harder to identify. After bull sharks attack, they often escape unseen.

- **Sharks with spines**, such as horn and dogfish sharks, are not deadly but can inflict painful injuries on people.

- **Not all dangerous sharks** are fast hunters. Nurse sharks and wobbegongs are usually placid and sluggish animals – but they can bite suddenly and hard if disturbed.

- **Stingrays**, which are related to sharks, can be killers – a few people die every year from their venom.

- **The wildlife expert** and TV personality Steve Irwin was sadly killed in 2006, when a stingray barb pierced his heart while he was filming an underwater documentary.

- **Of the many hundreds** of shark species, only about 12 are usually dangerous to people. The top four are the great white, the bull shark, the tiger shark and the oceanic whitetip shark.

- **Other dangerous sharks** are the great hammerhead, shortfin mako, porbeagle, sand tiger shark, Galapagos shark, blacktip shark, Caribbean reef shark and grey reef shark.

426

Sharks and people

◄ The deadly box jellyfish has 15 tentacles up to 3 m long, each one covered with half a million stinging cells. A single jellyfish contains enough venom to kill 60 adult humans.

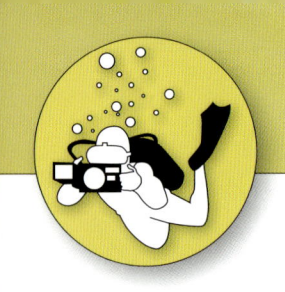

Attacks

- **Every year** there are fewer than 100 reported cases worldwide of sharks attacking humans. Of these attacks, fewer than 20 are fatal.

- **Most attacks happen** in shallow water near the shore. This is because that's where sharks and swimmers are most likely to be in the same place at the same time.

- **Most incidents happen** off the coasts of eastern North America, South Africa and eastern Australia.

- **The danger of a shark attack** increases at night, when sharks move inshore to feed and are most active.

- **Sharks usually only attack** if they are hungry, if they feel threatened or angry, or if they mistake a human for prey. Divers may provoke an attack if they grab a shark by the tail.

- **One of the worst shark** tragedies happened in 1945, during World War II. A US warship was torpedoed and sank in the South Pacific, leaving almost 1000 crew members in the water. Before they could be rescued, more than 600 had been eaten by sharks.

- **In the summer of 1969**, four people were killed in shark attacks within two weeks off the coast of New Jersey, United States.

- **People are more likely** to be killed by a lightning strike than a shark attack. Bees, wasps and snakes also kill many more people than sharks every year.

- **There are more deaths** from car accidents in one month than shark attacks in recorded history.

- **Most shark attacks** on people cause serious injuries, not death. Many deaths are due to blood loss from an initial bite, rather than repeated attacks.

Sharks and people

▶ *From below, a human surfer may look like a seal, causing a hungry shark to attack.*

DID YOU KNOW?
Experts have found that if a shark does take a bite of human flesh, it often spits it out or vomits it up later. Humans do not taste like a shark's normal prey.

Survival stories

- **In 1749, 14-year-old Brook Watson** lost a leg to a shark while swimming at Havana, Cuba. He later became Mayor of London and was famous for his wooden leg.

- **Rodney Fox** was grabbed by a great white while taking part in a spear-fishing contest in Australia in 1963. His body was bitten right open, but he survived and went on to become a shark expert.

- **A great white shark** bit off undersea photographer Henri Bource's leg while he was diving off the coast of Australia in 1964. He was soon back at work in the same job, and four years later another shark bit his artificial leg!

- **In 1996, surfer Joey Hanlon** was attacked by a great white shark while surfing in California, United States. The shark bit into his torso, but he recovered after being given over 300 stitches.

- **Another surfer, John Forse**, was on his surfboard in Oregon, United States, in 1998 when a great white shark grabbed his leg and pulled him deep underwater. He escaped by hitting the shark's dorsal fin until it let him go.

DID YOU KNOW?
In 2004, while snorkelling in Australia, Luke Tresoglavic was bitten by a wobbegong. He had to swim to shore and drive to get help with the shark still attached.

Sharks and people

◗ **In 2003, 13-year-old Bethany Hamilton** had her left arm bitten off by a tiger shark while surfing in Hawaii. She was surfing again within months.

◗ **Fishermen often get bitten** by sharks they have caught. Most of these bites are minor and go unreported.

◗ **Shark attack survivors** are often left with huge semicircular scars from the shape of the shark's mouth.

◗ **Today, shark attack victims** are more likely to survive thanks to fast boats and modern treatments, such as blood transfusions.

◀ *Bethany Hamilton is still a top surfer, despite losing an arm in a tiger shark attack.*

▶ Bethany Hamilton at a surfing competition in 2013. Bethany's courage has been an inspiration to many and her story was featured in a film in 2011, for which she did all the surfing stunts.

Sharks and people

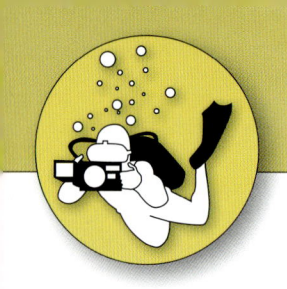

Staying safe

- **Humans have developed** several ways to try to stay safe from shark attacks.

- **Swimming beaches** in shark areas are sometimes surrounded with strong nets to keep sharks out.

- **Chainmail diving suits** protect divers from sharks' teeth, but their bodies can still be crushed by a bite.

- **Some ships carry shark screens** – floating sacks that shipwreck survivors can climb inside. The screen disguises a person's shape and hides their scent, making them less likely to attract sharks.

- **Anti-shark weapons** can be used to scare away sharks. They include electrical prods that confuse a shark's electrical sense, and bangsticks, which are like underwater guns.

- **Some divers wear** striped diving suits for camouflage, making them harder to spot.

- **You shouldn't swim** in a shark zone if you have a cut or wound as blood can attract sharks.

- **If you see a large shark** when you are in the sea, the safest thing to do is to stay calm, avoid splashing about, and swim steadily towards the shore.

- **If you are swimming** in an area where sharks could be present, it is a good idea to avoid wearing shiny clothing or metals, as the sharks may mistake these for fish scales.

- **It is also sensible** to avoid swimming at night when sharks are most active.

▶ *This diver is wearing a chainmail suit to protect against shark bites.*

Sharks and people

▶ A scuba diver wearing a chainmail shark suit touches a Caribbean reef shark. These suits are made of stainless steel or titanium, and provide a protective layer that reduces the potential harm from a shark bite.

Sharks and people

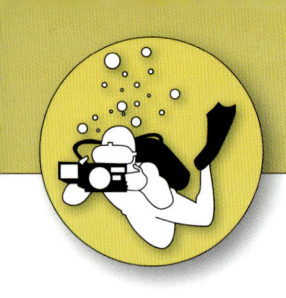

Fishing for sharks

- **Shark fishing** is a huge industry. Sharks are fished for food, and for several other uses too. Humans catch over 100 million sharks ever year, perhaps as many as 250 million. At least three sharks die every second.

- **Sea anglers** fish for sharks as a sport. Many coastal tourist resorts have special boats that take tourists sportfishing for sharks and other large fish. Sharks caught for sport are often thrown back alive.

- **Sport fishermen** like to catch fast-swimming species, such as mako sharks, because they struggle when caught.

- **Many sharks are killed** in fishing tournaments off the east coast of the USA every year.

- **Whale sharks and other species** are sometimes hunted for their fins. After the fins are cut off, the rest of the shark is thrown back into the sea to die.

- **Shark fin soup**, which is popular in Asia, is made by boiling shark fins to extract the gluey cartilage rods – the soup's main ingredient.

- **Millions of sharks** are caught by accident every year in nets meant for other sea creatures, such as squid.

- **Sharks are a nutritious food** because their flesh is very lean and full of protein.

DID YOU KNOW?
About 6–8 percent of all the sharks in the world are killed by people every year.

Sharks and people

- **Many people don't like** the idea of eating sharks. Therefore when they are sold as food, their names are often changed to things such as 'huss'.

- **Parts of sharks** are often made into health food supplements, which contain vitamins A and E.

▼ *A box of freshly caught sharks for sale at a food market.*

Tourist attractions

440

Sharks and people

- **People like to get close to sharks** because they can be exciting and fearsome.

- **In coastal areas** around the world, tourists pay to see sharks in their natural habitat.

- **Ecotourism is tourism** that helps preserve wild habitats and species. Some of the money generated is used for conservation work.

- **Cage-diving allows** people to view dangerous sharks in their natural habitat. Tourists are lowered into the sea inside a metal cage.

- **Sometimes, sharks have been known** to head-butt the metal shark cages or even bite the bars.

- **If sharks are being filmed** or photographed outside a cage, safety divers should be present to watch out for sharks that the film-maker or photographer cannot see.

- **On shark-feeding tours**, tourists go diving to the sea bed, where a guide uses fish to attract species such as whitetip reef sharks.

- **Sharks come to rely** on the free hand-out of food and may become aggressive if it stops.

- **Undersea photographers** use special cameras to take pictures of tourists with sharks as part of the experience.

◀ Tourists line up to take close-up photographs of blacktip reef sharks. The sharks have learned that they will get a free meal of fish if they swim in this area.

► Shark handlers wearing protective shark suits feed Caribbean reef sharks, while ecotourists watch and take photographs. These sharks do not have a history of attacking people, but are still potentially dangerous.

Sharks and people

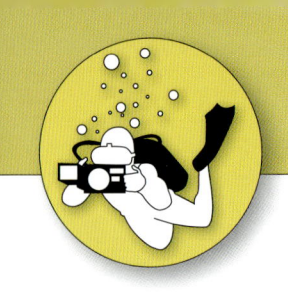

Sharks in captivity

- **Some sharks**, such as lemon sharks, sand tigers and sandbar sharks, are able to survive in sea life centres and aquariums.

- **Giant tanks and walk-through tunnels** allow people to stand right next to sharks, and learn about their bodies and behaviour.

- **Watching sharks close-up** helps people to appreciate and respect them, and understand why it is necessary to protect sharks.

- **Most species of shark** don't survive well in captivity, and many die within a year of being captured. Some refuse to be fed by humans, and large sharks are very hard to handle.

- **It is very expensive** to keep sharks in captivity as they need a large space in which to move around and they eat a lot of food every day. Captive sharks are usually fed 1–3 percent of their body weight weekly.

- **Many scientists** think that the intelligence of sharks and their keen senses (especially their electrical senses) make them feel confused and stressed in captivity.

- **Sharks that usually migrate** long distances may become aggressive and refuse to eat when they are unable to go on their usual migration journeys in captivity.

- **Monterey Bay Aquarium** in California is developing ways to collect and exhibit great white sharks in a safe and sustainable way that educates visitors about the threats to sharks in the wild.

- **They have kept young great white sharks** successfully and released them back into the wild. All the released sharks have been tracked to make sure they are doing well in their natural environment.

Sharks and people

⯈ **One of the most common reasons** for keeping sharks in captivity is to care for injured sharks and help them to recover, so they can be returned to the wild.

▼ *Standing in an aquarium to watch a whale shark – the largest fish in the world – as it glides slowly past is an awesome experience that these visitors will remember for ever.*

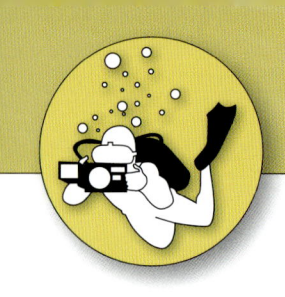

Shark products

- **Some shark species**, such as the spotted wobbegong, are still hunted for their skin. It is made into items such as belts, wallets, shoes and handbags.

- **Polished shark skin leather** was once used to cover books and scientific objects such as telescopes.

- **Dried but untreated shark skin** makes a rough substance called 'shagreen', which is used to make sandpaper and a non-slip binding for sword hilts.

- **Squalene is an oil** extracted from shark livers. It is used in cosmetics, perfume and skin care.

- **Shark liver oil** is also used in some candles and paints.

- **Shark liver oil** has traditionally been used to waterproof boats, for lighting and for machine oil in industry.

- **Shark teeth** are often made into necklaces and other jewellery for people to wear.

- **Shark teeth** were once thought to be dragon's teeth in China. They were traded a long way from the ocean and people did not realize they were connected with sharks.

- **Shark fin soup** is a clear soup that has been prepared from dried shark fins for over 2000 years. It was once so rare and precious that it was eaten only at the banquets of Chinese emperors to honour special guests.

▶ Hunting sharks to make their teeth into jewellery is placing many sharks in danger of extinction. This jewellery was made from the teeth of the rare great white shark.

Sharks and people

DID YOU KNOW?
Some shark teeth were often used as tools by early humans because of their sharp edges.

447

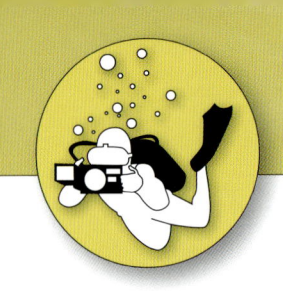

Sharks and medicine

▼ *Some of the most popular shark products are dried shark's fin for homemade soup, tinned shark's fin soup and shark liver oil capsules.*

Sharks and people

- **The ancient Greeks** used burnt angelshark skin to treat skin diseases, and shocks from electric rays as a painkiller during medical operations.

- **A type of medicine** for heart disease is made from chemicals extracted from shark blood.

- **Scientists have worked out** how to use shark corneas (the transparent protective covering in front of the eye) to make cornea transplants for humans.

- **Shark cartilage** can be used to make artificial skin for burn victims who have had their own skin burned away.

- **Shark cartilage** has been used in human and pet health supplements to treat joint problems. However, similar products are available that do not contain shark cartilage.

- **Shark cartilage pills** have been marketed as a cancer cure because sharks were not thought to get cancer. However, scientists now know that sharks do suffer from many cancers, and these pills are not effective at treating cancer.

- **Taking too many** shark cartilage pills can result in harmful side effects.

- **A shark's liver** contains high levels of vitamin A and many sharks were killed in the past so that their livers could be used to make health supplements. Today, vitamin A can be made artificially.

- **An antibiotic called squalamine**, found in a shark's liver, could be used as a new type of drug to treat human viruses, from yellow fever to hepatitis. However, squalamine can be made artificially.

Legends and beliefs

- **There are many legends** involving sharks. Most come from parts of the world where sharks are common.

- **Hawaiian legends** tell of a shark king and a shark queen who controlled all the other sharks in the sea.

- **In legends from the South Pacific**, 'shark men' were sharks that could take human form and come ashore to cause mischief and steal things.

- **In the past**, many cultures around the world worshipped shark gods.

- **People from the Solomon Islands**, in the Pacific Ocean, believed that the spirits of people who had died lived on in sharks.

- **In Fiji, in the Pacific Ocean**, people used to catch sharks, roll them onto their backs and kiss their stomachs. This behaviour was believed to make the sharks harmless, so people could fish safely.

- **In Greek mythology**, Odysseus was killed when his son, Telegonus, struck him with a spear tipped with the poisonous spine of a stingray.

- **The scientific name for mackerel sharks**, Lamniformes, comes from the serpent-like monster from Greek myths, called Lamia, who liked to eat human flesh.

- **The goblin shark** is named after the goblin-like creature Tengu, from Japanese folklore.

Sharks and people

◗ **Inuit legends refer** to the smell of urine that Greenland sharks tend to have. One legend says that the shark lived in the urine pot of the god Sedna and was created as a helping spirit. Another legend tells how an old woman washed her hair in urine, dried it with a cloth and threw the cloth into the sea, where it became the Greenland shark.

▼ *A shark features in this Australian Aboriginal art, which has been painted on an urban brick wall.*

DID YOU KNOW?
The legend of Ina and the shark was so popular in the Cook Islands that it was shown on their bank notes in 1992.

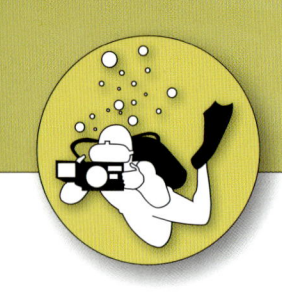

Books and films

- **In his 1851 novel *Moby-Dick***, Herman Melville described how a character named Queequeg almost lost his hand to a shark.

- **Another famous novel**, *20,000 Leagues Under the Sea* by Jules Verne, features man-eating sharks.

- **The best-known shark novel** of all is *Jaws* by Peter Benchley, published in 1974. It tells of a great white shark attacking swimmers off the east coast of the United States.

- **In 1975**, *Jaws* was made into a film by Steven Spielberg. Much of *Jaws* was filmed using a 7-m-long artificial shark, known on set as Bruce.

- **In a later movie**, *Deep Blue Sea* (1999), the shark sequences were partly created using computer animation. It tells the story of a group of scientists who use genetic engineering to create super-intelligent sharks – which then turn against them.

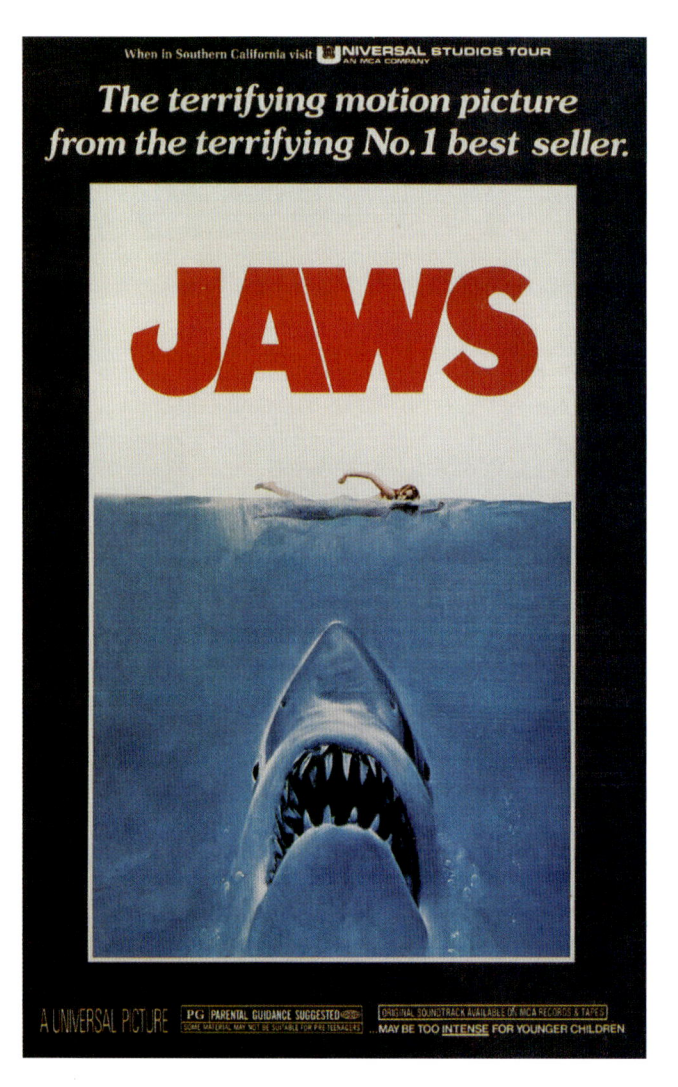

▲ The thriller Jaws broke box-office records and is still one of the biggest-grossing films of all time. It has won several awards.

Sharks and people

- **The film *Bait* (2012)** tells the story of a group of shoppers trapped in an underground supermarket in Australia after a tsunami. They have to confront a killer tiger shark on the prowl, as well as the threat of drowning.

- **In the film *Open Water* (2004)**, two scuba divers are accidentally left behind by a tour boat in the ocean and battle to survive in shark-infested waters.

- **The 2009 film** *Mega Shark versus Giant Octopus* chronicles the epic battle of two prehistoric sea creatures awoken from a frozen tomb as a result of global warming.

▲ *A still from a shark attack sequence in the film* Deep Blue Sea.

- **The film *Dark Tide* (2012)** tells the story of a professional dive tutor who returns to deep waters nine years after he was nearly killed by a great white shark. The nightmare from the deep is still lying in wait for him.

- **Although many shark books** feature scary, man-eating sharks, the children's book, *The Shark Who Was Afraid of Everything* (2006) tells the story of a fictional shark who has to overcome his fears and help a new friend get home safely.

- **Great whites** have had more books written about them than any other species of shark.

453

454

Sharks and people

◀ A scene from the film Finding Nemo, where a great white shark called Bruce tries to eat Nemo's father, Marlin, and his friend Dory, a blue tang fish.

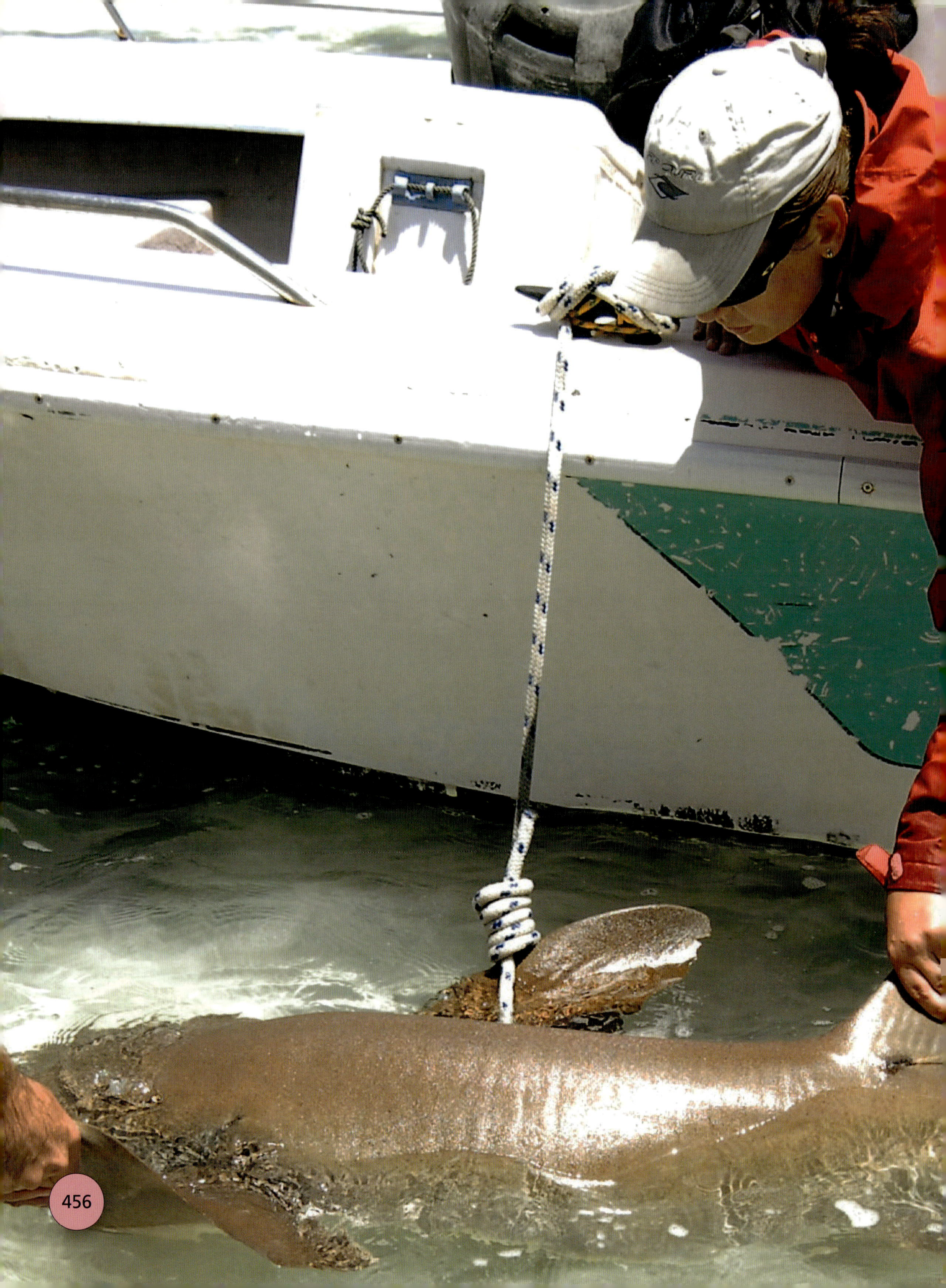

Shark science

Studying sharks

- **We know relatively** little about sharks. Scientists are trying to find out more about them.

- **The study of sharks** is sometimes called elasmobranchology.

- **Knowing more about sharks** – such as how they breed and what they need to survive – will help us to conserve them and stop shark species from dying out.

- **To find out how sharks live**, scientists have to study them in the wild. This is called 'fieldwork'.

- **Scientists also catch sharks** so they can study them in captivity. This lets them look closely at how sharks swim, eat and behave.

- **In laboratories**, scientists study shark blood, skin and cartilage to find out how their bodies work.

- **Some scientists study shark cells** to try to find out why they get so few diseases. This information could help to make new medicines.

- **In aquariums**, scientists test shark reactions to see how their brains and senses work.

- **Genetic analysis of shark DNA** helps scientists to identify closely related shark species, which look very similar and are difficult to distinguish from their appearance alone.

- **Dried shark tissue** from ancient sharks in museums can even be examined genetically to confirm the species and find out more about sharks that lived hundreds of years ago.

▶ *Some sharks, such as great whites, take an interest in diving cages, and seem to become more familiar with humans after coming into contact with them.*

Shark science

DID YOU KNOW?
After scientists found out how shark denticles reduced drag, a swimming costume company designed a swimsuit that worked in the same way.

Shark scientists

- **Biologists are scientists** who study living things. Many shark scientists are marine biologists, which means they study sea life.

- **Zoologists are scientists** who study animals, and ichthyologists are scientists who study fish. These scientists also work with sharks.

Shark science

- **Other scientists called geneticists** study shark genes and DNA – the instructions inside cells.

- **Palaeontologists study fossils** of animals and plants. Shark fossils are very important in revealing how sharks evolved over time. Some scientists specialize in studying just shark fossils.

- **Oceanographers study** the sea. They know about habitats and how sharks live with other animals.

- **Most shark scientists** work for universities or research centres such as the Woods Hole Oceanographic Institute in Massachusetts, United States.

- **One of today's most famous** shark scientists is American zoologist Dr Eugenie Clark. She has studied shark behaviour and deep-sea sharks.

- **The famous French** undersea expert Jacques Cousteau was one of the first people to study sharks underwater. He invented scuba diving equipment, which scientists still use today.

- **The American Elasmobranch Society (AES)** is the world's largest association of shark and ray scientists.

- **If you'd like to be a shark scientist**, choose subjects such as biology and chemistry at school, and study biology or zoology at university.

◀ A marine biologist attaches a transmitter to the dorsal fin of a tiger shark before releasing it into the sea. The shark's movements can then be tracked to learn more about its biology.

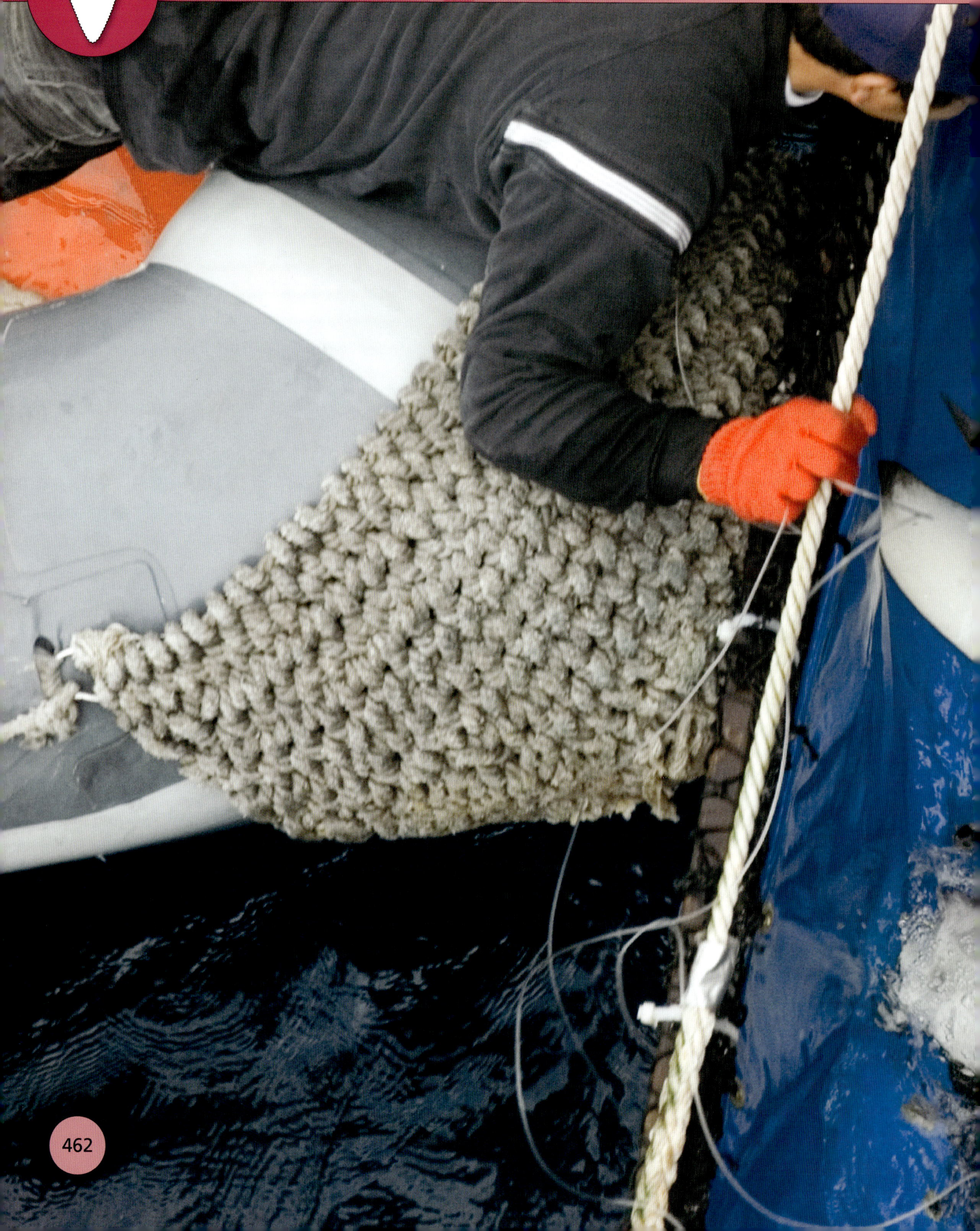

Shark science

◀ A scientist preparing to tag a scalloped hammerhead. The information gathered from tagging sharks is very important, helping scientists to learn about shark movements in their natural environment and plan protected areas to aid their survival.

463

Observation

- **To learn more about sharks**, scientists need ways of finding, following and catching them.

- **Most shark scientists** have to be strong and good at diving to get up close.

- **Scientists often use diving cages** or protective chainmail suits to study sharks underwater.

- **They can also study sharks** such as great whites without going in the water, using cameras on the ends of long poles.

- **Some shark scientists** dissect dead sharks to find out about their bodies or what they have eaten recently.

- **To follow sharks**, scientists use radio-tracking devices. They catch a shark and attach a transmitter that gives out radio signals. Wherever the shark goes, scientists can pick up the signals and work out the shark's location.

- **Scientists sometimes attach tags** to sharks they catch. The tag states where and when the shark was last caught. The same shark may then be found again somewhere else, giving scientists information about the shark's range.

- **A camera can be attached** to a shark to record its travels. The strap holding the camera gradually dissolves, and the camera floats to the surface to be collected.

Shark science

DID YOU KNOW?
In 2014, a great white tried to take a bite out of an underwater shark camera set up by the Woods Hole Oceanographic Institute.

▲ *A diver swims alongside a shark and records its movements and activities.*

- **Satellite tags help scientists** to track shark migration journeys by reporting the position of the shark to the satellite whenever the shark comes to the ocean's surface.

- **Acoustic tags** give off coded signals that identify individual sharks. These signals are picked up by a network of receivers on the sea bed.

▶ Scientists sometimes coax sharks into a temporary relaxed state by turning them over and rubbing their belly or massaging their nose. This stops the shark struggling and reduces the risk of injury to shark or scientist.

Shark science

Discoveries and mysteries

- **Shark scientists** are still finding out new information about sharks, and puzzling over unanswered questions.

- **Experts may disagree** about shark facts. For example, some think that the prehistoric shark *Megalodon* was closely related to the great white, while others disagree.

- **Scientists did not used to know** where basking sharks disappeared to at certain times of the year – but in 2008 tagged basking sharks revealed that they go on long migrations deep underwater.

- **The dwarf lanternshark** was discovered in 1985. New species of shark are still being found.

▲ *Nicolas Steno (1638–1686) believed that objects known as tongue stones were in fact the teeth of ancient sharks.*

Shark science

- **Scientists don't always** find new shark species in the sea. Instead, they are often seen in fish markets or reported by local people.

- **In 2004, scientists learned** that Greenland sharks eat giant squid. Before this, only sperm whales were thought to eat these creatures.

- **In 2002, scientists worked out** how to test the DNA in shark fin soup to see which species it contains. This helps to stop people hunting protected sharks.

- **Scientists studying** whale sharks found that they don't just eat plankton – they also feed on fish eggs.

- **In 2001 scientists studying** shark fins discovered they sometimes contain very high levels of mercury (a type of metal), which comes from pollution in seawater.

DID YOU KNOW?
In 2011, scientists discovered a new species of dogfish shark – not in the sea, but in a fish market in Taiwan.

▼ The ornate wobbegong was found to be a separate wobbegong species in 2006.

Evolution of sharks

- **The oldest fish** with a shark-like body shape lived in the ancient oceans about 450 million years ago. These 'spiny sharks' were not true sharks, but had jaws and a lateral line system similar to that of modern sharks.

- **One of the first true sharks** was *Doliodus*, which was about 50–75 cm long and probably looked like a modern angelshark.

- **By about 360 million years ago**, sharks of many shapes and sizes had developed. This was called the 'golden age of sharks'.

- **About 150 million years ago**, the sharks of the golden age began to die out. The ancestors of modern sharks began to take over.

- **These sharks were active**, fast-swimming hunters, with more flexible jaws that could be moved forwards, making it easier for them to catch food.

- **Fossil teeth from relatives** of today's mackerel sharks, such as ancient porbeagle sharks, have been found in rocks dating back about 100 million years.

- **Some sharks today**, such as goblin sharks and frilled sharks, look very similar to their prehistoric cousins, and have hardly changed over millions of years.

- **About 65 million years ago**, about 70 percent of all living things were wiped out, but some of the new sharks, such as basking sharks and requiem sharks, survived.

- **The most recent shark family** to evolve is the hammerhead shark family.

Shark science

Evolutionary tree of vertebrates

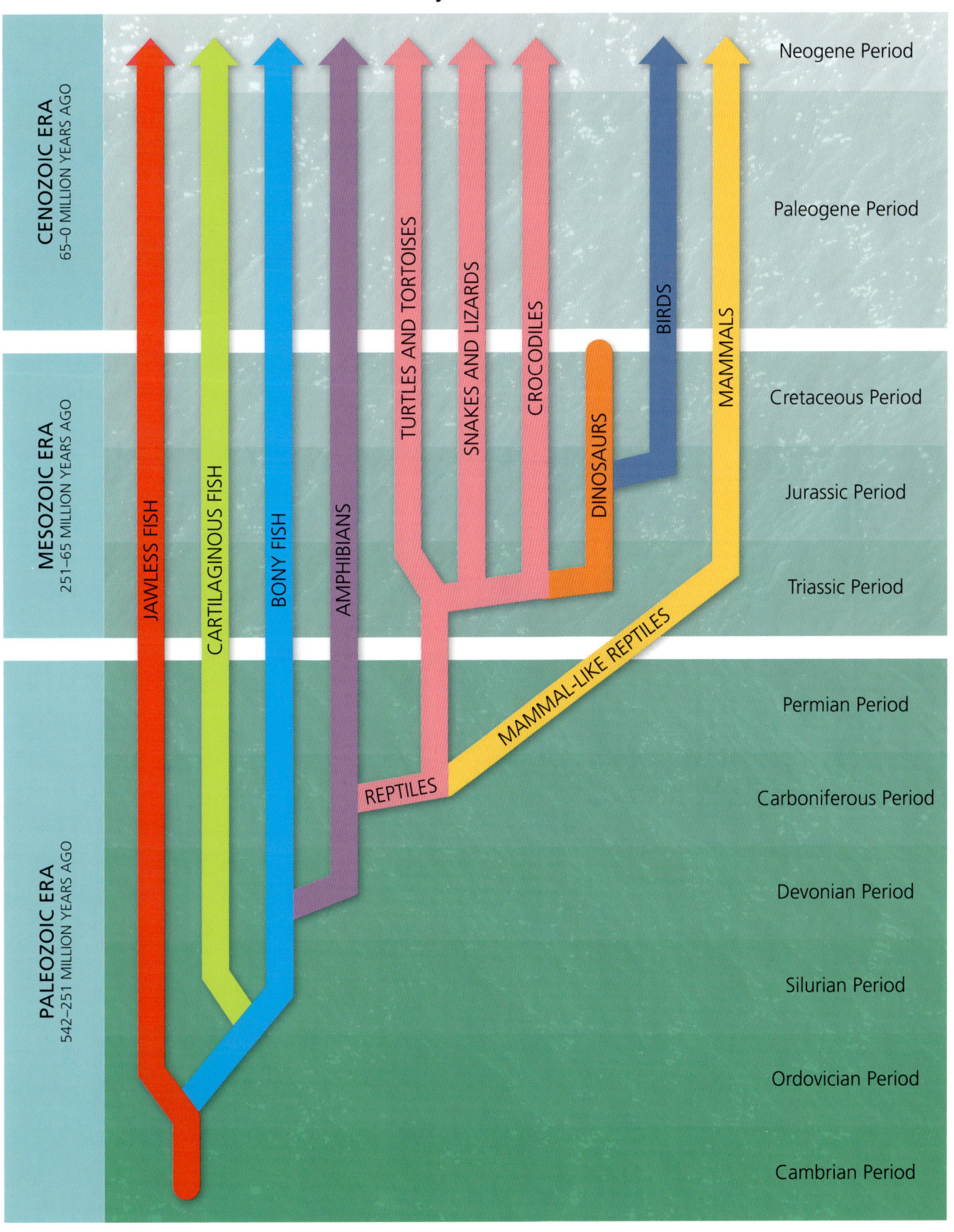

▲ The first true sharks were cartilaginous fish that appeared over 400 million years ago, about 200 million years before dinosaurs walked the Earth.

Early sharks

- **One of the earliest sharks** of all was *Cladoselache*, which lived about 370 million years ago. It was around 1.5 m in length and had a powerful tail, like a modern mako shark.

- *Cladoselache* **had large eyes**, a short snout and many three-pointed teeth, just as frilled sharks have today.

- *Stethacanthus*, **which lived** about 350 million years ago, had a helmet of small teeth on its head and a spiny brush sticking out of its back. This may have been used during courtship or for defence.

- **Like many modern sharks**, *Hybodus* had both sharp cutting teeth and flat, blunt, chewing teeth.

- **The biggest shark** ever was probably *Megalodon*. It first appeared about 20 million years ago. Some scientists think it looked like a great white shark, only bigger – maybe 20 m in length (as long as two buses).

- *Tristychius* **was similar** to a modern dogfish, but lived about 350 million years ago. It had a strong spine on each dorsal fin.

- **The unicorn shark**, *Falcatus*, had a strange, L-shaped spine on the top of its head. Only males had this spine, which may have been used to fight rival males or to attract females.

- **The whorl-tooth shark**, *Helicoprion*, did not lose its teeth. They moved along in a spiral and then were stored in a special chamber under its bottom jaw.

- **The giant scissor-toothed shark**, *Edestus giganteus*, had a mouth one metre wide. Its teeth were replaced in rows, but the old teeth stuck out in front of the shark's head and did not fall out.

Shark science

DID YOU KNOW?

In 2003 scientists found the world's oldest complete shark fossil, which was of Doliodius problematicus. This shark was the size of a large trout and lived about 409 million years ago.

▲ Hybodus *lived about 160 million years ago in the Jurassic Period, during the age of the dinosaurs.*

Shark fossils

- **Fossils are** the remains of, or the shape of, an animal preserved in rock. Often only the hardest parts of an animal, such as its skeleton, become fossilized.

- **When an animal dies**, its flesh and other soft parts start to rot. The harder parts, such as bone, rot more slowly and last longer. Over time, sediment layers settle on the remains. Minerals and salts replace the once-living parts and turn them and the sediments into solid rock.

- **As sharks have** soft skeletons made from cartilage, there are few whole shark fossils.

- **Scientists use** shark fossils to find out what sharks looked like long ago and how they lived. They often use tooth fossils to guess how big an entire shark was.

- **Shark fossils are** often found on land in places that used to be seas millions of years ago.

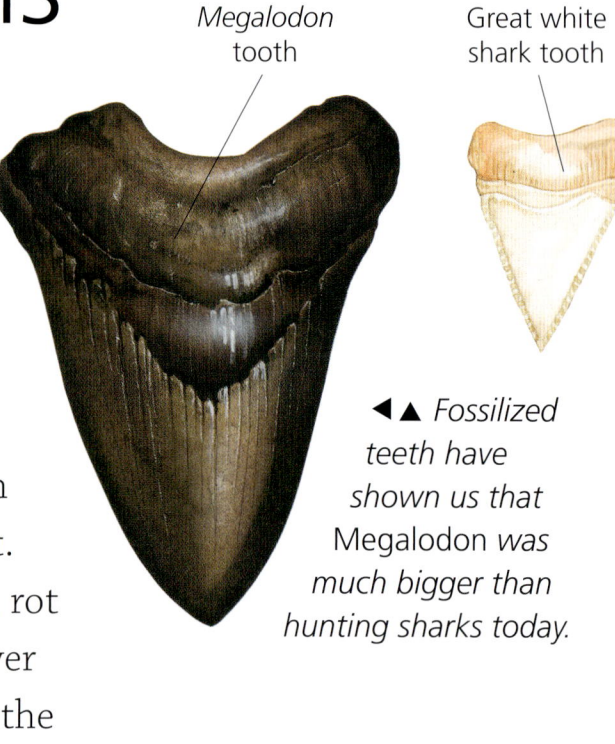

Megalodon tooth

Great white shark tooth

◀▲ *Fossilized teeth have shown us that* Megalodon *was much bigger than hunting sharks today.*

▲ Megalodon *shown to scale alongside a great white shark.*

Shark science

- **Some of the best** shark fossil areas are in parts of the United States, such as California, Maryland and Oklahoma.

- **Fossils of *Cladoselache***, one of the earliest known sharks, have been found with fish preserved in their stomachs.

- **Fossil shark teeth** are common because ancient sharks shed many teeth in a lifetime, like living sharks. Shark teeth are as hard as human teeth and do not rot away.

- **The earliest fossil teeth**, resembling those of great white sharks, have been found in rocks about 65 million years old.

- **Fossil *Megalodon* teeth** date from over 15 million years ago to less than 2 million years ago.

▶ *Fossil shark teeth preserved in a rock from the Sahara desert, in Africa.*

Sharks in trouble

- **Shark populations** are falling mainly because of human activities, such as hunting and overfishing.

- **Overfishing may mean** that many shark populations can't recover.

- **Sharks are also** in demand because other fish caught for food, such as cod, have become scarce. They have also been overfished.

- **Many sharks are killed** when they get caught in nets put up to protect swimmers from shark attacks, or nets meant to catch other fish.

- **Sharks caught for sport** are usually released, but often die from exhaustion soon afterwards.

- **Sharks mature slowly** and don't always bear many young, so it can be hard for a species to build up their numbers again after being overfished.

- **Sharks are** at the top of the food chain. Poisonous chemicals from pollution collect in sea creatures, which the sharks eat. The poison then builds up in the sharks' bodies. Scientists think this may make sharks ill and make it harder for them to reproduce.

- **Some sharks live** near the coast and young sharks often use shallow coastal waters as nursery areas. These areas are regularly polluted by human sewage and other waste, as well as by agricultural and industrial chemicals washed into the sea from rivers.

DID YOU KNOW?
Many shark species are so hard to study that scientists have no idea how many of them are left in the wild.

Shark science

- **The demand for shark fin soup** in parts of Asia is responsible for the deaths of millions of sharks every year, including hammerheads, which have large fins.

- **The fins may be removed from the shark**, which is then thrown back into the sea while still alive. The shark dies soon afterwards because it can't get enough oxygen to breathe or hunt for food. This cruel practice is banned in about one third of shark-fishing countries.

▼ *Many sharks die when they become tangled up in fishing or safety nets.*

Endangered species

- **An endangered species** is in danger of dying out completely and becoming extinct.

- **When a species becomes extinct**, all the members of that species die and the species can never exist again.

- **Scientists try to find out** if a shark species is at risk by counting the number of sharks seen in a particular area and measuring how much this changes over time.

Shark science

- **Experts found** that sandbar shark sightings on America's east coast fell by 20 percent over 20 years. This shark is now classed as vulnerable.

- **Overfishing is the main reason** that sharks become endangered.

- **International organizations** such as the IUCN (International Union for the Conservation of Nature and Natural Resources) compile lists of endangered species to raise awareness.

- **According to the IUCN** over 50 shark species are now endangered, and 30 percent of sharks and rays are threatened with extinction in the wild. Several species of sawfish are critically endangered and may die out very soon.

- **Well-known sharks** that are at risk include great whites, whale sharks, basking sharks, makos, porbeagles, sand tigers, dusky sharks, oceanic whitetips and thresher sharks.

- **Some sharks are threatened** when natural coastlines and estuaries are developed and built on. This destroys nursery areas where sharks lay eggs or bear their young.

- **Some of the rarest sharks** are the river sharks, the daggernose shark and several species of angelsharks. Several deep-water sharks, including the gulper shark and Harrisson's dogfish, are also vulnerable to extinction.

◀ Even though basking sharks are protected in some parts of the world, these large sharks are still at risk because they grow and mature slowly, and take a long time to reproduce.

▶ The whale shark is listed as 'vulnerable' on the IUCN's Red List, meaning it faces a high risk of extinction in the wild in the future. The large size, slow growth and long lifespan of this shark mean that it is slow to recover from problems caused by fishing and pollution.

Shark science

Saving sharks

- **Ecotourism helps** to save sharks by encouraging local people not to kill them, as they can make money from sharks as tourist attractions.

- **Some shark-fishing** countries have imposed quotas to limit how many sharks fishermen can catch.

- **Governments can ban** the killing of some sharks altogether. The UK has passed a law making it illegal to catch or disturb a basking shark.

- **Some countries** have set up marine wildlife reserves where hunting wildlife is banned.

- **Conservation charities** such as the WWF (World Wildlife Fund) and the Shark Trust work to educate people to help them avoid killing sharks unnecessarily.

- **By banning trade** in shark products, governments can help to stop unnecessary killing of sharks.

- **To help protect sharks**, people should avoid buying products such as shark fin soup.

- **Modern aquariums and sea life centres** help to explain the importance of shark conservation to their visitors. They also look after injured sharks, which can be returned to the wild when they recover.

▲ *The Shark Trust is a respected advocate for shark management and is part of a global collaborative movement in shark conservation. It works to safeguard shark, skate and ray populations through science, education, influence and action.*

Shark science

- **Many sharks could be saved** from extinction if we work towards keeping the oceans clean and free of pollution, and try to preserve important shark habitats, such as coral reefs, near the shore.

- **More scientific research** into sharks would help us to understand more about their biology and behaviour, and work out the best ways of helping sharks to survive in the future.

▼ *Steve Backshall swims with the sharks at the London Aquarium, demonstrating that many sharks are not as dangerous as people imagine. People are in fact more dangerous to shark survival than the other way around!*

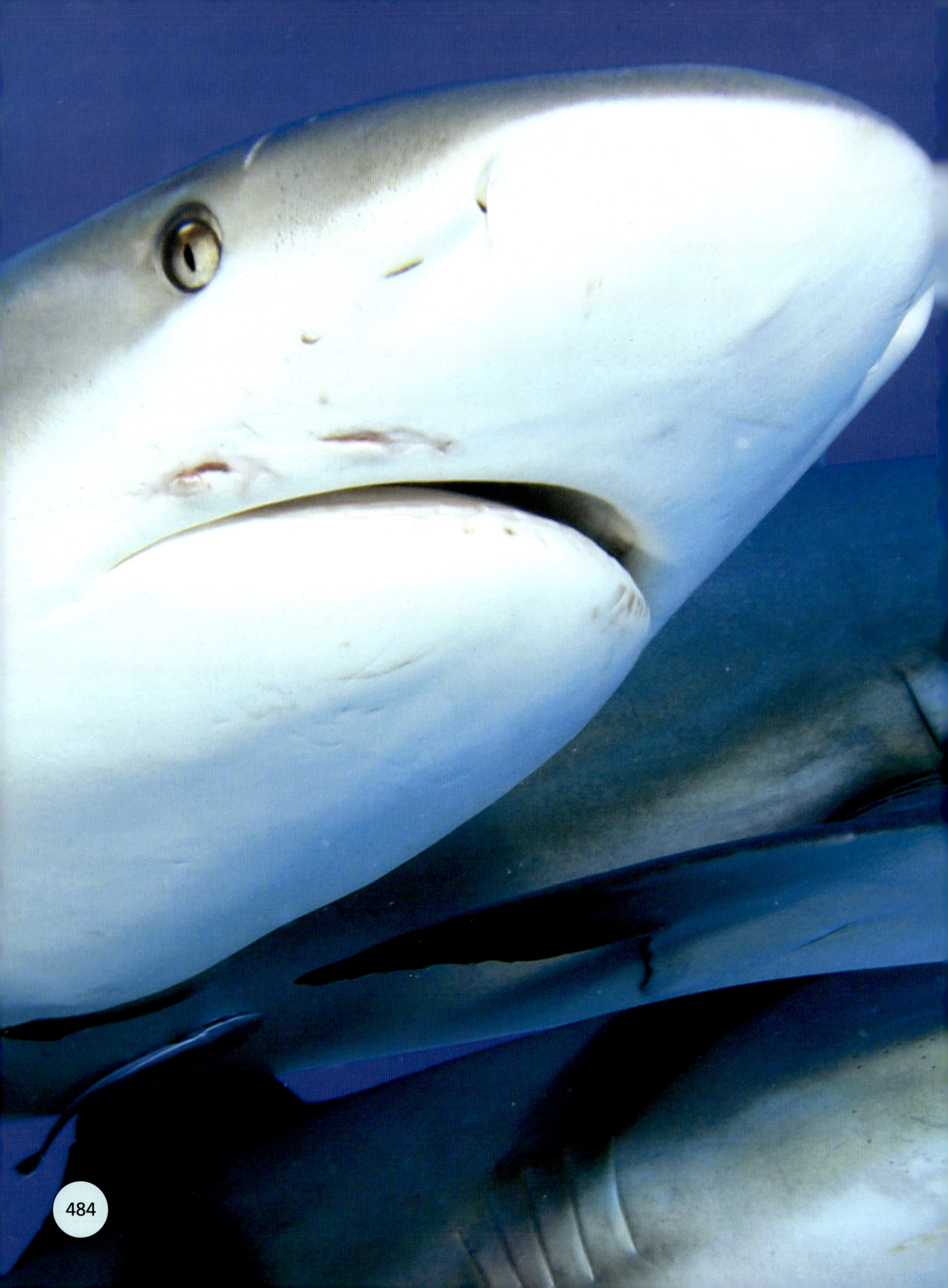

Glossary and Index

Glossary

acoustic tags Scientific transmitters fitted to sharks, which give off sound signals to help scientists identify individual sharks, and track their movements and behaviour.

aggression An act or threat of action by one individual against another. Sharks such as the dusky shark, silky shark, silvertip shark and grey reef shark often behave aggressively.

ampullae of Lorenzini Tiny, jelly-filled pits in the head of sharks and rays that detect electrical signals sent out by other animals or objects in the water. The ampullae of Lorenzini can also pick up changes in the temperature or salinity of the water.

anal fin A single fin underneath the body between the pelvic fins and caudal fin of some sharks. Dogfish, sawsharks, angelsharks, batoids and some chimaeras do not have an anal fin.

anatomy The structure of a living thing, including the size and shape of its internal parts, or organs.

angelsharks Sharks with a flat body, a short snout and wide, wing-like fins. Angelsharks live on the sea bed and often have camouflaged patterns on the top of their bodies.

angler A person who catches fish with a hook on the end of a long line attached to a fishing rod.

Antarctica The frozen continent surrounding the South Pole. Antarctica is the fifth largest continent and has very little ice-free land, even in summer.

aquarium An artificial tank or pond, usually with transparent sides, for keeping live plants and animals that inhabit water. Many sharks do not survive well in aquariums, but some that do include catsharks, the blacknose shark, the dusky shark, lemon sharks, sand tiger sharks and sandbar sharks.

Arctic The area around the North Pole, which includes the Arctic Ocean and the northern edges of Europe, Asia and North America.

artery A blood vessel (tube) that carries blood away from the heart to the rest of the body.

backbone A common name for the spine in vertebrates.

barbel A long, thin strip of fleshy skin near the mouth of some fish (including some sharks and catfish), which they use to feel for food or find their way around.

batoid A cartilaginous fish related to sharks, which usually has a flat body, wide fins and gill openings underneath the body. Batoids include rays, skates, sawfish and guitarfish.

benthic The base of a watery habitat, such as the sea floor.

Glossary

biologist A scientist who studies living things.

bioluminescence The production of light by living things without heat. The word means 'living light'. Some sharks can make light like this, including lanternsharks and the cookie-cutter shark.

blood vessels Tubes, such as arteries, veins and capillaries, which carry blood around an animal's body.

blubber Thick layer of fat under the skin of marine mammals (such as seals), which helps to stop them losing body heat to their surroundings. This keeps them warm when they swim in cold oceans.

body language The way in which an animal positions its body or body parts in order to communicate information. It's rather like speaking without words.

bony fish Fish with skeletons made of bone. Most of the fish alive today are bony fish, apart from sharks, batoids and chimaeras.

bullhead sharks Small sharks, named after their chunky bodies and pig-like snouts. They live on the sea bed and have sharp spines to protect them from predators. Females lay eggs in screw-shaped egg cases.

camouflage Colours or patterns that help an animal to blend in with its surroundings. This helps an animal to avoid predators or move close to its prey without being seen.

cannibal An animal that eats others of its own kind. Some sharks, such as great hammerheads and tiger sharks, are cannibals.

cardiac muscle Muscle forming the walls of the heart, which keeps the heart beating.

carnivore An animal that feeds on other animals, usually their flesh or meat.

carpet sharks A varied group of sharks, many with a flat, well-camouflaged body, such as wobbegongs. The whale shark is included in this group, as are nurse sharks and the zebra shark.

cartilage A lightweight, bendy, but very strong, material, sometimes called gristle. Shark and ray skeletons are made of cartilage, rather than bone like most other animals with backbones. In humans, cartilage forms the end of the nose and outer ears.

cartilaginous fish Fish, such as sharks, which have a skeleton made of cartilage.

catsharks The largest shark family. These sharks are named after their cat-like eyes and many of them have striking markings on their skin.

caudal fin The fin on the end of the tail in fish. In sharks, the caudal fin has two lobes, one of which may be larger than the other.

chimaera A fish with a cartilaginous skeleton that looks like a cross between a shark and a bony fish. The name means 'a mixture'. The elephant fish is a chimaera.

claspers A pair of extensions to a male shark's pelvic fins, which are used to transfer sperm to a female shark. The elephant fish has claspers on his head to help him hang on to a female while mating.

classification The system scientists use to put living things into groups according to features that they have in common. From biggest to smallest, the groups are called: kingdom, phylum, class, order, family, genus and species.

cloaca A single opening on the underside of a shark, near the tail, where waste materials, eggs, sperm and young pass out of a shark's body.

cold-blooded An animal whose body temperature changes with its surroundings. Most sharks are cold-blooded, but a few, such as the great white shark, are warm-blooded.

computer animation Using computer programmes to make still images appear to move on the screen and images of animals, such as sharks, look as if they are alive.

conservation Protecting and preserving our natural surroundings, and the plants and animals living in them, from threats caused by humans.

continent One of the seven large areas of land on Earth. The world's continents are: Europe, Asia, Africa, North America, South America, Australia and Antarctica.

copepods A large group of crustaceans, mostly living in the oceans. It includes many external parasites that live on sharks and other fish.

coral reef A structure built up from the skeletons of tiny animals called corals. Coral reefs are rich in a variety of animal life and are sometimes called the 'rainforests of the sea'.

cornea The transparent covering at the front of the eye.

countershading In animals, having a lighter colour underneath and a darker colour on top. This helps with camouflage because it hides the shark against the light sky (when seen from below) and the dark ocean (when seen from above).

courtship Behaviour that helps to form a bond between a male and a female before mating. Female blue sharks have skin twice as thick as

Glossary

males to protect them from a male's courtship bites.

cow sharks A small family of sharks with six or seven pairs of gill slits – most sharks have five pairs.

crepuscular Animals that are active at dusk, during twilight hours, or before sunrise.

crustaceans Hard-bodied animals without backbones, such as crabs, lobsters, shrimps, copepods and barnacles. Crustaceans have jointed legs and two pairs of antennae (feelers).

denticles Tiny, tooth-shaped scales. Dermal denticles are the thorn-like hooks on a shark's skin, making it feel like sandpaper to touch. Much larger, stronger denticles form a shark's teeth.

digestion The process of breaking down food into chemicals that can be absorbed into an animal's body. In sharks, digestion takes place inside a long tube that stretches from the mouth to the cloaca.

dissect To cut up an animal in order to examine its body parts.

DNA (deoxyribonucleic acid) The chemical code that carries all the information needed to build an individual and keep it alive. DNA is inside every cell of an animal's body and is passed from one generation to the next when living things reproduce.

docile Submissive and easy to manage. Whitetip reef sharks, manta rays and tawny nurse sharks all have a docile nature.

dogfish sharks Small, relatively common sharks with a spine in front of their dorsal fin. Some dogfish sharks hunt in packs, like dogs, hence the name of the group. Sharks in this group include: gulper sharks, lanternsharks, roughsharks and kitefin sharks.

dominance A type of behaviour in which certain individuals behave aggressively towards others and become more important than others, or perhaps the leader of a group.

dorsal fin A large, triangular fin on a shark's back, which helps it to stay balanced while swimming. Most sharks have two dorsal fins; some batoids have only one dorsal fin, or no dorsal fins at all.

drag The resistance to movement in water or air.

ecotourism Tourism that conserves the environment, helps to preserve wildlife and improves the well-being of local people.

elasmobranchology The study of sharks, skates and rays.

endangered species Species that are in danger of dying out in the wild very soon. Many sharks are endangered, including the scalloped hammerhead, sawfish (types of rays), river sharks, the daggernose shark and several species of angelsharks.

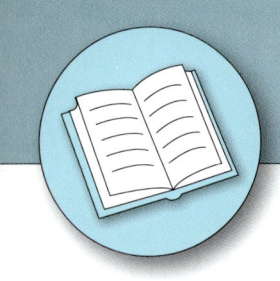

epaulette An ornamental shoulder piece on a uniform. Epaulette sharks are named after the distinctive spot-like markings on their 'shoulders'.

Equator An imaginary line running east-west around the middle of the Earth at 0° latitude.

evolution The gradual process by which plants and animals adapt to changing environmental conditions through natural selection.

extinction The process whereby a species of living thing completely dies out and disappears forever.

feeding frenzy The way a group of sharks can become over-excited while feeding, slashing or biting anything that moves, including each other.

fertilization The process by which a male sex cell (e.g. sperm) and a female sex cell (e.g. egg) join together to form a new living thing. Fertilization in sharks happens inside the female's body.

fieldwork The way scientists study animals, including sharks, in their natural habitat.

filament A slender, thread-like structure, such as the hair-like structures in a shark's gills, which help to absorb oxygen from the water.

filter-feeding Eating by filtering tiny particles of food (such as plankton) from the water, often using gill rakers. The biggest sharks, such as the basking shark and the whale shark, are all filter-feeders.

fluoride The active ingredient in most toothpastes and dental care mouthwashes, which helps to stop tooth decay. The outside of a shark's teeth is made up of fluoride, so sharks don't get holes in their teeth.

food chain A sequence of feeding actions, when an animal eats a plant and is then eaten by another animal, and so on. Food chains can be linked together to make food webs, which show how the living things in a habitat are connected through what they eat.

fossil The remains of a living thing preserved in rock. The cartilage of a shark's skeleton is not often preserved in rock because it is not as hard and solid as bone. However, shark teeth are common fossils because they are hard and do not decay easily.

freshwater Water that is not salty, like the water in seas and oceans. Very few sharks can survive in freshwater, but river sharks and the bull shark are exceptions.

Glossary

gene The basic unit of biological inheritance, consisting of a sequence of chemical code in the DNA molecule.

genetic engineering Any change in the genetic make-up of a living thing that has been brought about artificially and which would not usually occur in nature.

geneticists Scientists who study the genetics of living things.

gestation period The period of time between conception and the birth of an animal, while it is developing inside its mother.

gill arch A bony or cartilaginous arch, which supports an individual gill in fish, including sharks.

gill rakers Comb-like bristles on the gills of filter-feeding sharks, which are used to trap food as water flows over the gills.

gills Breathing organs used by fish and some other water-dwelling animals to extract oxygen from the water.

gill slit Long, narrow opening in the side of a shark's head (or under the body in batoids), where water exits the body after flowing into the mouth and over the gills. Most sharks have five gill slits on each side.

global warming Gradual increase in temperatures all over the world (the globe), which has been speeded up by human pollution.

ground sharks The largest, most varied and most widespread order of sharks. It includes nearly 300 species, from catsharks, houndsharks and weasel sharks to requiem sharks and hammerhead sharks. Most ground sharks are small and harmless, but this order also contains the largest and most dangerous sharks, such as the bull shark.

habitat The natural home where a group of animals or plants lives.

hammerhead sharks Nine species of shark with very wide heads, which are shaped like a hammer.

hemisphere Half of the Earth, which is divided into the northern hemisphere and the southern hemisphere by the Equator.

hormones Chemicals produced by animals, which circulate around the body in the bloodstream and help to control their life processes. Lanternsharks use hormones to switch their photophores (light spots) on and off.

houndsharks Small sharks, such as the leopard shark, which usually live on shallow sea beds and have flat teeth for crushing prey.

intestines Part of an animal's digestive system, or gut, where food is broken down and absorbed into the body.

Inuit The native peoples living in Arctic regions of northern Canada, parts of Greenland and Alaska.

keel A narrow ridge (like the keel on a boat) near the tail of some sharks, such as the salmon shark, mako shark and great white shark. It probably helps them to twist and turn easily in the water.

lamellae Thin, plate-like structures in the gills of fish, which provide a large surface area for absorbing oxygen from the water.

lanternsharks The largest family of dogfish sharks, which are named after their ability to glow in the dark. The smallest sharks (the dwarf lanternshark and the pygmy lanternshark) are in this family.

lateral line A pair of sensory tubes along each side of a fish's body, just under the skin. The lateral line detects ripples, currents and other water movements, including those made by prey.

lifespan The length of time that a living thing remains alive.

liver A very large organ in the abdomen with many important jobs, including making proteins, storing and processing fats and carbohydrates, and removing harmful chemicals from the blood. It also produces bile, which helps with the digestion of fats. A large, oily liver helps sharks to float, but also threatens their survival as people catch many different sharks (such as the kitefin shark, the gulper shark and the blacktip shark) for their liver oil.

lobe Rounded and flattened part of the body. In sharks, this refers to part of the tail, which is often divided into two lobes.

luminescent Giving off a cold form of light.

luminous Giving off light, shining or glowing. Many sharks, such as lanternsharks, are able to glow in the dark.

mackerel sharks A small family of sharks, which are mainly fast, open-ocean sharks, such as the mako and the great white shark. The mackerel shark family also includes the filter-feeding megamouth and basking sharks, and the strange, deep-water goblin shark.

magnetism An invisible natural force given off by some pieces of metal, rock or stone, which have the power to attract or repel certain materials. Scalloped hammerhead sharks use the magnetic force given off by lava (very hot rock) pushing through the sea bed as a magnetic highway.

mammal An animal with fur or hair that can control its own body temperature. Female mammals feed their young on milk. A few mammals,

Glossary

such as seals, dolphins and whales, live in the oceans.

mangrove A tree or shrub that grows in dense swamps on tropical coasts. It has thick, tangled, arching roots, which grow above warm, shallow water, forming safe hiding places for young fish, such as lemon sharks, nurse sharks, sawfish and the mangrove stingray.

marine Something found in the seas or oceans, or having something to do with saltwater habitats.

migration A regular movement from one place to another, usually to find food, mates or better living conditions. Some migrations are linked with the seasons; others are daily migrations, such as sharks moving from deep water to the surface to feed at night.

mineral A natural crystalline solid with a constant chemical composition and regular internal structure. A mineral is not alive and does not come from animals or plants.

navigate Finding the way along a particular route.

nictitating membrane Thin, lid-like layers of skin that can be drawn across the eyes for protection in some sharks, such as houndsharks, weasel sharks and requiem sharks.

nocturnal Animals that come out at night.

nursery areas Safe, warm, shallow water areas near the coast where sharks lay eggs or give birth to their pups. Young sharks may grow up in these nursery areas before moving out to the open ocean.

nutritious Nourishing food that is full of goodness.

oceanographers Scientists who study the oceans and the plants and animals that live there.

ocellated Having eye-like spots or markings, such as those of the ocellated angelshark, and some rays and bamboo sharks. These large pigment spots may help to frighten predators away because they look like the huge eyes of a big animal.

offspring An animal's young or descendants.

olfactory lobes Parts of the brain that process the sense of smell.

organ A structure within an animal's body, such as the heart or stomach, which performs a particular function.

ovaries A female's reproductive organs, which produce eggs.

over-fishing Catching too many fish so that the species cannot replace its numbers and is in danger of dying out. Many sharks are endangered because of over-fishing.

oviducts Tubes that carry eggs from a shark's ovaries into two enlarged parts of the oviducts, each called a uterus (womb).

oviparous An animal that lays eggs. Some female sharks, such as bullhead sharks, lay eggs inside leathery egg cases.

ovoviviparous An animal in which the young develop inside eggs in the mother's body, feeding off the egg yolk until they are ready to be born. The young are not nourished by the mother's body.

oxygen A highly reactive element that is extremely abundant on Earth where it occurs naturally as a gas in the atmosphere, as well as forming many chemical compounds with other elements. Oxygen gas is essential to almost all living things. Sharks need to take in oxygen from the water to stay alive.

palaeontologists Scientists who study living things that were alive long ago, in prehistoric times.

parasite A living thing that lives in, or on, another living thing, which is called its host. A parasite obtains food from its host, causing harm to the host in the process.

pectoral fins The pair of fins at the front of a shark's body, one on either side, just behind the gill slits.

pelagic Open water in a watery habitat, such as the open ocean, rather than the sea floor.

pelvic fins The pair of small fins on the underside of a shark's body, behind the pectoral fins and just in front of the anal fin.

pheromones A chemical substance produced by one animal, which affects the behaviour or body of another animal. Sharks produce pheromones to attract mates during courtship.

photophores Tiny round organs that produce light by a low temperature chemical reaction. These glowing spots appear on the bodies of most lanternsharks and some kitefin sharks.

pigment Colouring matter.

placenta See yolk sac placenta.

plankton Tiny plants and animals (less than one centimetre in length) that float on the surface of the water and are eaten by many larger animals, such as basking sharks and whale sharks.

Polar Something relating to the cold regions around the North Pole and the South Pole.

pollution Wastes produced by people, which builds up and harms plants and animals, as well as the environment they live in.

Glossary

population A group of individuals of a species living in a particular area.

predator An animal that catches and eats other animals.

pregnant A female animal with one or more developing young in the uterus (womb).

prehistoric The time before written history.

prey An animal that is caught and eaten by other animals.

pup A young shark, particularly when it has just hatched out of its egg or been born.

rays Close relatives of sharks with a cartilaginous skeleton and large, wing-like fins. Most female rays give birth to live young.

red blood cells Cells which transport oxygen in the blood. Leopard sharks have extra red blood cells to help them absorb enough oxygen because they live in water that contains small amounts of this vital gas.

reproduction The process by which living things create offspring.

requiem sharks An important family of large, active sharks, including tiger sharks, bull sharks and reef sharks. Female requiem sharks usually give birth to live young.

rostral teeth The teeth on the long 'saw' at the front of a sawshark's body.

rostrum The long beak-like snout of a sawshark.

roughsharks Small sharks with a tough, prickly skin and two sail-like fins on their back.

salamander Small amphibians with long tails and four legs that stick out at the sides of the body. The epaulette shark crawls around on the sea bed rather like a salamander crawls around awkwardly on land.

satellite tags Scientists fix these tags to a shark in order to pinpoint its position via a satellite whenever the shark comes to the surface of the sea.

sawfish A family of rays with a long, saw-like snout.

sawsharks A family of small, slender sharks with a saw-like snout and a pair of long, sensory barbels in front of the nostrils.

scavenger An animal that feeds on the remains of dead plants or animals, or food thrown away by people. The tiger shark is a scavenger.

schools A group of sharks, or other fish or water creatures, travelling together in an organized fashion. The tope shark is also called the school shark as it usually swims in schools.

scuba divers Divers that carry air tanks on their backs so that they can breathe underwater. The name 'scuba' stands for 'self-contained underwater breathing apparatus'.

season A change in the weather that occurs at the same time each year. Some parts of the world have two seasons, summer and winter, while others have four seasons, spring, summer, autumn and winter.

sediment Small particles of rocks, soil or living things that are carried along for a while and then dropped by rivers or ocean currents in a different place.

shark fin soup An expensive soup that uses shark fins to add texture, rather than flavour. About 73 million sharks are killed each year just for their fins, but sales of this soup have dropped by up to 70 percent in recent years.

sharpnose sharks Small, shy sharks with a long snout that usually live in shallow water.

shoal Group of fish swimming together.

siphon Funnel-shaped structure in shellfish, such as clams, which is used to draw water in and out of the body. Leopard sharks sometimes feed on the siphons from clams.

skate A close relative of sharks and rays, which is usually smaller than a ray, with a large dorsal fin, small teeth and a shorter, fleshier tail. Skates lay eggs, while rays give birth to live young.

skeletal muscle A type of muscle attached to the skeleton, which makes an animal move.

skeleton A strong framework providing support and protection for an animal's body. In sharks, the skeleton is made of cartilage and is inside the shark's body.

skull A bony framework inside an animal's head which protects the brain.

snorkel A special tube fixed to a diving mask, which sticks out of the water and allows a swimmer to breathe with their head underwater.

snout The pointed nose of an animal, in front of its eyes and mouth.

species The basic unit for the classification of living things. A species consists of all the individuals who share the same characteristics and can interbreed. Each species has its own scientific name, which is made up of two Latin words, such as *Megachasma pelagios*. This is the name for the megamouth shark and it means 'huge yawner of the open sea'.

sperm A male reproductive cell that combines with a female egg cell during reproduction.

Glossary

spine Backbone.

spiracle An opening between the eye and first gill opening of most sharks and rays, which allows them to take in water containing oxygen without opening their mouth.

squalamine A chemical found in the liver of dogfish sharks, which helps to fight viruses, and can be used to treat cancers and eye problems. It can be made synthetically to save killing sharks.

squalene An oil found in a shark's liver, which is used to make cosmetics, medicines and machine oil. The livers of deep sea sharks, such as gulper sharks, kitefin sharks and Portuguese dogfish, as well as chimaeras, contain a lot of squalene, but many of these sharks are now over-fished and rare. Squalene can be produced synthetically or from vegetable sources.

stingray A type of ray with one or more poisonous spines on its tail. Most stingrays live on the sea bed, and crush shellfish and crabs with their teeth.

streamlined Something that has a smooth, slim shape, which cuts through water or air easily, enabling fast movement.

submersible A small submarine used by scientists to work deep down in the oceans. It protects the scientists from the huge water pressures at great depths.

sub-species A smaller group than a species in biological classification. Members of a single sub-species are similar to each other, but are sufficiently different to need their own group.

sustainable Something that can be kept at a certain rate or level, without being used up or destroyed.

symbiosis The close relationship between two different species that live together to the advantage of both.

symmetrical Having sides or halves that are the same. Some sharks, such as mako sharks, have symmetrical tail lobes, which helps them to swim fast.

tag To attach a label or marker to an animal in order to follow its movements and learn more about its lifestyle.

tapetum lucidum A layer at the back of a shark's eye, which reflects light back into the eye and helps the shark to see better in dim light or darkness.

tapeworms A group of flatworms that are internal parasites of animals. They attach themselves to the wall of the animal's gut via their head end and steal the animal's food.

tastebud A taste organ found mainly on the upper surface of an animal's tongue.

temperate A mild area that is neither too hot, nor too cold. The parts of the world in between the hot tropics and the cold poles have this type of weather.

temperature The measurement of how hot or cold something is.

territory A special area where an animal lives that may provide living space, food and shelter, and which it guards and defends against intruders. Some animals only defend a territory during the breeding season.

tissue Cells of a particular type that are packed and held together in an organized way, such as nervous tissue.

tropics The warmest part of the Earth's surface, extending about 22° north and south of the Equator, between the tropic of Cancer and the tropic of Capricorn.

tsunami A giant, fast-moving ocean wave, which is usually triggered by an earthquake under the sea and travels across the ocean. A tsunami can be very destructive when it hits land.

uterus (plural uteri) One of a pair of enlarged parts of a female shark's oviducts, where the eggs or young develop. Some sharks have two uteri, while others have only one working uterus.

vein A blood vessel that carries blood towards the heart.

venom Poisonous fluid produced by some animals, including some sharks (such as the spiny dogfish) and stingrays, which is used to kill or injure other animals.

vertebrae (singular vertebra) The bony or cartilaginous segments that make up a backbone. In the middle of the vertebrae is a channel for the spinal cord, which links the brain to the rest of the nervous system.

vertebrate An animal that has an internal skeleton with a backbone and spinal cord.

vibrations Tiny movements of air or water, caused by very small changes in pressure. Sound travels in the form of vibrations. It travels five times faster in water than in air.

vitamin A A vitamin found in the liver oils of certain fish (including sharks), as well as in milk and eggs. Vitamin A is essential for growth, keeps skin healthy and helps animals to see in dim light.

vitamins Natural substances that are needed in tiny amounts for the health of most animals and some plants. Vitamins are found in natural foods or are sometimes produced within the body of a living thing.

viviparous An animal in which the young develop inside the mother's body, so she gives birth to live young.

Glossary

vulnerable An animal that faces a high risk of extinction in the wild in the near future, but is not likely to die out immediately.

warm-blooded Being able to maintain a more or less constant body temperature, which is usually above that of the surroundings.

whaler sharks Another name for requiem sharks.

womb A common name for uterus.

yolk A liquid inside eggs that provides food and nutrients for a developing animal.

yolk sac A bag-like structure surrounding the yolk of an egg.

yolk sac placenta An organ in the uterus of most requiem sharks, which is formed from the yolk sac and lining of the mother's uterus. Nutrients from the mother shark pass through the placenta to the developing shark.

zoologists Scientists who study the biology of animals and how they behave.

Index

Page numbers in **bold** refer to main subject entries; page numbers in *italics* refer to illustrations.

A

Aboriginal art *450–451*
acoustic tags 465
AES (American Elasmobranch Society) 461
air bubble sounds 78
American Elasmobranch Society (AES) 461
ampullae of Lorenzini **84–85**, 101, *280–281*, 376
anal fins 43, 44
anatomy **50–57**
ancient Greeks 401, 422, 449, 450
angelsharks 28, 39, 124, *126–127*, **198–203**, *200–201*
anglers 423, 438, 441
angular rough sharks *188–189*
antibiotics 449
aquariums 444–445, 458, 482
armoured skins 121
arteries 64, 65
Atlantic sharpnose sharks *372–373*
attacks 403, **424–435**
Australian angelsharks 202

B

balance 79
balloon sharks *120–121*, **292–293**
bamboo sharks 28, *82–83*, *146–147*, **236–237**, *238–239*
barbels 25, 81
　blind sharks 231
　brown-banded bamboo sharks *82–83*
　carpet sharks 227, 231

barbels (*cont.*)
　mandarin dogfish 170
　nurse sharks 240
　Pacific angelsharks *200–201*
　sawsharks 206, *207*, *208–209*
　spurdog sharks 172
　whiskery sharks 298
　wobbegongs 232
barbelthroat carpet sharks 227
barndoor skates 407
basking sharks 24, *26–27*, *62–63*, *104–105*, 112, 128, 150, **268–269**, *270–271*, *478*
batoids 17, 392–393
bat rays 216
beliefs **450–451**
benthic sharks 23
bigeye sixgill sharks 160
bigeye thresher sharks 14, 260, 261
biggest sharks **16–17**
bigmouth sharks 268
biologists 460, 461
bioluminescence 16, **118–119**, 131, 178–179, 192, 195
birdbeak sharks 176
birthing **142–143**, 145
biting 134, 194–195
blacknose sharks **318–319**
blacktail spurdog sharks 173
blacktip reef sharks 34, 35, 91, *92–93*, 108, **340–341**, *342–343*
blacktip sharks **344–345**
blacktip spinner sharks 329
blind sharks **230–231**
blood **64–65**, 449
blood vessels 64
blue-grey carpet sharks 230
blue sharks *12–13*, 14, *32–33*, *46–47*, *96–97*, *98–99*, 145, 148, 314, **366–367**, *368–369*

Index

blue-spotted stingrays *402, 404–405*
blue whales 113
bluntnose sharks 160–161
body language **130–131**
bone sharks 268
bonnethead sharks **380–381**
books **452–453**
Borneo river shark 360
bottom dwellers **28–29**
bowmouth guitarfish 408, *410–411*
box jellyfish *425, 426–427*
brains 76–77, 80, **86–87**
bramble sharks 48, **164–165**, *164–165*
breaching *67, 68–69*
breathing **60–61**
breathing holes 61
broadnose sevengill sharks 160, 161, *162–163*
bronze whaler sharks 103, **330–331**
brown-banded bamboo sharks *82–83, 146–147, 238–239*
bullhead sharks 15, 28, **214–221**
bull sharks 314, *314–315*, **338–339**, 425

C

cage-diving 441, *458*, 464
cameras 441, 464
camouflage **124–125**, *126–127*, 198
cannibalism 103, 387
captive sharks **444–445**, 458
cardiac muscle 66
Caribbean reef sharks *35, 436–437, 442–443*
Caribbean sharpnose sharks *372, 373*
caring for sharks 444–445
carnivores 12
carpet sharks 39, **226–249**
cartilage 12, 50–51, **54–55**, 393, 449

catsharks 24, 28, *139*, **288–289**, *290–291*
caudal (tail) fins 15, 42, **44–45**, 55
cell studies 458
chemical poisons 476
chimaeras 392, 393, **414–419**
Cladoselache 472, 475
claspers 132, 134
cleaning stations 150, 151, 398
cloaca 70, 134
coffin-rays 401
Colclough's shark 230
cold-bloodedness 51
cold water sharks 23, 31
common skates *406*
common smoothhound sharks 304
common thresher sharks 15, 260, 261
communication **130–131**
conservation 458, 476–477, 482–483
cookie-cutter sharks 14, 107, 118, 125, 168, **194–195**
coral reefs 22, **34–35**
cownose rays 403
cowsharks **160–161**
crocodile sharks **266–267**
Cyrano spurdog sharks 172

D

Deania species 176
death 149, 476–477
deep-sea sharks 24–25, *74–75*
denticles **48–49**, 122, 176, 209, 459
  see also skin
devil rays 398
diets see feeding and food
digestion **70–71**
discoveries **468–469**
disguise **124–125**, 198
dissections 464

diving cages 441, *458*, 464
DNA 469
dogfish sharks 24, **168–195**, 288–289
   hunting 108, *109*, 128
   spines 122–123, *174–175*
   travel distances 100
Doliodus 470
dorsal fins 42, 170, 362
dried tissue 458
droppings 71
duckbilled rays 403
dusky sharks 144, 335, **350–351**
dusky smoothhound sharks 305
dwarf lanternsharks 17, 468

E

eagle stingrays 402, *403*
early sharks **472–473**
ears **78–79**
ecotourism 441, 482
Edestus giganteus 472
eel-like sharks 38, **158–159**
eggs 13, 132–133, **138–139**, 142, 145
   bamboo sharks 236
   bullhead sharks 215
   carpet sharks 227
   catfish sharks 289
   chimaeras 415
   elephant fish 418–419
   epaulette sharks 228
   horn sharks 216
   laying eggs **138–139**
   Port Jackson sharks 220–221
   skates 406–407
elasmobranchology 458, 461
electrical senses **84–85**, 101, 208, 357, 376, 377, 418
electric rays **400–401**
elephant fish **418–419**
elephant sharks 268
endangered species 177, **478–479**
enemies **150–151**
environments **22–35**
epaulette sharks 23, *42*, 43, *227*, **228–229**
Eqalussuaq sharks 184
evolution **470–473**
extinction 203, 478, 483
eyelids 72
eyes 14, **72–73**, *74–75*, *193*, 315, 360–361, 366, *416–417*

F

Falcatus 472
family types **154–165**
fatspine spurdog sharks 173
feeding and food **102–115**
   see also hunting
   bamboo sharks 236
   basking sharks *26–27*, *104–105*, *270–271*, 268
   batoids 392
   blacktip sharks 344–345
   blue sharks 366
   bronze whaler sharks 330
   bullhead sharks 15
   bull sharks 339
   captive sharks 444
   carpet sharks 227
   cookie-cutter sharks 194
   crocodile sharks 266
   digestion **70–71**
   dusky sharks 351
   elephant fish 418
   Galapagos sharks 334
   goblin sharks 256
   great white sharks 274–275
   Greenland sharks 184, 185, 193

feeding and food (*cont.*)
   guitarfish 408
   hammerhead sharks 382, 387
   leopard sharks 307
   mackerel sharks 254, 262
   manta rays 398
   megamouth sharks 262–263
   night sharks 355
   nurse sharks 240
   oceanic whitetip sharks 346–347
   porbeagle sharks 284
   Port Jackson sharks 220
   reef sharks 324, 370
   salmon sharks 282
   sand tiger sharks 258
   sharpnose sharks 372
   silky sharks 332
   silvertip sharks 321
   sleeper sharks 182
   smoothhound sharks 304
   spinner sharks 328
   tawny nurse sharks 242
   thresher sharks 261
   tiger sharks 356
   whale sharks 193, 248–249
   winghead sharks 379
   wobbegongs 232
   zebra sharks 245
feeding tours 441
female sharks **132–143**
fertilization 133
fieldwork 458
films **452–453**, *454–455*
filter-feeders 103, **112–113**
   basking sharks 268
   mackerel sharks 254, 262
   manta rays 398
   megamouth sharks 262
   whale sharks 248–249, *250–251*

fins **42–45**, 55
   batoids 393
   frilled sharks 158
   gulper sharks 176
   hammerhead sharks 376
   kitefin sharks 191
   mandarin dogfish 170
   oceanic whitetip sharks 346
   reef sharks 43, 370
   requiem sharks 315
   rough sharks 188
   silky sharks 332
   skates 406, 407
   soup 300–301, 438, 446, 448, 469, 477
fishing 423, **438–439**, 441, 482
flake sharks **298–299**
flapper skates 406–407
flexible skeletons 54–55
floating ability 94–95, 190
fluoride 57
food industry 438–439
fossils 470, 473, **474–475**
fox sharks 261
freshwater sharks 315, 338, 339, **360–361**
friends and enemies **150–151**
frilled sharks 38, **158–159**
frog sharks 183

G

Galapagos sharks *316–317*, **334–335**, *336–337*, 351
Ganges sharks 360
genetic analysis 458
geneticists 461
ghost sharks 393
ghouls 393
giant guitarfish 408
giant lanternsharks 178

giant oceanic manta rays *394–395*, 398
gills *52–53*, 55, 60–61, *62–63*, 199, 209, 414
goblin sharks 254, **256–257**, 450
'golden age of sharks' 470
governments, saving sharks 482
great hammerhead sharks **386–387**, *388–389*
great lanternsharks *74–75*
great white sharks 23, 30, 66–67, 68–69, *136–137*, **272–275**, *276–277*, 425, 453, *459*
   attacks 424
   hunting 107, 108, 128
   messaging 131
   scavenging 114
   speed 96
Greek history 401, 422, 449, 450
Greenland sharks 31, 148, *151*, **184–185**, *186–187*, 451, 469
green sawfish 412, *412–413*
grey reef sharks 34, 35, 79, **324–325**, *326–327*
grey sharks 184
ground sharks **288–311**
groups **128–129**
growth **148–149**, 171, 190, 192, 208
guitarfish 124, 392, **408–409**, *410–411*
Gulf of Mexico smoothhound sharks *304–305*
gulper sharks 25, **176–177**
gums 56
gurry sharks 184

H
habitats **22–35**
hammerhead sharks 17, 30, 39, *76–77*, 103, *128–129*, **376–387**, *384–385*, *388–389*, *462–463*

hammerhead sharks (*cont.*)
   anatomy 55
   birth 143
   brains 86
health foods 439
hearing ability **78–79**
heart **64–65**
Helicoprion 472
Henry's epaulette sharks 229
hiding 121, 198
hormones 179
horn sharks 57, 122, **216–217**, *218–219*
houndsharks **296–297**, **304–305**
hunting 16, 102, **106–109**, *128–129*, *274–275*, *368–369*
   blacktip reef sharks 108, *128–129*
   dogfish sharks 108, *109*, 128
   great white sharks 107, 108, 128, *274–275*
   pygmy sharks 108, 128
   shark size 16
   whitetip reef sharks *110–111*
Hybodus 472, *473*

I
intelligence **86–87**
internal organs **50–57**
International organizations 479
intestines 51
Inuit people 184, 185, 451
Irrawaddy river sharks 360

J
Japanese angelsharks 202
Japanese history 423
jaws **56–57**, 189, 191, 274
jellyfish *425*, *426–427*
jumping heights 14

Index

K
keels 44
kidney-headed sharks **382–383**
kitefin sharks **190–191**, 192

L
labyrinth tubes 78
Lamniformes 450
lanternsharks 17, *74–75*, 118, 123, **178–179**, *180–181*, 468
large spine velvet dogfish 183
large-tooth cookie-cutter sharks 194
large-tooth sawfish 413
lateral line **80–81**
Latin names 154
legends and beliefs **450–451**
lemon sharks *50–51*, *156–157*, 314, **362–363**, *364–365*
  brains 86, *87*
  giving birth *142–143*
  growth *148–149*
  hunting *107*
  mating 134
  pups 144
leopard sharks 29, 125, 244, **306–307**, *308–309*
lesser electric rays *400–401*
life expectancy 148–149, 172
lifespans 15
lighting up **118–119**, 131, 178–179, 192, 195
lined lanternsharks 179
liver oil 422, 448, 449
livers 177, 249, 257, 269
living with sharks **422–453**
loners **128–129**
long-distance travel **100–101**
longfin mako sharks 279
longnose sawsharks **208–209**, *210–211*

luminescent copepods 184
luminous species 16, **118–119**, 131, 178–179, 192, 195

M
mackerel sharks 24, **254–285**, 450
magnetism 382
mako sharks 101, 144, **278–279**, *280–281*
  see also shortfin makos
male sharks **132–143**
mandarin dogfish **170–171**
mangrove stingrays 397
manta rays 17, *392*, *394–395*, 397, **398–399**
marbled catsharks 124
mating **134–135**, 145, 352
  scars *136–137*
mechanisms **38–87**
medicine 422, **448–449**
meeting and mating **134–135**
Megachasma pelagios 263
Megalodon 16, 472, 475
megamouth sharks 43, 112, **262–263**, *264–265*
mercury levels 469
messaging **130–131**
Michael's epaulette sharks 229
migration **100–101**, 192, 255, 387
mizuwani 266
monk fish 39, 124, **198–203**
movement 50, **66–67**, **90–102**
muscles 50, **66–67**
mysteries and discoveries **468–469**

N
newborns *142–143*, **144–145**, 148
New Guinea river sharks 360

Nicaragua sharks 339
nictitating membranes 72, 299, 310, 315
night sharks **354–355**
nocturnal hunting 106
noise detection **78–79**
nostrils **76–77**, 188, 376, 378
novels **452–453**
nurseries 91, 128, 148, 300, 330, 363, 476, 479
nurse sharks *29*, *60*, **240–243**, *466–467*
nutcracker rays 403

O

observation **464–465**
oceanic manta rays *394–395*, 398
oceanic whitetip sharks **346–347**, *348–349*, 425
oceanographers 461
ocellated angelsharks 203
oil 190, 422, 446
oil sharks 300–301
olfactory lobes 77
organs 50–51
ornate wobbegong *469*
ovaries 132
overfishing 476, 478
oviducts 132
ovoviviparous species **138–139**, 142, 397
oxygen 51, **60–61**

P

Pacific angelsharks *126–127*, *200–201*, 203
Pacific sleeper sharks 182–183
pack hunters **108–109**
palaeontologists 461
parasites 71, 150–151

patterns **124–125**, 198
pectoral fins 42, 43, 94, 330
pelagic sharks 23, 260, 261
pelagic stingrays 403
pelvic fins 42, 94
people and sharks **422–453**
pheromones 130, 134
photography 441, 464, 465
photophores 119, 178–179, *179*
piked dogfish 122–123, **172–173**
pineal eyes 73
plankton 103, **112–113**
plough-nosed chimaeras **418–419**
poisonous chemicals 476
poisonous flesh 15
polar species **30–31**
pollution 476, 483
population numbers **476–477**, 478–479
porbeagle sharks 24, 31, *254–255*, **284–285**
Port Jackson sharks *56*, *123*, **220–221**, *222–223*
Portuguese sharks 24, 183
precaudal pits 311
pregnancy **142–143**, 202
prey 102–109
prickly sharks 24, **164–165**
products from sharks 438–439, **446–449**
protection **120–121**
pupil shapes 73
pups 142–143, **144–145**, 148
pygmy sharks *16*, 17, 108, 122, 128, 168, **192–193**

R

rabbitfish 415
rare species 13, 478–479

Index

ratfish 393, *414–415*, *416–417*
rays 13, 17, 392, *392*, **396–403**
records **14–17**
red muscle 66–67
reef manta rays 398
reef sharks **34–35**, 314
    blacktip reef sharks 34, 35, 91, *92–93*, 108, *128–129*, **340–341**, *342–343*
    Caribbean reef sharks 35, *436–437*, *442–443*
    fins 43, 370
    grey reef sharks 34, 35, 79, **324–325**, *326–327*
    whitetip reef sharks 34, 108, *110–111*, 134, *135*, 340, 346, **370–371**
relatives of sharks **392–419**
released sharks 444–445
remoras 151
requiem sharks 24, 103, **314–373**
research studies **458–483**, 483
research submersibles 79
river sharks 73, 315, 339, **360–361**
river stingrays 402
rock cod 172
rock salmon 172
rostrum 206
rough sharks 121, **188–189**
round stingrays 402

S

safety **120–121**, **434–435**
sailback houndsharks 297
salmon sharks **282–283**
sandbar sharks *101*, **352–353**
sand devils 202
sand tiger sharks *58–59*, 131, 144, **258–259**
satellite tags 465

saving sharks **482–483**
sawback angelsharks 202
sawfish *393*, **412–413**
sawsharks 29, 121, **206–209**, *210–211*
scalloped bonnethead sharks 380
scalloped hammerhead sharks *30*, 86, **382–383**, *384–385*, *462–463*
scavenging food **114–115**
scent detection **76–77**
scent release 130
schools **128–129**, *168–169*, 300, *326–327*, 380
school sharks **300–301**
science studies **458–483**, 483
scientists **460–469**
scissor-toothed sharks 472
sea leeches 150
sea-life centres 444–445, 482
seaweed forests 22
sending messages **130–131**
senses **72–85**, **106–107**
    electrical **84–85**, 101, 208, 357, 376, 377, 418
    hearing **78–79**
    hunting skills **106–107**
    sight **72–73**
    sixth sense **84–85**
    skin **80–81**
    smell detection **76–77**
    taste **80–81**
    touch **80–81**
sevengill sharks **160–161**, *162–163*
Seychelles gulper sharks 177
shallow dwellers 24–25
shapes **38–39**, 44–45, 176
sharkfin guitarfish 408, 409
shark fin soup 300–301, 438, 446, 448, 469, 477
shark relatives **392–419**
shark suckers 151

Shark Trust *482*
sharpnose sevengill sharks 160
sharpnose sharks 160, **372–373**
sharptooth smoothhound sharks 305
shortfin mako sharks 14, 15, 96, *97*, 254, 255, 278–279, *280–281*
short-nose electric rays 400
shortspine spurdogs 172
short-tail nurse sharks 248
shovelnose guitarfish 124, 408, *408–409*
shy-eye sharks 73
silky sharks *44–45*, **332–333**
silvertip sharks **320–321**, *322–323*
sixgill sawsharks 206
sixgill sharks *24*, 25, **160–161**
sixth sense **84–85**
sizes **16–17**, 72, 198, 206, 209
skates 392, **406–407**
skate wings 407
skeletal muscle 66–67
skeleton (cartilage) 12, 50–51, **54–55**, 393
skin **48–49**, **80–81**, *98–99*, 121, 422, 446
  see also denticles
skulls 55
sleeper sharks **182–183**, 184
smallest sharks **16–17**
smalleye pygmy sharks 168
smallspotted catsharks *289*, *290–291*
small tooth sawfish *393*
smart sharks **86–87**
smell detection **76–77**
smooth hammerhead sharks *376–377*
smoothhound sharks **304–305**
snake-like sharks 38, **158–159**
snaky sharks **298–299**
snouts 38, 172, 206, 412–413
sound detection **78–79**, 130–131

soup, shark fin 300–301, 438, 446, 448, 469, 477
souvenirs 422
speartooth sharks 360, *360–361*
species 12–13, **154–165**
  batoids 392
  bullhead sharks 214
  catsharks 288
  chimaeras 393, 414
  cookie-cutter sharks 194
  gulper sharks 176
  hammerhead sharks 376
  houndsharks 296
  lanternsharks 178
  mackerel sharks 254
  mako sharks 279
  manta rays 398
  requiem sharks 314
  rough sharks 188
  sawsharks 206
  sharpnose sharks 372
speed 15, 45, **96–97**, 366
sperm 132–133
spikes **122–123**
spines 54–55, 121, **122–123**, 425
  chimaeras 415
  dogfish sharks 168, *174–175*
  sleeper fish 183
  spurdog sharks 122–123, 172–173
  stingrays 402
spinner sharks **328–329**
spiny dogfish sharks 24, *109*, 122–123, 168–169, **172–173**, *174–175*
spiracles 165, 189, 230
spitting sharks 242–243
spook fish 393
sports anglers 423, 438, 476
spotted eagle stingrays 402, *403*
spotted houndsharks *296–297*
spotted ratfish *414–415*, *416–417*

Index

spotted wobbegongs *81*
spring dogfish 172
spurdog sharks **172–173**
squalamine 449
squalene 446
squat-headed hammerhead sharks **386–387**
starry smoothhound sharks 304
statistics **14–21**
staying safe **434–435**
Stethacanthus 472
stingrays 123, 396, **402–403**, *404–405*, 425
stomachs 50, 70–71
striped smoothhound sharks 305
studying sharks **458–483**
submersibles 79
Suez Canal 340
sundowner sharks **298–299**
sunfish 268
survival 23
survival stories **430–431**, *432–433*
swellsharks 28, *120–121*, *140–141*, **292–293**, *294–295*
swimming skills **94–95**, 195, 396
symbiosis *348–349*, *364–365*

T

tagging sharks 464, 465
tail (caudal) fins 15, 42, **44–45**, 55
tails *46–47*, 55, 192, 260–261, 393, 396
tapetum lucidum 72–73
tasselled wobbegongs 39, *40–41*, 232, 234–235
taste senses **80–81**
tawny nurse sharks 60, **242–243**
teeth **56–57**
    baby sharks 148

teeth (*cont.*)
    basking sharks 268
    bonnethead sharks 380
    bronze whaler sharks 330
    bullhead sharks 215
    chimaeras 414–415
    cookie-cutter sharks 194–195
    crocodile sharks 267
    dusky sharks 350
    elephant fish 418
    fossils 470, *474–475*
    frilled sharks 158
    goblin sharks 257
    great white sharks 274
    grey reef sharks 324
    gulper sharks 177
    horn sharks 216
    houndsharks 296–297
    kitefin sharks 191
    leopard sharks 306
    mako sharks 278
    mandarin dogfish 171
    night sharks 355
    nurse sharks 240
    porbeagle sharks 284
    pygmy sharks 192
    requiem sharks 315
    river sharks 361
    rough sharks 189
    sand tiger sharks *58–59*, 259
    shark products 422, 446–447
    silvertip sharks 321
    smoothhound sharks 305
    spinner sharks 328
    swellsharks 293
    tiger sharks *52–53*, 356
    whiskery sharks 298
    wobbegongs 232
temperate water sharks 30
Texas skates 407

threat displays 130–131
thresher sharks *14–15*, 45, 108, 121, **260–261**
tiger sharks *39*, *52–53*, *57*, *72*, *116–117*, 314, **356–357**, *358–359*, 372, 425
  food 103, 115, 356
tissue studies 458
tongue stones *468*
tope sharks **300–301**, *302–303*
touch senses **80–81**
tourism 325, 422, **440–445**, 482
tracking devices 464
trade bans 482
travel **90–102**
  see also migration
Tristychius 472
tropical species **30–31**
types of sharks **154–165**

U

umbilical cords 142
unicorn sharks 472

V

valves 64, 71
veins 65
velvet belly lanternsharks *118*, 123, *180–181*
Venezuelan dwarf smoothhound sharks 305
vertebrate evolution *471*
vertical migration 101
vibration 76–77, 80
viper dogfish 179
viperfish *119*
vision **72–73**
vital organs 50

vitamin sharks 300–301
viviparous sharks 142–143

W

warm-bloodedness 23–24, 51
weasel sharks **310–311**
whale sharks 16–17, *18–19*, 24, 43, 112–113, 150, 244, **248–249**, *250–251*, *480–481*
whaler sharks 24, 103, **314–373**
whiskers 81
whiskery sharks **298–299**
white muscle 66–67
white-spotted bamboo sharks 237
white-spotted dogfish 172
whitetip reef sharks 34, 91, 108, *110–111*, 134–135, 340, 346, **370–371**
whitetip sharks **346–347**, *348–349*, 425
whorl-tooth sharks 472
winghead sharks **378–379**
wing-like fins 43
wobbegongs 28, *39*, *40–41*, 81, 124, *226*, **232–233**, *234–235*, *469*

Z

Zambezi River sharks 339
zebra sharks **244–245**, *246–247*
zoologists 460, 461

Acknowledgements

All artworks are from the Miles Kelly Artwork Bank.

The publishers would like to thank the following sources for the use of their photographs:

Front cover WaterFrame/Alamy Stock Photo **Spine** Brandelet/Shutterstock.com
Back cover (t) Kjersti Joergensen/Shutterstock.com, (l) Michael Bogner/Shutterstock.com, (r) magnusdeepbelow/Shutterstock.com

Alamy 98–99 F1online digitale Bildagentur GmbH; 208–209 Stephen Frink Collection; 254–255 Doug Perrine; 300–301 Charles Hood; 316–317 Stephen Frink Collection; 451 Suzanne Long

Ardea.com 133 Ron and Valerie Tayor; 308–309 Ken Lucas; 440 Ron and Valerie Tayor; 469 Valerie Taylor

Corbis 58–59 Norbert Wu/Science Faction; 60 Dave Fleetham; 62–63 Alex Mustard/Nature Picture Library; 66–67 Keren Su; 68–69 Thomas Kokta/Masterfile; 87 Keren Su; 102 Tui De Roy/Minden Pictures; 196–197 P. Sutter; 243 Jason Isley – Scubazoo/Science Faction; 270–271 Alex Mustard/Nature Picture Library; 423 Chris Rainier; 483 Mike Kemp/In Pictures

Dreamstime.com 61 & 357 Naluphoto; 226 Jamiegodson

FLPA 16 Jeffrey Rotman/Biosphoto; 29 Peter Verhoog/Minden Pictures; 92–93 Fabien Michenet/Biosphoto; 110–111 OceanPhoto; 149 Brandon Cole/Biosphoto; 162–163 Bruno Guenard/Biosphoto; 200–201 Photo Researchers; 203 Gerard Soury/Biosphoto; 204–205 Kelvin Aitken/Biosphoto; 212–213 Fred Bavendam/Minden Pictures; 215 Fred Bavendam/Minden Pictures; 222–223 Fred Bavendam/Minden Pictures; 237 Bruno Guenard/Biosphoto; 246–247 Imagebroker, Norbert Probst/Imagebroker; 282–283 Mathieu Pujol/Biosphoto; 288 Fred Bavendam/Minden Pictures; 289 Ingo Arndt/Minden Pictures; 293 Norbert Wu/Minden Pictures; 296–297 Imagebroker, Norbert Probst/Imagebroker; 320–321 Fred Bavendam/Minden Pictures; 322–323 Photo Researchers; 324–325 Norbert Probst/Imagebroker; 331 Norbert Wu/Minden Pictures; 333 /Imagebroker; 342–343 Fabien Michenet/Biosphoto; 344–345 Reinhard Dirscherl; 384–385 Norbert Probst/Imagebroker; 394–395 OceanPhoto; 416–417 Norbert Wu/Minden Pictures; 436–437 Â© Biosphoto, Jeffrey Rotman/Biosphoto; 462–463 Pete Oxford/Minden Pictures; 475 Juan-Carlos Munoz/Biosphoto

Fotolia.com 477

Glow Images 90 Norbert Probst

Imagequestmarine.com 190–191 Kelvin Aitken/V&W; 304–305, 306–307, 353, 410–411 and 412 Andy Murch; 326–327 James D. Watt; 336–337 Andre Seale; 419 Kelvin Aitken/V&W

iStock 362–363 Rainer von Brandis; 364–365 NaluPhoto

Jillian Morris 456–457

National Geographic Creative 435 Brian J. Skerry; 460 Paul Sutherland

Naturepl.com 26–27 Chris Gomersall; 30 Michele Westmorland; 31 Doug Perrine; 46–47 Chris & Monique Fallows; 56 Jeff Rotman; 74–75 David Shale; 82–83 Visuals Unlimited; 101 Doug Perrine; 104–105 Alex Mustard/2020VISION; 122–123 Ian Coleman (WAC); 123 Jurgen Freund; 126–127 Brandon Cole; 136–137 Pascal Kobeh; 140–141 Brandon Cole; 142–143 Doug Perrine; 144–145 Jeff Rotman; 146–147 Georgette Douwma; 178–179 Florian Graner; 218–219 Brandon Cole; 229 Alex Mustard; 234–235 Alex Mustard; 238–239 Georgette Douwma; 244–245 Jurgen Freund; 258–259 Chris & Monique Fallows; 264–265 Bruce Rasner/Rotman; 275 Chris & Monique Fallows; 276–277 David Fleetham; 290–291 PhotographerAlex Mustard/2020Vision; 376–377 Chris & Monique Fallows; 368–369 Chris & Monique Fallows; 407 Jeff Rotman; 442–443 Jeff Rotman; 447 Jeff Rotman; 478 Alex Mustard/2020Vision

OceanwideImages.com 12–13 C & M Fallows; 109, 173, 174–175, 176–177, 302–303 and 319 Andy Murch; 210–211 Rudie Kuiter; 233 Justin Gilligan; 280–281 C & M Fallows; 328–329 Michael Patrick O'Neill; 334–335 Gary Bell

Photo Discs/Digital Vision 130–131

Photo Discs/ImageState (panel)

Photoshot 125 Oceans Image; 152–153; 250–251 NHPA; 448 NHPA

Rex 452 Everett Collection; 453 Moviestore Collection

Science Photo Library 84–85 Jeff Rotman

SeaPics.com 118 Espen Rekda; 151 Doug Perrine; 180–181 Florian Graner; 186–187 Saul Gonor; 294–295 Andy Murch; 373 Doug Perrine; 378–379 Stephen Kajiura

Shutterstock.com Endpapers Kozachenko Maksym; 1 frantisekhojdysz; 2–3 Yann hubert; 4 & 420–421 Amanda Nicholls; 5, 22 & 100 ilolab; 6 & 138 BMCL; 10–11 Fiona Ayerst; 14–15 nicolas.voisin44; 16–17 Krzysztof Odziomek; 18–19 Nicolas Aznavour; 20–21 Specta; 23 Elsa Hoffmann; 24 Greg Amptman; 32–33 Dray van Beeck; 35 frantisekhojdysz; 36–37 Rich Carey; 38–39 Matt9122; 40–41 Teguh Tirtaputra; 43 cbpix; 44–45 Sergey Dubrov; 52–53 Matt9122; 57 Photon75; 72 Greg Amptman; 73 Dray van Beeck; 76–77 Matt9122; 78–79 Pommeyrol Vincent; 84 Matt9122; 88–89 A Cotton Photo; 94–95 Fiona Ayerst; 106–107 A Cotton Photo; 113 Dudarev Mikhail; 116–117 Matt9122; 120 NatalieJean; 128–129 (& banner) Brandelet; 156–157 Greg Amptman; 166–167 Boris Pamikov; 199 Stephen Nash; 224–225 stockpix4u; 227 iliuta goean; 241 Sergey Dubrov; 245 aquapix; 252–253 Mogens Trolle; 263 maodoltee; 286–287 Susana_Martins; 312–313 Fiona Ayerst; 338 Ian Scott; 339 Fiona Ayerst; 340–341 Micha Rosenwirth; 341 Ian Scott; 346–347 orlandin; 348–349 Dray van Beeck; 350–351 Ian Scott; 358–359 Greg Amptman; 363 A Cotton Photo; 367 Fiona Ayerst; 374–375 Matt9122; 383 Ian Scott; 387 frantisekhojdysz; 388–389 Shane Gross; 390–391 Rich Carey; 392 Isabelle Kuehn; 396–397 Durden Images; 401 Ethan Daniels; 403 Ethan Daniels; 404–405 LauraD; 414–415 Greg Amptman; 424 kbrowne41; 426–427 Daleen Loest; 429 Alex Pix; 430–431 Gustavo Miguel Fernandes; 432–433 Brian A. Witkin; 439 hainaultphoto; 445 tororo reaction; 459 kbrowne41; 465 Greg Amptman; 466–467 Durden Images; 480–481 Soren Egeberg Photography; 484–485 Rich Carey

Topfoto 454–455 Disney/Pixar

Every effort has been made to acknowledge the source and copyright holder of each picture. Miles Kelly Publishing apologizes for any unintentional errors or omissions.

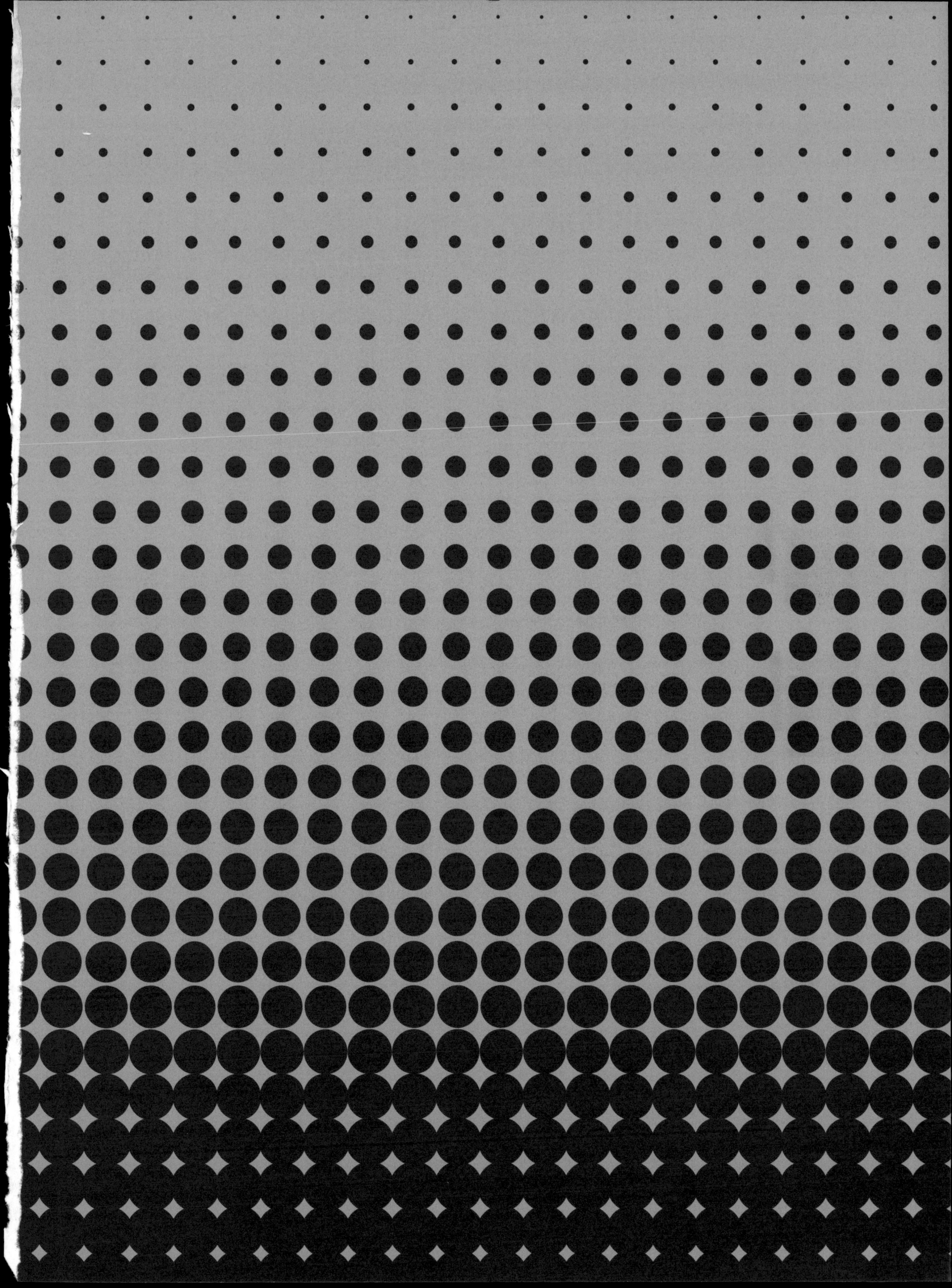